OPERA OFFSTAGE

OPERA OFFSTAGE

Passion and Politics Behind the Great Operas

Milton Brener

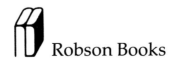

Robson Books

First published in Great Britain in 1996 by Robson Books Ltd,
Bolsover House, 5-6 Clipstone Street, London W1P 8LE

British Library Cataloguing in Publication Data
A catalogue record for this title is available from the British
Library

Design by Ann Gold

ISBN 1 86105 025 9

Printed in Great Britain by WBC Book Manufacturers Ltd.,
Bridgend, Mid-Glamorgan

To Eileen,
and
to Lisa, Ann, Neil, and Mat

CONTENTS

Contents

ACKNOWLEDGMENTS

For almost all of the factual material used I am indebted to the authors and editors of the volumes listed in the references. Apart from their value as research tools, these sources make fascinating reading. I recommend them to those who are interested in delving further into the matters touched on in this book. My original research, confined to only a few of the chapters, is very limited, and I have relied almost entirely on the authors and editors of these works.

Special thanks are due to Ray Anthony Delia, Director of Development, Marketing and Public Relations of the New Orleans Opera Association, and to Esther Nelson-Ulken, its former Public Relations Director, both of whom encouraged, assisted, and afforded me the opportunity to write opera history; to Dean M. Shapiro, Director of Media and Publicity at the New Orleans Opera Association, for his help over the years with my articles, many of which became chapters in this book, and also for his review of the book's final proofs and his helpful suggestions; to Mary Kennen Herbert, formerly of Walker and Company, for her help and interest in publication of the book, and to George Gibson of Walker and Company for publishing it and working with me on the final product; and to The Metropolitan Opera's *Opera News* magazine for permission to include the chapter on Wagner's *The Flying Dutchman,* which first appeared in its December 1989 issue. Special thanks also to my wife, Eileen, and to my daughter, Ann, whose interest and editorial skills were a tremendous help in smoothing out many rough spots, and to my son, Neil, whose knowledge, and keen sense of history, more than once pointed me toward fertile ground.

PREFACE

In the year 1206, when notions of romantic love were quite new in the world, a group of "minnesingers" held a contest of song. Talented as both poets and songsters, these minnesingers were the German version of the French troubadours. The setting for the contest was the Hall of Minstrels in the historic Wartburg Castle in central Germany's Thüringian mountains. The event, with some poetic license, was immortalized in the second act of Richard Wagner's *Tannhäuser*.

Viewed from the selective and narrow perspective of a late twentieth-century opera devotee, it may seem that the entire nineteenth century, including a few decades before and after, was one long contest of song, and that all of Europe was the hall. Hundreds of composers wrote thousands of operas, almost five hundred new ones reaching the stage in one nine-year period in mid-century Italy alone. It was a time when giants with names like Mozart, Verdi, Wagner, Puccini, and Strauss walked the streets of Europe's cities and towns. They eclipsed the minnesingers, and almost everyone else who had set verse to music, and by the time their line disappeared, they had raised the state of opera to artistic heights previously unimagined. To no small degree they were stimulated and inspired by other giants with names like Beaumarchais, Alexandre Dumas, Victor Hugo, and Oscar Wilde.

This bloom of creative genius that was nineteenth-century opera, including some works from a few bordering decades, may well have been the most powerful explosion of artistic expression ever known—

from the prehistoric cave paintings in southwestern Europe, to the tragedies of fifth century B.C. Athens, to the paintings of the Italian Renaissance and the poetry of Elizabethan England. And the reason may be opera's uniquely great potential for artistic expression. A strong case for such a statement was made by one who was well qualified to do so.

In his 1851 book-length essay, *Opera and Drama*, Richard Wagner argues that music, unlike words, goes directly to the seat of emotion. According to him, the "primal organ-of-utterance of the inner man is tone speech," which is the primitive expression of pure emotion, namely, the vowel sounds. These are, still today, the intense expressions of joy, fear, or anger. But as humans became civilized, and society more complex, these cries of emotion gave way to the "clang of talk," and we lost "the instinctive understanding of our own speech roots." Words must first be absorbed by the intellect, and their meaning "delineated in a thousand details" before they may be conveyed to the heart. The artist can master these primitive roots only through music, which, like the primal sounds themselves, expresses and evokes raw emotion.

According to Wagner, however, even music standing alone does not reach its full potential as a form of expression. It is only by enhancing the poetry and action of the drama with music that the artist can most effectively bypass the intellect and directly reach the emotions of the spectator.

While Wagner's essay may, in some respects, be valid for him and his work alone, some important aspects of it may be borne out by all opera. If Wagner is right, we will get more of the feeling of gypsy life, or Bizet's concept of it, from the drama, poetry, and music of his *Carmen* than from any painting, novel, poem, spoken play, or music alone. The cobblestoned streets and gabled roofs of medieval Germany will be more roundly portrayed as the combination of music, poetry, and drama that is *Die Meistersinger* than by any other art. And to many of us, so it seems.

I can think of no more appropriate form of tribute to the great composers who are the glory of opera than by recording the intensely human circumstances that surrounded the creation of some of their finest works. It was my intention to do this with material that is factual, as the facts are far more fascinating than anything I could create in imagination. These stories are based entirely on correspondence, diaries, autobiographies, published reminiscences, contemporary news articles, or works by reputable biographers or historians. They are listed in the references section.

Because this golden age was also, in a sense, an artistic and economic jungle, interesting stories abound behind the creation of the operas of the time. Each chapter of this book concentrates on only one story for each of the works I included. And I included the ones I did, not because they are the greatest, the most important, or even the most popular, but because the stories behind them seemed to me the most interesting, and tell us most about the human beings involved in their creation. Each offers a unique insight into the creative functioning of the composers, and, in many instances, of the men of letters whose works were their source materials. The composers, remarkable as their talents may have been, did not work in a vacuum.

It is hoped that this book will convey something of the emotional upheaval that often goes into the creative process. Those of us whose lives have been so tremendously enriched by these operas often feel a deep sense of obligation. If this book enhances your appreciation of opera, especially of those readers for whom opera is a new experience, I will feel that the debt has been partially repaid.

—Milton E. Brener

Mozart. Oil painting by Barbara Krafft in 1819. According to Wolfgang Hildesheimer, a Mozart biographer, the composer's contemporaries still living in the
nineteenth century claimed this portrait to be the best likeness of him. (Collection
of the Society of Friends of Music in Vienna.)

1

THE MAN WHO
WAS FIGARO

THE MARRIAGE OF FIGARO

THE PLOT: *Figaro and Susanna, attendants to Count Almaviva and the Countess Rosina, plan to marry. Susanna believes the count has designs on her, though the peasants thank the Count for renouncing his traditional right to the first night following the wedding of any of his servant girls. Susanna and the Countess plot to trap him. A tryst is arranged by Susanna, but the women disguise themselves, each as the other, and the rendezvous is kept by the Countess herself. Despite complications, it works, and results in repentance by the Count for his infidelity.*

"This is detestable. It will never be played . . . This man laughs at everything that ought to be respected in a government."

So bellowed King Louis XVI of France to his queen, Marie-Antoinette. The year was 1780, and the queen was reading to the king *The Marriage of Figaro*, a new play by Pierre-Augustin Caron de Beaumarchais, once the watchmaker to the king's predecessor.

Beaumarchais's career as a watchmaker was short-lived. He left to become, at various times, an inventor, adventurer, adviser to the king, publisher, and playwright. At the age of forty-one he was imprisoned for over two months in the midst of litigation resulting from disastrous business reverses. It was an experience that left him with a fierce hostility to the legal system and did nothing to dampen his distrust of authority in general.

Two years later his fortunes rebounded with the successful run of his play, *The Barber of Seville*. He used part of his newly acquired wealth to organize aid for George Washington's Revolutionary Army, enlisting the help of the French king in the process. It is typical of the controversy surrounding Beaumarchais that, for his efforts, he was termed by some a defender of liberty, by others an arms merchant for profit.

The Barber of Seville is more than a touch autobiographical. The barber, Figaro, like Beaumarchais, is a clever and enterprising commoner who assists and advises a nobleman. In the play it is Count Almaviva who is aided in winning the hand of Rosina. Like his creator, Figaro wins fame for himself, rises above his station, and is alternately praised and condemned while "mocking the foolish, braving the wicked." A comparison of this fictional character with the life of the author leaves little doubt but that Beaumarchais is Figaro, and Figaro is Beaumarchais.

Soon after the first performance of *The Barber*, Beaumarchais started work on a sequel involving the same characters. In the sequel, *The Marriage of Figaro*, the barber has become a valet to Count Almaviva.

Age and the travails of the intervening years had saddened and matured the playwright. *The Marriage* is more serious in its conception and more biting in tone. The bursts of pent-up anger in the Barber are now deft and rapierlike thrusts at nobility, government, and the legal system. "Be obedient and obsequious," Figaro advises the Count, "and you'll succeed at everything." And he has something to say about lawyers: "A party to a suit who is but a little educated always knows his case better than some attorney, shouting his head off and knowing everything but the facts, boring the court and putting the jury to sleep. Afterwards he is more puffed up than if he had composed the oration of Cicero."

In a lengthy and revealing fifth-act soliloquy, Figaro says to the absent Count: "What have you done to earn so many honors? You have taken the trouble to be born, that's all."

By comparison with today's merciless garroting of public officials, the text of *The Marriage* seems tame. But in its time it lighted sparks. The reaction of the king and the difficulties in having the play produced give some insight into the prevailing political atmosphere nine years before the savagery of the French Revolution. So does Figaro's description of the then-current "free press" in the play itself: "Provided I do not write about the government, or about religion, or ethics, or people in power or with influence, or the opera, or other theatre, or about anybody connected with anything, I can print whatever I choose under the supervision of two or three censors."

For *The Marriage of Figaro* there was a succession of five such censors. The problems were twofold: There was not only the ridicule of nobility but also the risqué character of the story, centered as it was around the attempts of the Count to reimpose, with respect to Figaro's intended bride, the "droit du seigneur." This was the right of a medieval nobleman to spend, with any of the servant girls of his estate, the first night following her wedding. Descriptions of this "right" abound in works of fiction, going back to one of the earliest epics known, *Gilgamesh,* from ancient Babylon. Evidence for its actual historic occurrence is a good deal less certain.

There were a number of changes made to win the approval of the king and censors, but Beaumarchais fought primarily with other resources. He stirred up public interest with repeated readings of his play in the salons of Paris. Vivid descriptions of these readings have been preserved for us: the author on a raised stool, opening a ribboned manuscript; those in the rear standing on tiptoe, the better to see his gesticulations; the large circles of young girls in hoops; the blushing of well-bred ladies at the erotic plot and suggestive dialogue; the rustling of rich materials; the men in the rear with their tricorn hats in hand, their snickering laughter punctuated by loud guffaws.

The number of readings grew. "Every day," wrote a lady of rank, "persons were heard to say, 'I was present, or I shall be present, at a reading of Beaumarchais's piece.' " The more King Louis thundered, the more curious became the courtiers. The ranks of Beaumarchais's admirers and supporters reached into high places. They included a close friend of the queen's, the king's youngest brother, and Empress Catherine of Russia.

The king and the bevy of censors still demanded small changes; Beaumarchais grudgingly made even smaller ones. Emboldened by the growing public support, Beaumarchais made arrangements along with a few friends for a production at a small theater. On the day of the planned performance, when carriages were already converging on the theater entrance, it was canceled by direct order of the king, causing much resentment at court—muted and otherwise.

Rare murmurings of "oppression" and "tyranny" and the urging of Marie-Antoinette finally compelled the king to consent to a performance on the private property of a nobleman. The courtiers were amused to see themselves mocked and ridiculed, each apparently assuming the jibes to have been aimed only at the others.

The king finally relented. He had been assured that the play would fail, whether by friends or enemies of Beaumarchais is not certain, and he yielded in the hope that the feverish public demand for it would be dissipated. The first public performance was on April 27, 1784. Only half of those besieging the theater from eight in the morning were able to get tickets. About three hundred persons of rank shut themselves up in the players' dressing rooms as a means of assuring access. When the box office opened, so great was the crush that three persons were reported to have suffocated. Many forced their way in, throwing money at the doorkeepers as they did.

The president of the high court asked Beaumarchais if he could exchange his box tickets for ones on the ground floor. He was, he explained, taking several ladies who did not approve of the play and would only come if their presence could be concealed. Answered Beaumarchais: "I have given my piece to the public for their amusement, not their instruction; nor to offer prim fools the pleasure of thinking well of it inside a box on condition of speaking ill of it in society. I greet you, Mr. President, and keep your box."

The play was a tremendous success. Far more than *The Barber,* it won fame for its author and a fortune that he donated to a home for destitute mothers.

Living in Vienna at the time was the twenty-nine-year-old Wolfgang Amadeus Mozart. Like Beaumarchais, Mozart was a rebel. He had come to Vienna two years earlier after having been expelled from his employment by the archbishop of Salzburg. He left with a literal kick in the pants from the cleric who had lost patience with his musician's impudence.

Though performances of *The Marriage of Figaro* were banned in

Lorenzo da Ponte, librettist for Mozart's *Marriage of Figaro* and *Don Giovanni*. His weakness, and heedless quest, for beautiful women resulted in his expulsion from two countries. (Schenk, Erich. *Mozart and His Times*. New York: Alfred A. Knopf, 1959.)

Vienna by Emperor Joseph II as "too outspoken for a polite audience," he permitted its publication later that year. The translator exhibited a talent for humor himself by dedicating the book to the two hundred ducats he lost as a result of the emperor's prohibition on performances.

It also happened about this time that the musically oriented emperor experienced a growing distaste for the heavy German opera then in vogue. He called for the establishment of a first-rate Italian opera venture, which had been long neglected. The director of the Italian opera was Antonio Salieri, who was also court composer. The official theater poet was Lorenzo da Ponte.

Da Ponte's life had also not been dull. Born a Jew in a small Italian town, he, his brother, and his father were converted when da Ponte was only fourteen so that his father could remarry a Christian girl. Da Ponte studied for the priesthood, and was ordained at the age of twenty-four. He soon left it for a life of amorous adventure that would rival that of the fictitious Count Almaviva or da Ponte's real-life friend, Casanova. Nonetheless, he could describe in his memoirs his brief status as a priest as the only embarrassing incident of his life.

He left Italy hurriedly in 1779 following a scandal involving a married woman, for which he was convicted in Venice of adultery and public concubinage. He was sentenced to banishment for fifteen years, and threatened with seven years' imprisonment in a dungeon should he be apprehended in Venice. By the time the judgment was handed down, however, he was long gone, having been tried in his absence and having already taken up residence in Austria.

While still in Italy he made a mark as a promising literary talent, and when he arrived in Vienna in 1782 he was armed with letters of introduction to Salieri. His first collaboration as an opera librettist with Salieri was a failure for which Salieri blamed da Ponte. Salieri was thereafter only too happy to permit the poet to peddle his services elsewhere.

Da Ponte had met Mozart shortly after the composer's arrival in Vienna and had developed a respect for what he later described as "the sweep of Mozart's genius." He asked the composer for permission to write a libretto for him. Mozart agreed and had his own idea about what the libretto should be. He was familiar not only with the text of *The Marriage of Figaro* but also with an opera recently performed in Vienna, *The Barber of Seville* (the music was by Giovanni Paisiello; Rossini was not yet born), based on the earlier Beaumarchais play. Da Ponte was quick to accept the suggestion.

By November 1785 Mozart was working on the music, composing, Da Ponte said, as fast as he could write the verses. Writing twenty years after the fact, da Ponte claimed that it was he who persuaded the emperor to allow the performance of Mozart's opera in preference to two others submitted at the same time, including one by Salieri. He had, said da Ponte, given the emperor assurances of both the beauty of the music and the sanitary nature of the text.

Da Ponte's libretto follows the basic structure of the Beaumarchais play. It is tighter and shorter, but retains most of the play's story line and action, even much of the dialogue. However, with the exception of centering around the droit du seigneur and the manipulation of the Count by his valet, nearly everything that could have been considered objectionable by the aristocracy has been removed. In exchange for the satire, we have character portrayals that are deeper, more rounded, and more human.

Gone are the biting sarcasms. Gone also is the long fifth-act soliloquy, biographical in nature and full of bitter irony. It would be a trifle presumptuous to second-guess Mozart and da Ponte, but one is entitled to a fleeting regret for the absence of the aria those two could have made of it. It was the queen's reading of this very soliloquy that precipitated King Louis's outburst.

The opera was performed in Vienna on May 1, 1786. Audience reaction was described by one observer as lukewarm to cool, though it was repeated a number of times in that city. In December, however, it was performed to wildly appreciative audiences in Prague under the auspices of Pasquale Bondini, the theater director who had previously successfully produced Mozart's *The Abduction from the Seraglio*. The enthusiastic reception in Prague spoke well for the level of musical sophistication in that city. *The Marriage* was something new in opera, a kaleidoscope of intricate harmonies, far more complex than anything that had previously been heard on the operatic stage.

In January, Mozart was invited by a "company of distinguished connoisseurs and lovers of music" to hear a performance of the opera in Prague. He was heartened by the rousing reception of his opera in the Bohemian capital, and he and his wife, Constanze, had little hesitancy in making the three-and-one-half-day journey.

That Mozart's finely worked orchestration and vocal lines met with a better reception in Prague than in Vienna was not mere accident. Far more than Vienna, Prague was steeped in musical tradition; it exuded from every pore of Bohemian life. For centuries, families of wealth and nobility eagerly patronized young men who distinguished themselves in music, placed them in institutions to continue their education, then supported them until they found employment. The headmasters of schools were each obliged to write a new Mass every year to be performed with the students. Knowledge of music was often considered a prerequisite to employment as a servant, and even to service in the military. Until he could blow a bugle perfectly, a rifleman was not permitted to wear the uniform.

It is little wonder that the audiences of Prague could immediately appreciate this music that at the time was so avant-garde, intricate and complex beyond anything they had previously heard.

Mozart was lionized and idolized during what must have been among the happiest days of his short life. On January 15 he wrote a friend about a ball he had attended several days previously: "I was quite pleased to see all these people hopping about to the music of my

'Figaro' turned into waltzes and country dances; nothing is talked of here but 'Figaro.' " But even the Prague audiences could not have guessed that this was the first of many great operatic masterpieces that would become part of a permanent repertoire, a repertoire destined to last through the twentieth century, and that now seems poised to last for centuries more. After *The Marriage of Figaro* there followed a steady flow of such master works for about a hundred and fifty years; this one has held its own with the best of them.

The play has not fared so well. It is now a curiosity piece, and, except for Mozart's opera, might be played even less. Though Napoleon Bonaparte himself is said to have called it the "first shot" of the French Revolution, from the vantage point of 200 years it is difficult to take such claims literally. More likely, the same factors that fomented revolution made the play so popular. It was a timely play, but times change.

Many of the works of Beaumarchais are still widely read. But through the timeless art of Mozart and da Ponte, an even wider public sees the man himself, or as much of himself as he put into his Figaro, still portrayed on the living stage.

2

TIRSO DE MOLINA AND
THE DUKE OF OSUNA

DON GIOVANNI

THE PLOT: *Don Giovanni surreptitiously enters the apartment of Donna Ana, whose screams bring forth her father, the Commendatore. He challenges, then is killed by Giovanni, who proceeds on his way of amorous escapades. Hiding in a cemetery, he hears a statue of the Commendatore speak, swearing vengeance. He brazenly invites it to dinner. It actually appears, grasps Giovanni's hand, and demands that he repent his ways. When Giovanni refuses, he is dragged down to hell before the astonished guests.*

Just how late in life can a sinner repent and still avoid purgatory? Does a last-minute confession nullify a lifetime of wanton behavior? These were troubling questions on the minds of clerics and many laymen in sixteenth- and seventeenth-century Spain.

For a single offense, especially for a minor one, confession was certain to bring absolution. This belief was the theme of a legend of long standing in both Italy and Spain, and was the subject of popular ballads. They involved, in one form or another, a young man who kicks a skull that he finds lying near a cemetery, mockingly invites it to dinner, and is shocked when the ghost actually appears. In the course of the meal, the offender is either dragged down to hell for his sacrilege or is saved through confession, sometimes with the invoca-

9

Tirso de Molina, author of *The Trickster of Seville and the Stone Guest*. A sixteenth-century friar, the alleged profanity of his dramas often brought him into conflict with the religious order to which he belonged. (Edwards, Gwynne. *Tirso de Molina; The Trickster of Seville*. Warminster, Wiltshire, England: Aris & Phillips Ltd., Teddington House. Used by permission of Aris & Phillips Ltd., Wiltshire, England. Source of credit Anthony Stones.)

tion of some religious relic. In the latter case, of course, he learns an important lesson.

As with all legends, there is no one correct version, and this one showed up in many forms. A skull, skeleton, or statue may be the offended party, and, particularly in Spain, there was often a return invitation by the ghost or statue to its tormentor to dine with it. It is at this second meal, hosted by the supernatural figure, that the offender often faces his moment of truth.

In one of these versions, still told early in this century in the Spanish province of Segovia, the young man pulls the beard of a statue and brashly invites it to dinner. He is chilled to the bone when the statue arrives at his home, still more so when it offers a return invitation. Before going to the cemetery to keep the engagement, he makes his confession to a priest, and is given a cross for his protection. The meal, served by the black-robed servants of the dead man, is one of scorpions and vipers. The young man is stricken with fear, but escapes with a warning. Had he not partaken of the holy bread, says the ghost, he would have been obliged to join the other dead souls. Don't make fun of the dead, he adds to the world at large, or you, too, will be invited to dinner.

But what if the offense is more serious? Can a lifetime of criminal behavior be atoned for so easily? Therein lay the religious question, and therein lay a tale—quite literally.

The teller of the tale was Fray Gabriel Téllez. About 1620, give or take a few years, writing under the pseudonym of Tirso de Molina, he wrote a play, *The Trickster of Seville and the Stone Guest*, which had a point to make. What better way for an accomplished playwright to make it?

It was first published in 1630, but was probably performed a few years earlier. This was at the very midpoint of the golden age of Spanish drama, a time of a prodigious output of stage plays. Garcia Calderón penned at least 120; Tirso de Molina, 300; Lope de Vega, 800. This was the time also of Cervantes and Velázquez, of proliferating theaters with ingenious technical innovations, and traveling groups of itinerant actors.

In an age of very many great Spanish dramatists, Molina was, by all accounts, among the best half dozen of them. He was born in Madrid about 1580. In 1600 he joined the Mercedarian Order in Guadalajara, ultimately becoming a friar. His prolific output of dramatic works, which began not too long thereafter, more than once brought him into conflict with the Order, profanity being the main issue. Through various transfers commanded by the Order, he became familiar with a number of Spanish cities, including Seville, the setting for his *Trickster*.

Unlike the legend, the subject of *The Trickster of Seville* was not to be an innocent youth, guilty merely of a momentary indiscretion. Pulling the beard of a statue would be the least of his crimes.

Forty years before 1616, the earliest date on which it is believed *The Trickster* could have been written, there was born in the town of Osuna, near Seville, one Don Pedro Téllez-Girón, Marquis of Peñafiel, later to become known as the Duke of Osuna. He apparently cut a wide swath through the neighborhood, including especially Seville, marking his way with sexual escapades, swindling, cheating, brawling, and, finally, killing. His specialty seems to have been the sexual "trick," the word apparently carrying a different connotation from what it does today. To those familiar with the Mozart opera, the meaning, namely, disguising oneself as the husband or lover of the intended victim, will be clear enough.

The identity of the true name of Molina, namely, "Téllez," with one of those of the errant duke has not escaped notice, and, although the matter is by no means settled, the intriguing possibility exists that the author and the duke may be half-brothers. It is intriguing because, according to the researches of Gwynne Edwards, a scholar of Spanish literature, it is quite likely that the infamous Duke of Osuna is the model for Molina's Don Juan, the central character of the *Trickster*. The duke was notorious enough that shortly after his death in 1624 a play, *The Carefree Escapades of the Duke of Osuna*, centering around his sordid career, was written by a little-known playwright, Monroy y Silva.

Molina's play, however, was not a mere tale of the adventures of a murderous villain, any more than it was a mere retelling of the legend of the sacrilegious young man; he combined the two. It was a combination that was to have an impact on the literature of Europe with explosive force, and would become a legend of its own.

Molina's subject, Don Juan Tenorio, is frequently, throughout the drama, called upon by various characters to repent of his odious ways. His consistent response: There is plenty of time to pay the debt. In the climax of the play, Tenorio is impelled to pull the beard of a statue because the stone figure is a likeness of the elderly Don Gonzalo. Gonzalo had been murdered by Tenorio as he attempted to defend his daughter against Tenorio's designs, and Gonzalo's statue bears an inscription calling for vengeance against his murderer. As Tenorio plucks the stone beard, he cynically invites the statue to dinner so that it may there obtain its vengeance. At the dinner, the appearance of the statue panics everyone but Don Juan Tenorio, who, whatever his inward state, calmly finishes his meal. When he does, he is invited by the stone guest to dinner in the chapel.

As in the Spanish ballad, Tenorio accepts. He resolutely keeps his appointment, though he is obviously stricken with terror. We hear voices offstage offering advice to the world: Avoid the boast that there is time to pay the debt, for no sooner is it said than the debt must be paid. As in the ballad, Don Juan is served scorpions and snakes and a stew of fingernails. When the statue takes his hand, Tenorio begs, "Tell me who can I call to take my confession and absolve me." Answers the statue: "There is no time; you are too late."

The vision of a villain roasting in hell must be immensely satisfying to some need of the universal psyche. By all odds, the two most popular and enduring myths that have taken root in modern times are those of Faust and Don Juan, and the title characters of both are consigned to the flames before our very eyes. Like Faust, Molina's Don Juan hit a universal nerve, and the story of the reckless philanderer, finally getting his comeuppance from the statue of one of his victims, was irresistible. It was seized upon with a vengeance. Only thirty-five years after Molina's play, Molière authored *Don Juan or The Stone Guest,* and through the next century and a half, the story, in one form or another, spread across Europe.

For much of that time it was often treated as a burlesque and was a subject for low comedy. One example was a practice, usually improvised, in the late seventeenth-century Paris performances of a translation of the Molina play, under the title *The Invitation of the Statue.* It involved the scene that has come to be depicted in *Don Giovanni* by the "Catalogue Aria," the piece sung by Leporello to Donna Elvira as he unrolls, to the lady's horror, the interminably long list of names of his master's conquests. In these French performances of the play, it was the custom to allow the end of the roll to fall, as if by accident, into the audience. The roll was filled with the actual names of ladies from the town, and the audience would scramble to get a glimpse of the names on the list, getting a good laugh in the process.

At the beginning of the eighteenth century, *Don Juan or The Dinner Guest* became a vehicle for improvisation throughout Germany, reaching Vienna in 1716 and lasting there for fifty years as burlesque and puppet shows. In Paris, in 1713, came the first operatic treatment, a comedy known as *The Feast of the Statue.* In 1761, a ballet, *Don Juan,* by Gluck, was performed in Vienna, and sixteen years later, in Vienna and Prague there were performances of an opera called *The Stone Guest.* Two other operas of that name appeared in Italy in the 1780s and made their way throughout Europe.

In most of these representations, unlike in the Molina play, Don Juan is warned by the statue to repent, with the clear implication that repentance of his lifelong debauchery will save him much grief in the next world, to which he will shortly be dispatched. It is only through his own stubborn refusal that, as we soon hear, he is burning in hell. An unrepentant Don Juan was apparently more appealing than a contrite one.

The later of these two Italian operas of the eighties, first performed in Venice, was composed by Giuseppe Gazzaniga to a text by Giovanni Bertati, a famed and prolific librettist. According to Goethe, it was given in Rome every evening for a month, and, in the words of the great poet, "no one was satisfied who had not seen Don Juan roasting in hell, and the late lamented Commandant rising to heaven in a disembodied spirit." It is this opera that is the ancestor of the *Don Giovanni* we know today.

It was in the beginning of 1787, the same year in which the Gazzaniga opera was opening in Venice, that Mozart journeyed from Vienna to Prague to see his *Marriage of Figaro.* Following the discouraging reception of his opera in Vienna, Mozart found the enthusiasm of Prague exhilarating, and before leaving in early February, he signed a contract for a new opera to be produced in that city the following season.

Mozart was pleased with the libretto of *Figaro,* as he had every reason to be, and invited the librettist, Lorenzo da Ponte, to prepare one for his new opera. It was da Ponte who chose the story of the stone guest. He was very familiar with the libretto that Bertati had prepared for Gazzaniga, and he relied heavily on it. Although there are few incidents in da Ponte's libretto that are new, his three-dimensional characterizations and the tragicomic dramatic impact certainly are. Critics can, and do, find faults with the dramatic structure of the text, but as a poet da Ponte outclassed his competitors to almost as great a degree as Mozart did his.

He wrote the libretto together with two others, one for each of two other composers. Da Ponte has described for us how he worked during this period, twelve hours at a time, with a bottle of spirits on one side, his snuff on the other, and the inkstand before him. The landlady's daughter, a girl of sixteen, brought him coffee or cake, whenever he wished, according to him, and sometimes she brought just "her winsome little face, always gay and smiling, as if created to inspire poetical fancies and witty ideas." He wished, says da Ponte, that he could have felt only paternal affection for her. What an ideal librettist for *Don Giovanni*!

The completed libretto was delivered to Mozart in April. Though the composer was seriously ill in July, much of the composition was completed by September, at which time he returned to Prague. He stayed in the quiet solitude of the estate of a friend on the outskirts of the city, known as the Villa Bertramka, later a popular tourist attraction. There Mozart completed the rest of the composition except for the overture, which he did not complete until the early morning of October 28, the very day of the final rehearsal. The premiere was the following day.

Mozart's music won immediate, and lavish, praise in the Bohemian capital, where a reviewer for a major journal wrote that "its like has never before been heard in Prague." Scores of reviewers and thousands of opera patrons all across Europe, eventually including Vienna, were shortly to echo this judgment. Da Ponte's purple text earned some favorable comment in the Catholic south, but mostly condemnation in the Protestant north. Complained a Berlin reviewer in 1790: *Don Giovanni* "satisfies the eye, charms the ear, offends reason, insults morality, and treads wickedly upon virtue and feeling."

In Vienna there had been no public clamor for the opera, but it was performed nonetheless, beginning May 7, 1788, on the direct order of Emperor Joseph II. It was a dismal affair. The performances were less than satisfactory, and the audiences appreciated the music as little as they had *The Marriage of Figaro.*

The emperor himself did not see any of the first Vienna performances as he was soon to be off fighting a disastrous war with the Turks. He did not return until December 5, deathly ill and extremely unpopular. He attended a performance on December 15, but he was met with such icy hostility from the audience that he left before the conclusion. In matters of music he understood his subjects well. He sadly noted that *Don Giovanni* "is no food for the teeth of my Viennese," but whether intending to reflect on his Viennese or on Mozart's music is not clear. His own appreciation of the composer was greater, certainly, than that of the general public of that city; not so great, however, as that of the audiences of Prague. Mozart, like the apocryphal prophet, was honored everywhere except, at least in the beginning, in his own country.

Honored everywhere, but nowhere adequately paid, certainly not in Vienna, his city of residence. In December 1787 the emperor had appointed him chamber musician following the death of Gluck. No one seems to know exactly what that meant or entailed. His yearly salary was 800 florins. According to biographers writing in the mid-twentieth century, it amounted to about $360, hence some appropriate multiple of that figure in dollars of the 1990s. In any event, it was less than half that paid to Gluck, who had been given the title "orchestra conductor." Franz Joseph Haydn, whose admiration for Mozart was unbounded, pleaded with an official in Prague for a court appointment for "this unique Mozart," but to no avail.

Just a few months previously, a German traveling through Austria noted with chagrin the huge profits reaped by a mediocre soprano at a public concert, and wrote, "Artistic Talent, what can you expect of your fatherland, where people fight to hear a few arias poorly sung, while Mozart . . . is not even paid so much for a good concert as will cover his costs for it."

It fell on deaf ears. Within the space of one year, Mozart had written two of the supreme masterpieces of the operatic repertory. Both met with extraordinary popular success, and rendered stale, if not obsolete, everything that had gone before. His fee for the Prague performances of *Don Giovanni* was 100 ducats (about 200 mid-twentieth-century dollars); in Vienna, 50 ducats, not as bad for the times as it sounds today. But, inexplicably, *Don Giovanni* marks the beginning of the period of his direst financial straits. His correspondence becomes laced with pleas to friends seeking loans of small amounts, and forbearances for monies due.

In part, his problems were due to the protracted and costly war with the Turks, the financial burden of which fell on all, including musicians. But that explains only a small part of it. He was still receiving for his court concerts only half of what his rival, Antonio Salieri, received for his.

Some of his many biographers attempt to explain the reasons for such a bitterly ironic situation. They have not succeeded very well, probably because it is not explainable.

One treasure, however, he has kept all for himself. Faust, that other great modern legend, has been appropriated for all time by Goethe through his poetry, and by Gounod through his music. But the legend of Don Juan has never had its Goethe. It belongs only to Mozart.

3

THE FREEMASON OPERA

THE MAGIC FLUTE

THE PLOT: *Three ladies give Prince Tamino a picture of Pamina, daughter of the Queen of Night, telling him he may marry her if he can free her from her sorcerer captor. They give him a flute with magic power over human emotions. At the Temple of Reason, he learns that the High Priest, Sarastro, is not evil, but noble, and that Pamina is protected there from the sorceries of her mother. Pamina falls in love with Tamino, but they must pass ordeals of silence, fire, and water before being united, which they do with the aid of the magic flute.*

*T*he setting for Mozart's last opera, with its air of ethereal mystery, is the Temple of Isis in Egypt during the reign of Ramses I, who lived more than 3,300 years ago. He was the father of Seti I, without whom we might never have heard of the Temple of Isis. It stands at the once holy city of Abydos, about 275 miles south of Cairo.

It was Seti, sometimes called Sethos, who enlarged the Temple to its present grandiose scale, and elevated the god Osiris, his wife, Isis, and their child, Horus, to the loftiest niches in the Egyptian pantheon. Within the huge shrine, Seti constructed separate and splendid sanctuaries for each of the three deities, and, of course, did not forget to build a fourth one for himself. As completed after his death, the struc-

17

Emanuel Schikaneder, librettist for Mozart's *The Magic Flute.* The eccentric and mercurial entrepreneur ended his days in an insane asylum. (Schenk, Erich. *Mozart and His Times.* New York: Alfred A. Knopf, 1959.)

ture has often been called the most magnificent hall of pillars to be seen anywhere.

In *The Magic Flute,* homage is paid to the god and goddess by the chorus, and by Sarastro in his hauntingly majestic second-act aria, "O, Isis und Osiris." Osiris, in particular, was many things to the ancient Egyptians, including the god of the dead. Aided by magic spells, the souls of the deceased were obliged to seek his permission to enter the underground kingdom. It was to celebrate the many important dates in his legendary life that mysterious rites were performed by priests. And it was Osiris, according to the legends, who invented the flute that was to accompany ceremonial song, and who was the enemy of all violence. By flute and song alone, he subjugated nation after nation, winning over and disarming their inhabitants, a feat similar indeed to one of the more playfully humorous ones in Mozart's opera.

Thanks in large part to Seti's towering monument, the legends still captivated the minds of many Europeans in the time of the Enlightenment, three thousand years later. In the early part of the eighteenth century, visions of the flowing Nile, palm trees, sandy wastes, and majestic pyramids filled the imaginations of millions. It was inevitable that books on Egypt and things Egyptian would proliferate. One of the most popular was a novel, *Sethos,* published in 1731. It was claimed, falsely, by its author, Abbé Jean Terrasson, a French professor of philosophy, to be a translation of a book in Greek written in Roman times.

The novel was translated into several languages and was widely read half a century before the composition of *The Magic Flute.* The claim of Greek authorship was never believed, but it appears nonetheless that Terrasson was quickly accepted as an authority on the ancient initiation rites, and on the philosophy and world view of the priests.

The novel concerns an Egyptian prince, Sethos, who lived about the time of the real Sethos, or Seti, and includes an account of his education and initiation into the religious mysteries. Numerous incidents and characters of the opera, too many for mere coincidence, have counterparts in the novel. That the author of the opera libretto was familiar with the novel seems certain.

But there is more in the opera than story and characterizations. It is filled with esoteric rituals and exotic symbols. Where do they come from? They could have come from the novel. But they could also have come from the Secret Brotherhood of the Masonic Order, then a potent, if infamous, force in Europe. It is difficult to tell which, as the Masonic rituals themselves came in large part from that very book. The interest of the Brotherhood in the religious practices and symbolism of ancient Egypt stems from one of its oldest legends, reduced to writing in about 1390, in which the origins of the Order are traced back to that land about the fourth century B.C.

In 1717, just fourteen years prior to the publication of the Terrasson novel, Freemasonry began its highly organized existence with the formation of the Grand Lodge in England, and later took its rituals largely from *Sethos,* the then-popular novel. When *The Magic Flute* was first performed in 1791, a public controversy erupted. What excited the controversy was not its similarity to the fictional episodes of the sixty-year-old, little-remembered novel, but the public display of the supposedly secret rites of the living active organization of Freemasons.

Why should that have been controversial? Because Freemasonry, then a potent political force, was considered dangerous by both church and state, and was discouraged, outlawed, and often persecuted by both. Their enmity was only heightened by the Freemasons' well-guarded secrecy. Royal suspicion had reached its peak at the time of the French Revolution, just two years before the opera was produced. Many a crowned head thought that revolution was fomented, at least in part, by the lodges.

The suspicion had begun early on, and was intensified by the wildfirelike spread of the Order. Within fifty years following the founding of the Grand Lodge, others sprang up in all parts of the world. In 1742 came the first Vienna lodge, The Three Firing Glasses. Among the members was Francis of Lorraine, the husband of the Archduchess Maria Theresa. That did not stop her from closing it the following year with a raid on the lodge, obliging her husband to escape by the back stairs. The members, her husband included, continued to meet in secret. Two more lodges had been formed by the time of her death in 1780, and four more in the balance of the reign of her more liberal son, Emperor Joseph II.

What caused the suspicion in the first place? As we know from *The Magic Flute,* such concepts as reason and wisdom are very much enmeshed in the Masonic scheme of things. A letter, published and distributed by a lodge in Bordeaux shortly after the French Revolution, spoke of the basic Masonic precepts of freedom, equality, justice, and tolerance. In the eighteenth century these were dangerous ideas. Benjamin Franklin and Alexander Hamilton were Freemasons, and neither they, nor the ideas espoused in the new American Constitution endeared themselves to the European monarchy. As for the Church, it could not tolerate the secrecy and placed the Order off-limits to its flock.

In 1784 Mozart joined the Lodge Zur Wohltätigkeit, or the Lodge of Benevolence. Despite the name, it was, according to at least one biographer, considered a "gorging and boozing lodge," a description at odds, however, with those of some other writers. Shortly thereafter the lodge was merged with another where Mozart attained the grade of master.

It was in May 1791 that a theatrical jack-of-all-trades, Emanuel Schikaneder, approached Mozart in Vienna with the idea of an opera on a theme involving magic. The subject was one of great attractive power, he claimed, and Mozart was just the man to compose the music. The opera was to be presented by Schikaneder's own troupe at his Theater auf der Wieden. Mozart accepted.

Both men were down on their luck. Mozart had just lost his great benefactor, Joseph II, who died in March 1790, and under the new emperor, Leopold II, was faring none too well. He was reduced to borrowing from friends and usurers.

There were probably other reasons that might, in any event, have prompted him to accept. He had known Schikaneder from Salzburg about eleven years previously. Like Mozart, Schikaneder was a Mason, and he was the employer of Mozart's sister-in-law, a soprano, Josefa Hofer. Then, too, his good friend and collaborator, da Ponte, had recently been obliged to leave Austria for much the same reason he had come to that nation from Italy in the first place—scandals with women. So he was in need of a librettist. And Mozart yearned to write a German opera, not having written one to a German text in eight years. But the prime motivation was undoubtedly his desperate need for money.

The forty-year-old Schikaneder was not doing too well himself, being then in the midst of one of his many periods of financial embarrassment. By turns a wandering musician, entrepreneur, actor, and poet, at heart he was always a showman, trying to keep his finger on the pulse of what the public wanted, whether a rodeo, low comedy, musical, or anything else to which paying customers might be attracted. Ancient mysteries and magic were very much in the air, and his showman's instincts had sensed that there was profit to be made from it.

Ancient mysteries and magic were one thing. But why would Schikaneder and Mozart choose to get it from sources whose secrecy they had sworn to uphold? Any answer is speculative. But political circumstances may give a clue.

The new emperor, Leopold II, had little tolerance for the Masons, and it appeared that in Vienna their days were numbered. In August 1790, a retired gubernatorial secretary complained bitterly that the "wheel of the . . . revolutions in Europe is driven by the Brotherhood of Freemasons." Four months later, an official memorandum of the Viennese government made the same accusation. "The defection of the English colonies in America," it claimed, "was the first operation of this secret ruling élite . . . and there can be no doubt that the overthrow of the French Monarchy is the work of such a secret society." And, the memorandum added ominously, there was no reason to believe the Masons intended to rest there.

Two possibilities come to mind. First, that the public display of the secrets by Schikaneder and Mozart resulted from a desire to make a statement about the benevolent nature of the society and thereby combat the fierce hostility. The second possibility was a perception that the Freemasons were an all-but-defunct society anyway, and that it no longer mattered; the Order was dead and they might as well take what profits they could from the carcass.

Neither Mozart nor Schikaneder ever showed much revolutionary zeal or inner fire for any cause other than opera or theater. So it is the latter motivation that seems a better bet. If this was the motivation, their premonition was correct. The official hostility was too great. The Austrian lodges disbanded in 1792, less than a year after the first performance of the opera.

Whatever the rationale for making the secret rites public, by no means were all other members of the Brotherhood in accord. It was a fateful decision, causing bitterness for some, and it hounded Mozart to the grave and beyond.

That was not the only controversy sparked by this problematic libretto. Credit for the text, or blame, depending on the point of view, is almost universally ascribed to Schikaneder alone in opera programs and publications. But in the middle of the nineteenth century, a German opera director publicized a claim made in 1818 by one Karl Gieseke, a gentleman of avowedly unblemished reputation, to have written practically the entire libretto himself. Some believe it; some don't. Few cared, as for many decades the text was dismissed as second-rate. In recent times, however, the argument has heated up a bit as scholars have begun to claim, as scholars will, to see in it some very important and profound philosophical thought concealed in intricate symbolism. Others still see nothing but nonsense.

The most convincing comment may still be that of the great English musicologist, Ernest Newman, writing in the 1920s. He dis-

missed the question as one of no importance, noting that "The greater part of the text is miserable hack work that would be within the powers of anyone who could handle a pen." His remarks were arguably the pithiest, though not the first of their kind. Before him, Professor Edward J. Dent, a Mozart scholar, termed the libretto "one of the most absurd specimens of that form of literature in which absurdity is only too often a matter of course."

The premiere came on September 30, 1791, at Schikaneder's Theater auf der Wieden, sometimes known as the Freihaus Theater, located in a huge complex of houses connected by large courtyards. A resident of the area who attended a performance there a few years later described how, in order to get a cheap ticket, it was necessary to arrive at mid-afternoon and sit for three hours "bathed in heat and sweat and impregnated by the garlicky fumes of the smoked meats being consumed."

Despite a lukewarm first-night reception, the opera ran for a hundred straight performances in the Freihaus and was quickly picked up by houses throughout Europe. Of all of Mozart's operas it was his greatest popular success. Prospects of new commissions gave promise for a brighter future, but it came too late. In mid-November, Mozart, depressed and ill, took to his bed. Watch in hand, he would follow in his imagination the performances of his *Magic Flute*.

Both the use of the previously secret rituals, and its inherent acknowledgment of his status as a Mason caused problems for him in his remaining few months of life, and another at his death. Just hours before he died, his sister-in-law, Sophie Weber, at the insistence of his wife, Constanze, left the house to seek a priest at St. Peter's. "I did this," said Sophie later, "but the priests long refused, and I had a great deal of difficulty persuading one of those inhuman clerics to come." Neither those in attendance nor Mozart's biographers doubted that it was his openly avowed Masonic membership that made them pause.

Shortly after midnight on December 5 he brushed aside Constanze's assurances of a favorable report from the physician: "Now I must die when I could care for you and the children. Ach, now I leave you unprovided for." A few moments later he was dead, at not quite thirty-six years of age.

The nemesis of the publicized rituals followed him to his unmarked pauper's grave. The theory, thoroughly discredited, that Mozart died from poisoning by the court composer Antonio Salieri is well known. Those who have not heard of it otherwise have heard of it through the play *Amadeus,* no less effective as drama for its lack of factual basis. Not so well known is the suspicion in some dubious quarters that he was murdered by the Brotherhood of Freemasons.

In 1861 a book was published by one Georg Friedrich Daumer, a vocally religious researcher into whatever matters of antiquities seized his fancy. Its thesis was that through his rather harsh portrayal of the Queen of the Night, intended, it was claimed, as a portrayal of Maria Theresa, and use of religious music in his choral pieces, Mozart had provoked a revenge death plot among the Masons. There the matter rested until 1936, when Mathilde Ludendorff, wife of the Nazi general Erich Ludendorff, took up the cause. She suggested the composer's participation in an intricate plot, in which his opera played an important part, to rescue Marie-Antoinette from her captors, allegedly Masons. This resulted in a remarkably convoluted and successful counterplot against him.

In 1958, a Dr. Gunther Duda expressed his professional dissatisfaction with the medical cause given for Mozart's death, proposing that the evidence of both death and burial was consistent only with an execution, probably by the Masons. For good measure he credited them also with the death of Schikaneder in 1812, by then hopelessly insane, some twenty years after the Masons were disbanded in Vienna. He also pinned on them the death of Gieseke in 1833.

In 1966 came Dr. Johannes Dalchow and two more books, coauthored by Dalchow, Duda, and a German physician, Dr. Dieter Kerner. In these, the interesting element of ritualistic sacrifice to Masonic deities surfaces.

In recent years these claims have been proved to be as absurd as they sound. All of the medical records of Mozart's illnesses, not only his terminal one, as well as accounts of his symptoms and behavior, have been examined by respected medical professionals. All likely poisonous agents existing at Mozart's time and their effects have been considered. The most definitive work is that of one Dr. P. J. Davies, the results of which were published by him in 1984.

Mozart died of streptococcal infection, renal failure, bronchopneumonia, and cerebral hemorrhage. He was not poisoned by the Masons or anyone else. But the Masonic Order played a role in his life, and a huge one in his final opera. And it will apparently continue to do so in the legends that survive this unique, and still mysterious, musical genius.

Beethoven. A portrait in oils by Isidor Neugass ca. 1806 depicts the suspicious, contentious composer at the time of the first revision of his much revised *Fidelio*. (Solomon, Maynard. *Beethoven*. New York: Shirmer Books, 1977.)

THE RELUCTANT
OPERA COMPOSER

FIDELIO

THE PLOT: *Pizzaro, the prison governor at Seville, has imprisoned Florestan, a political enemy. Florestan's wife, Leonora, disguised as a boy, Fidelio, obtains work with the jailer. She plans secretly to rescue him. The Prime Minister plans to inspect the prison, and Pizzaro, fearing discovery of his mistreatment of Florestan, plans to kill the prisoner. Leonora accompanies the jailer, who is ordered to dig a grave, and when Pizzaro attempts to stab Florestan, she stops him with a drawn pistol. The Minister arrives, discovers the persecution, and frees Florestan.*

*I*t was late October 1805 and Napoleon's armies were bearing down on Vienna. On the thirtieth they entered nearby Salzburg and many persons of wealth and nobility fled the Austrian capital. On November 13 a vanguard of the French army, fifteen thousand strong, entered the city in full battle order, flags flying and bands playing. Routine activities came to a halt as crowds gathered to watch. Mingling among them may have been Ludwig van Beethoven as the rehearsal for *Fidelio*, then called *Leonora*, scheduled to open on the twentieth, had undoubtedly been suspended. If so, he probably watched with a good deal of bitterness and resentment, for he had become deeply disillusioned with the French emperor and his promise of liberty.

27

So it was that under these worst of circumstances *Fidelio* was performed at the Theatre an der Wien. The usual audience had either fled or was unable to reach the theater as the city had been closed to the suburbs. The entire attendance consisted of a few close friends and admirers and a number of French officers who understood neither the German words nor the strange music. They had been looking for lighter fare. The original score was in three acts and was considerably longer than the revised and refined two.

Beethoven was the musical heir to Mozart, and with his *Eroica Symphony,* two years earlier, he had broken free of the restraints of any mold. His symphonies and other instrumental work bore the stamp of his own unique genius. But he had never written an opera; this was his first, and would be his last.

The first performance pleased the reviewers as little as it did the sparse audience. According to one periodical, the music was ". . . way below the expectation of amateur and professional alike," lacking that "happy clear magical impression" that abounded in Mozart. According to another report, the second performance, on the twenty-first, was played to an "empty house." The house could not have been completely empty, however, as it was obviously attended by a visiting Englishman, more perceptive than most spectators, who wrote in his journal that "intricacy is the character of Beethoven's music, and it requires a well practiced ear, or frequent repetition to understand and appreciate its beauties."

Whatever the reason, after the third performance, Beethoven withdrew the opera in disgust.

It might have died right then and there. But a few friends and wealthy patrons, led by Prince Karl Lichnowsky and his princess, Christine, conspired to convince the contentious, fiercely defensive composer that alterations and deletions were imperative. They knew it would not be easy. At the rehearsals, the singers had begged him to make changes, calling many of his lines unsingable, but he had been unwilling to make the slightest concession. Nonetheless, too much in the opera cried out to be saved to let it sink out of sight without a struggle.

They arranged a meeting with Beethoven at the home of the prince. The strategy was to perform the opera in its entirety, to make clear to him that cuts and changes were needed, and to discuss with him on the spot the most effective alterations. The performance began at 7 P.M., with Princess Lichnowsky at the piano, accompanied only by a violinist. Two male voices took all the singing roles.

The group was expecting resistance, but was not prepared for the ferocity of it. Even those closest to him had never seen the explosive composer quite so excited. He sat on a makeshift podium under a great chandelier, the massive score in his lap, refusing to make a single cut. The battle lasted until one in the morning. Extremely agitated and disgusted, he was about to flee when the princess, who had befriended him for many years, embraced him and pleaded with him to do what he must to save his "child," a term bound to strike home with the childless, unmarried Beethoven. She also invoked the name of his deceased mother, a reference that always brought tears to his eyes. Beethoven melted, returned the embrace, and gave her his promise to review the opera.

Shortly thereafter he went to work with Stephan von Breuning, another of the friends who had been present at the Lichnowskys and who undertook the task of altering the libretto. The three acts were made into two; three arias were eliminated from the first act, one of which, Rocco's "Gold Aria," was later restored, and the entirety was shortened and tightened considerably. A performance of the modified opera was scheduled for March.

The changes in the text apparently raised a ticklish problem. The librettist for the opera had been Joseph Sonnleithner, the manager of the theater, and an impresario of considerable reputation in Vienna. Sonnleithner's libretto was based on a French opera that had been produced five years earlier under the title *Leonora, or Conjugal Love.* It, in turn, was based on a reputedly real-life incident occurring in France during the reign of terror. It had already been translated into Italian and set to music by an Italian composer.

Copyright laws in much of Europe at the time were such that artists stole each other's themes with impunity. But despite the absence of any legal complications resulting from the change in the text, Beethoven needed, or wanted, the libretto to be printed with Sonnleithner's name. He wrote a hurried note to the librettist shortly before the scheduled performance, asking for a "small statement in writing" permitting the use of his name on the altered libretto. He claimed to have made all of the changes himself and did not mention von Breuning. Nor did he send Sonnleithner a copy of the new text, claiming that time was too short. In a postscript he asked that the permission be granted at once, claiming to need it to show to the censor. Much of the note appears contrived, and the motive is a mystery.

In addition to the other changes, Beethoven composed a new overture, the towering piece known as the "Leonora Overture No. 3," which is usually performed today before or between the scenes of the second act. Beethoven persisted in calling the opera *Leonora;* the theater managers persisted in *Fidelio* because of the similarity in the title *Leonora* with that of several other current operas. The managers ultimately won out.

The work in its new form was produced on March 29, 1806. Despite the enthusiasm of the small but growing audiences and the favorable reaction of the journals, it was withdrawn after five performances by the pathologically suspicious Beethoven. He had somehow become convinced that the opera had not only been ill-performed but that it had been bungled purposely. No one, including Beethoven, has suggested any possible motive for this.

Then, he grossly overestimated the receipts, finally accusing the theater director, Baron Peter von Braun, of cheating him. Von Braun's patient reasoning had little effect. In a boisterous confrontation, the baron tried to calm Beethoven. Up to now, only the relatively few higher-priced seats were occupied, he explained. Perhaps as the opera's popularity grew, the galleries would also be filled.

"I don't write for the galleries," roared Beethoven.

"My dear sir," responded the astonished von Braun, "even Mozart did not disdain to write for the galleries."

"I will not give my opera anymore. I want my score back."

The baron rang for his assistant and ordered the delivery of the *Fidelio* score. Beethoven left with it, and the opera was not heard again until 1814.

The 1814 revival was sparked by Georg Treitschke, a poet and stage manager active in the management of the Kärntnertor Theatre. He was seeking an opera to perform without cost and turned to the abandoned *Fidelio*. Beethoven's fame had spread in the intervening years, and it was felt certain that his opera would draw large crowds. Beethoven agreed, but over time he had come to see many of the work's faults. He wanted still more changes before any further performance. Treitschke, this time with Sonnleithner's permission, took up the libretto and rewrote it almost from beginning to end. Once more, scenes were adjusted and rearranged. The new version of the opera was performed at the Kärntnertor on May 23 with still another new overture, this being the one that opens modern-day performances.

This time it was an unqualified success. Beethoven was called out after the first act and greeted with a storm of applause. He later wrote in his daybook: "It is certain that one writes best when one writes for the public." That the man who wrote that had, nine years earlier, said "I do not write for the galleries" may not be so ironic as it has seemed to some biographers.

That summer Beethoven inserted an announcement in the Vienna *Friedensblätter* entitled "A word to his admirers." It read:

> How often in your chagrin that his depth was not sufficiently appreciated have you said that van Beethoven composes only for posterity? You have no doubt been convinced of your error since, if not before the general enthusiasm aroused by his immortal opera *Fidelio,* and also that the present kindred souls and sympathetic hearts for that which is great and beautiful without withholding its just privileges for the future.

The German syntax is no less fractured than this English translation, but the meaning is clear enough. One can only guess at the depth of Beethoven's frustration upon being repeatedly told, by even the most well-meaning of his admirers, that he was writing for the future and that he could not be understood in his own day. That beneath the contemptuous disdain of the opinion of others, this uncompromising, creative talent, no less than other mortals, craved the approval of living audiences, should come as a surprise to no one.

5

THE USELESS
PRECAUTION

THE BARBER OF SEVILLE

THE PLOT: *Rosina is the ward of the elderly Bartolo. Count Al-maviva, disguised as a commoner, courts her, but is frustrated by Bartolo, who wants her dowry for himself. The Count meets the barber, Figaro, an arranger. On his advice the Count enters the home, claiming to be Rosina's music teacher substituting for the real one, Basilio, who is supposedly ill. Basilio turns up, but the barber bribes him, first to feign illness, then to substitute the Count's name for Bartolo's on the marriage contract. But Bartolo is mollified when he is given her dowry.*

They were rolling on the floor with laughter that first night, but not for reasons that Rossini and his librettist intended. Even the most sympathetic audience would have had trouble restraining laughter at the unfolding series of disasters. But, for several reasons, this was no sympathetic audience.

First there was the circumstance that the Beaumarchais play, *The Barber of Seville*, had been the subject of an opera by the reigning master of the Italian genre, Giovanni Paisiello. True, that had been thirty-four years before. True also that the play had been the subject of two other musical efforts prior to Paisiello's work, four more between Paisiello's and Rossini's 1816 premiere, and that another offering in Dresden was opening at the same time. Nonetheless, the

Paisiello opera was still popular in Rome, and the dictatorial old composer still had a massive following in that city.

So Rossini and his librettist, Cesare Sterbini, inserted as a preface to the libretto a "Notice to the Public" avowing Rossini's respect and veneration for the older man. They also thought it best, in deference to Paisiello, to give the opera a different name: *Almaviva, or the Useless Precaution*. The irony of that subtitle could not later have been lost on them. Their own precaution was a waste. Admirers of Paisiello were obviously chagrined and were not to be placated by any announcement or change of name.

Then there was the annoyance of the regular patrons of the Theatre Valle at having to attend this performance at the Theatre Argentina instead of their usual haunt. The reason for the use of the Argentina was the manipulation by the owner to have it, rather than the Valle, designated as the theater for opera buffa for the 1816 season. He then contracted with the twenty-four-year-old Rossini for a new opera in an attempt to boost his sagging fortunes.

Neither theater was any bargain. This was Rome, not Milan or Dresden. The papal government did not recognize the existence of theaters at all, and they were designated as temporary structures. A recent petition by the city's theatergoers to improve them was met with the reply that Rome was a city of churches, not theaters. An Irish novelist, Lady Sydney Morgan, described the theaters of Rome at the time as "dark, dirty and paltry in their decorations" and "offensive to the senses; disgusting in details of their arrangements." And what does Lady Morgan offer as the prime example of these wretched conditions? "The corridors of the Argentina," she complains, "exemplify the nastiness of the Roman habits and manners more forcibly than volumes could describe."

Apparently the artistic standards were no better. Two years later, when Percy Bysshe Shelley, the English poet, attended the Theatre Valle to see a performance of Rossini's *Tancredi,* he wrote that it was the worst he had ever experienced. The orchestra consisted of all amateurs, and "Rossini did not know whether to be more appalled that his barber played the clarinet, or that the clarinettist turned out to be his barber."

Such was the background when Rossini took his place at the piano that night of February 20 wearing what was described as an ostentatious Spanish-style coat with gold buttons. Now it happens that many years later while living in Paris, Rossini met with Richard Wagner and boasted that he had written the music to *The Barber* in 13 days and had been paid for it with 1,200 francs and a nut-colored coat with gold buttons that the impresario had given him. According to Rossini, the coat was worth another 100 francs and he had thus been paid a hundred francs a day for his efforts, compared to the measly two and one-half francs a day his father had earned as a musician. But he did not tell the Meister of the uproar it caused when he showed up on opening night wearing it. It met with instant derision from the audience, complete with hoots and catcalls.

When the audience finally quieted, the overture began. As to what overture it was, Rossini's biographers cannot agree. The one we hear today was not the one Rossini first intended for the opera. That one has been lost, whether before the first performance or later seems much in doubt. The one he first planned to use had already been used by him with two other operas in two other cities in recent years. When it was lost, whether during the frenetic pace of the last days' rehearsals, or later, the resourceful Rossini simply substituted another overture that had been used in three of his other operas in three other cities. It is that overture that we hear today. The one that was played that opening night, whichever one it was, went well. It was the last thing that did.

After the curtain rises, Almaviva enters to serenade Rosina with his guitar. He starts to pluck at it, but a string breaks and the audience roars with laughter. They no sooner settle down than Figaro enters, and what is he carrying but another guitar! Will this one break too? More hilarity. Upon the first entrance of Rosina, played by Giorgi Righetti, to whom we are indebted for the best account of the evening's activities, she is roundly whistled at by the libidinous male members of the audience. Don Basilio trips over an open trapdoor, cuts his nose, and is distracted during his big aria, "La Calumnia," by attempts to stanch the flow of blood. The audience whistles, shouts, and laughs, as it does for the balance of the first act. When the act finally ends, Rossini rises from his seat amid the jeering of the audience and applauds the singers who undertook such a brave fight against hopeless odds. For this insolent dissent from the judgment of the audience he is loudly hissed.

The second act is barely heard above the laughter, talk, and shouting. During the finale, a cat enters. The audience is now in stitches as Figaro chucks it off to one side. It leaves. Big sighs of relief from the cast. A moment later it enters from the other side and hurls itself into the arms of Bartolo. The audience calls out to it, meows, and encourages it to take a more active role.

At the end Rossini quietly went home, got in bed, and either went to sleep, as he claimed, and some believed, or feigned sleep in order to avoid facing the cast members who came to offer their sympathy, as some others believed. According to friends who knew him best, Rossini was not so thick-skinned as he sometimes liked to pretend.

After that first night, remarkably, the revelers went home and the audience that came the second night came to listen. But Rossini was not there to witness this triumph. He pretended illness to avoid the experience of another debacle, but was awakened by cheering crowds approaching his hotel. Despite the assurances of his Almaviva, Manuel Garcia, that the noise was friendly enthusiasm, Rossini told the tenor what they could do with their bravos, and hid in the stable. The frustrated music lovers hit Garcia with an orange and broke two of the windows of Rossini's empty room.

The Barber of Seville has been the subject of countless accolades over the years, but the ultimate tribute must have been that delivered to Rossini personally, however grudgingly, during a visit to Vienna six years after its debut.

After many unsuccessful attempts to arrange a meeting with Beethoven, Rossini finally succeeded through the efforts of Giuseppi Carpani, an Italian poet living in Vienna. It must have been an interesting, but strange, meeting. Rossini was thirty, wealthy, ebullient, and cocky. Beethoven was fifty-two, in failing health, deaf, eccentric, cantankerous, and living in squalor, but now more than ever a giant among giants. It was 1822. This was the Beethoven of the *Missa Solemnis* and the final piano sonatas, and we may assume that Rossini, his outsized ego notwithstanding, was awed to be in his presence.

Owing to Beethoven's deafness, Carpani was obliged not only to translate but to write for him all of Rossini's remarks. When Rossini and Carpani entered, Beethoven was correcting manuscripts, apparently lost in his silent world. Finally he looked up and exclaimed:

"Ah, Rossini. So you're the composer of *The Barber of Seville*. I congratulate you. It will be played as long as Italian opera exists. Never try to write anything else but opera buffa; any other style would do violence to your nature."

Carpani interrupted with a scribbled note. Rossini had already composed a large number of serious operas, he reminded Beethoven. Carpani himself had sent him the scores to examine.

"Yes," grumbled the churlish Beethoven, "I looked at them. Opera seria is ill-suited to the Italians. You do not know how to deal with real drama."

Even in the best of days Beethoven was not renowned for his tact. He preferred to lay it on the line. After some further conversation he saw his guests to the door, then called out to the departing Rossini, "Remember, give us plenty of *Barbers*."

But seven years later, Rossini quit composing. He spent his time composing only short pieces for special occasions, nursing various illnesses, including a debilitating bout with gonorrhea, and enjoying his fortune. He gave lavish parties and entertained composers, singers, and critics, first in various cities in Italy, then in Paris, where he died at the age of seventy-six. He gave us no more *Barbers*.

6

AN OPERA IN TWO WEEKS

THE ELIXIR OF LOVE

THE PLOT: *Adina, a wealthy village girl, flirts with Nemorino and Belcore, an army sergeant. Dulcamara hawks a "love potion," really only wine. Nemorino enlists in his rival's unit for money for the potion. He does not yet know that his rich uncle has died, leaving everything to him, and thinks the sudden attention from the village girls is due to the potion. Adina, who loves him, fears she will lose him. But when she buys his release from the army, the couple confess their love. The crowd credits the potion, and deluges Dulcamara with orders for bottles of their own.*

*T*he manager of Rome's Canobbiana Theatre was extremely agitated. Rehearsals for a new opera were to begin in two weeks, and the composer who had promised the opera had failed to deliver. Only two weeks to find a substitute for it! He approached—who else—Gaetano Donizetti.

It was a logical move. At the age of thirty-five, Donizetti was known to work at a white heat and had already reached, in full measure, that prolific output that is awesome to contemplate. How prolific? Numbers tell the story: He wrote his first opera at nineteen, his last in 1844 at age forty-seven just before his complete mental collapse. Between those two works, he wrote seventy-five other complete operas and almost six hundred and fifty other musical compositions.

Throughout his career, he alternated continuously between comic and serious opera and he wrote at a furious pace. When told that Rossini claimed to have written *The Barber of Seville* in thirteen days, he replied: "Ah! Rossini always was a lazy fellow."

Numbers, of course, do not tell the whole story of Donizetti. Behind the statistics we see tantalizing hints of a fascinating individual. The wife of Felice Romani, his librettist, described Donizetti in a book published long after his death as a handsome man, tall and slender with curly black hair, "likeable beyond all description and the fair sex went mad for him."

He had shown musical talent early on in Bergamo, the city of his birth. At age eighteen, he was recommended for what was reputedly the finest music school in Italy, one from which Rossini had only recently emerged. But during the next few years, contributing to the support of his parents, about to marry and driven by a need for money, he wrote operas to second-rate texts. His ninth opera, *Zoraide di Granata,* was the first to catch fire with the public. But it was not until his *Anna Bolena* in 1830, to a text by Romani, that his success as a composer was sealed.

Romani had quit his budding career in law to write opera texts and had become the most sought-after Italian librettist of the time. Before his death in 1865 he had written over 100 of them for many composers, including Rossini, Bellini, and Meyerbeer. His first text for Donizetti was in 1822. He seemed to have an irritating habit of contracting for more work than he could handle, and for delivery on schedules that he could not possibly meet. This was to cause Donizetti much grief, though for *L'Elisir d'Amore,* Romani came through in splendid form for him and the manager of the Canobbiana Theatre.

To the manager of that theater it did not matter that two months earlier Donizetti and Romani had bombed at Milan's La Scala with the composer's thirty-seventh opera. In desperate circumstances, he begged Donizetti to come up with something, anything. Maybe some old score could be reworked, his or someone else's.

Replied Donizetti: "Who is making fun of me? I am not in the habit of patching up an opera of my own—and never that of other composers." He would, said Donizetti, write a brand-new opera in fourteen days! "I give you my word. Now send Felice Romani to me here."

Said the composer to his librettist: "I am obliged to set a poem to music in fourteen days. I give you one week to prepare it for me. We'll see which of us two has the more guts."

"It bodes well," he joked to Romani, "that we have a German prima donna, a tenor who stammers, a buffo who has the voice of a goat, a French basso who isn't worth much . . . courage, march on."

For this opera, Romani took his story from the text of *Le Philtre* by Augustin-Eugène Scribe, the best-known French librettist of the day. Scribe himself had "borrowed" the plot from elsewhere to prepare his libretto for Daniel Auber, who composed the music for *Le Philtre* in 1831, only a year before Donizetti's *Elixir*. *Le Philtre* was a popular opera, which was to be performed at the Paris Opéra over 240 times during the next 30 years. Romani's text, with some significant changes from Scribe's libretto, was entitled *L'Elisir d'Amore*, or, in English, *The Elixir of Love*.

On April 24, 1832, Donizetti advised his father that in the coming week he would start rehearsals for the opera even though he had not yet finished the composition. The general rehearsal was on May 11 and the premiere on the following night. It was an instant success. Many of Donizetti's operas were, but *L'Elisir* is only one of five or six of them to survive and continue as part of the standard repertory. Writing to his former music teacher in Bergamo four days after the premiere, Donizetti said that the Milanese journals judged his opera and spoke of it "too well, believe me, . . . too well."

The opera ran at the Canobbiana Theatre for thirty-two performances. Hector Berlioz, the French composer, saw one of them but walked out before the conclusion. His reasons for doing so tell us more about the state of the Italian theater at the time than about the opera. He had to strain his ears to hear the music, he complained, as, "The people talk, gamble, sup and succeed in drowning out the orchestra."

Perhaps one of Donizetti's most enduring legacies is one that would be impossible to describe or measure: his influence on the genius of Giuseppe Verdi. When Verdi began to compose, Bellini was dead, Rossini had almost quit writing, and Donizetti reigned as the master of Italian opera. In his adolescence, Verdi had gone again and again to Milan's La Scala to hear Donizetti's works. Verdi's wife-to-be, Giuseppina Strepponi, an accomplished soprano, also had a particular fondness for them and later sang in two of them, including *L'Elisir d'Amore.*

Verdi's admiration for the older composer continued throughout his life. To Donizetti's offer to supervise the rehearsals of one of his early operas, he responded at once: "My notes can only derive great benefit when Donizetti devotes his thoughts to them . . . to you, Signor Cavaliere, I will pay no compliments. You belong to the small number of men who have sovereign genius and need no individual praise."

But terrible times lay ahead. In 1837, at the age of twenty-nine, his wife, Virginia, died from complications following childbirth. The infant son also died. Within the previous eight years, Donizetti had lost two other children and both parents. Now he was desolate. Twelve days later he wrote his deceased wife's brother, "Why do I labor on . . . I beg you on my knees, come here in October. Perhaps you can be of some comfort to me . . . and I to you."

In mid-October 1844, Donizetti received a miniature portrait of himself and affixed to it these gloomy words: "Ah! It is not true, they lie. So young I am not. The days of rejoicing are past for my poor heart. In the future, I see only the tomb closing over me." He was forty-eight and living in Vienna. It was not the last time in the next few months he was to suffer premonitions of death before his complete breakdown in Paris the following year.

The final chapter of his life is one of dark tragedy, though the full story of it remains an enigma. The accounts of his life tell of increasing sexual excesses, his frequent company with the prostitutes of Vienna, and of his final mental and physical degeneration. Among his contemporaries, there is much mawkish sentimentalizing on the one hand and moral posturing on the other—and what each calls cause, the other calls result.

What is known is, that complaining bitterly of what the harsh Viennese winter had done to his nerves, he moved to Paris in July 1845, and that his friends there were shocked by his appearance. In January, after increasing symptoms of severe mental disorder, he was certified insane and confined to a mental institution at Livry, near Paris. Sixteen months later, paralyzed and semiconscious, the authorities, after much controversy, permitted him to move to a private home in Paris provided by his family. There they tried to arouse some faint sign of recognition from him. They were unsuccessful, even through the medium of music, except for an excerpt from the "Mad Scene" in *Lucia di Lammermoor.* According to an account by Giovanni Ricordi, his publisher: "At the first chords, he raised his head, opened his eyes and beat time. When it was over, his eyes closed, his head sank down again onto his chest and all glimmer of intelligence went out."

Verdi wrote in August 1847 that: "His eyes were always closed. It is devastating . . . too devastating."

Political intervention finally brought official permission to remove him to his home in Bergamo in September of that year. His physical condition continued to deteriorate, and he died on April 8, 1848.

He was autopsied three days later, and the report contains a curious passage that is, if nothing else, an interesting commentary on the state of medical knowledge in the mid-nineteenth century: "The brain showed very highly developed circumvolutions corresponding to the locality of the organs of music, of mentation and of genius." About 1960, a Dr. Victor de Sabata, Jr., of Milan reviewed the report and, after making due allowances for the primitive state of medicine at the time, commented to Herbert Weinstock, a Donizetti biographer: "Nevertheless, a retrospective diagnosis of quaternary syphilis— based on clinical evidence and the autopsy, is almost overwhelmingly probable. In fact, there appears to be no other possibility."

Twenty years after Donizetti's death, Verdi returned to the Italian minister of education a medal bestowed on him by the Italian government, for what he took to be a slight to the memory of Donizetti. The minister had expressed the opinion that Italy had had no composers since Rossini. Explained Verdi to a friend: "I have returned the cross not on my own account, but out of respect to the memory of those two men who are no more and who have filled the world with their melodies." His reference, he made clear, was to Bellini and Donizetti.

7

WAGNER, ROBBER,
AND THE THETIS

THE FLYING DUTCHMAN

THE PLOT: *Daland, a Norwegian sea captain, and the Flying Dutchman both anchor in Sandwike. The Dutchman, for having called on the devil to assist him against ill winds, must sail forever, coming ashore once every seven years to seek salvation. He courts Daland's daughter, Senta, who knows of his curse and that he can be saved only by a woman "true unto death." Through a misunderstanding, he fears she will be unfaithful, and starts to sail alone, but she flings herself into the sea, proclaiming that now she has certainly been true unto death; the Dutchman at last finds salvation.*

"*E*verywhere you open the score the incessant wind blows out at you." This was the tribute paid by Franz Lachner, conductor of the Munich Opera in the 1860s to Richard Wagner's *The Flying Dutchman*. Where does the salt air come from that so permeates this music?

In large part, by Wagner's own account, it comes from a sea voyage undertaken by the unknown, unsuccessful, voluble, tempestuous, impulsive twenty-six-year-old composer in July 1839. He was accompanied by his wife, Minna, then in the first stages of pregnancy. The voyage was from Pillau, on the Baltic coast of East Prussia, to London in a tiny schooner. It was one stage of a desperate flight from creditors in Riga, Latvia, then, as so often, under Russian domination. Wagner's goal was imagined fame and wealth in Paris.

His passport had been confiscated to avoid such a flight, a small matter that was overcome with the help of a close friend and admirer, Abraham Möller. Möller was a portly, talkative, aging impresario from Königsberg (now Kaliningrad) near Pillau. It was in Königsberg that Möller had met Wagner, who was employed there as music director before relocating to Riga. In early July, Möller rented a coach and driver in Königsberg, and drove across the Russian border. At a small town near Riga, he picked up Wagner, Minna, and the balance of their entourage, consisting of two black trunks and a shaggy white Newfoundland named Robber.

Why would the Wagners opt to travel to Paris by way of London and a perilous sea voyage? Part of the reason was money. The ship was cheaper. But the major reason was Robber. Minna refused to ride any farther with him in Möller's cramped coach. It is quite possible that, except for Robber, this earliest of Wagner's repertory operas might be of a different character entirely.

Wagner was not about to leave Robber. They had been friends for too long. At the start, Minna had insisted there was no room for him in the coach, so the dog trotted behind it the best part of the first day. Wagner sat in a rearward-facing seat to keep an eye on him. As the dog's steps grew shorter with the rise of the blazing afternoon sun, Wagner gave a shout, the coach stopped, and, to Minna's chagrin, they shared their already crowded seats with the exhausted, panting beast.

They reached the Prussian border on the afternoon of the second day, and only then did Möller reveal his plan for smuggling them across. If Wagner was surprised, Minna was undoubtedly horrified to learn that they were to run several hundred yards, under cover of darkness, down a hill from a deserted Russian guard hut to a road on the Prussian side of the border. There, Möller, free to ride across the border with his passport, would pick them up. The hut was deserted as several Cossack guards had been bribed by the resourceful Möller to desert it. Not all of the white-uniformed sentries had been so corrupted, however, and one untimely bark from Robber could well have deprived the modern operatic repertory of *The Flying Dutchman* and nine other prized numbers as well.

While the Wagners waited in the small border town of Arnau, Möller returned the rented coach to Königsberg and made arrangements at nearby Pillau for the sea voyage to London. For the trip to Pillau, he rented a primitive wagon and an apparently inept driver. They could not follow the main road as that path lay through Königsberg. Königsberg, like Riga, and every other town where the spendthrift composer had lived since leaving his native Leipzig, was alive with his creditors and, at his insistence, they took a more circuitous, less-traveled road. He was determined to go to Paris, not a debtors' prison.

On one of the back roads, the clumsy wagon toppled, throwing passengers, dog, and trunks to the ground. Wagner landed in a heap of manure, but Minna suffered a more substantial blow. She was taken to a nearby farmhouse, though Wagner himself was first refused admittance due to the pungent odor he exuded. Minna lost the baby she was carrying and probably her child-bearing capacity as well. In any event, she and Richard remained childless throughout their marriage, though Minna, at sixteen, had borne an illegitimate daughter, and Wagner, late in life, fathered three children with his second wife.

Nowhere in his voluminous writings does Wagner mention Minna's pregnancy or her injuries. Not until after his death were the facts related to a Wagner biographer by the illegitimate daughter who had heard the tale from her mother.

Upon reaching Pillau, the Wagners and their dog said good-bye to Möller, who, Wagner tells us, assured them of his willingness to render financial assistance to them in Paris should the need arise. The couple was still without passports, and as arranged, crawled through mud and high weeds to the shore where they were picked up by a small boat and rowed to the ship, for whose comparative spaciousness Minna undoubtedly yearned. From all evidence, Minna craved little from life other than peace and security. With her fiery, impetuous husband, she was to find precious little of either.

The ship was the *Thetis,* a two-masted merchant schooner of the smallest type with an approximate gross weight of only 106 tons. The cargo on this trip was ninety-nine bushels of oats and two of peas, behind a few of which the Wagners possibly hid while customs inspectors made their rounds. The ship had a crew of seven, including the captain, an R. Wulff, a member of an old East Prussian family. The

Wagners shared his quarters. Wagner's bed was a seat, in the hollow of which was the brandy cask that the crew members used to fortify themselves from time to time.

The voyage to London, expected to last eight days, took over three weeks. First, there was an unusual calm in the Baltic. Then, upon rounding the Jutland peninsula and entering the Skagerrack, a violent west wind arose, making westward progress impossible and leaving the Wagners miserably seasick. Wagner, trying to get relief from his torments by stretching out full-length on his undersized berth, was further harassed by crew members, particularly one Koske, seeking to refresh themselves with the brandy. Koske's visits were particularly troublesome as the normally peaceful Robber took a dislike to him and would fly at Koske with a rage requiring Wagner's intervention.

Finally, the captain ordered the ship to turn north to seek shelter among the tiny islands and sea lanes that lace the southeast coast of Norway. With the wind abeam, they were driven at high speed and reached their haven in the early morning of July 29.

Thirty years later, when dictating his autobiography to his second wife, he described how the enormous granite walls of the cliffs that bordered the sea lanes echoed the shouts of the crew "like an omen of good cheer and shaped itself presently into the theme of the seamen's song in my 'Flying Dutchman'."

It would have been surprising if the haunting stories of *The Flying Dutchman* had not filled Wagner's mind at that moment and throughout the entire sea voyage. From an early age, he had been obsessed by spirits, ghosts, and wild creatures. At his uncle's home in Leipzig, he had slept in a four-poster beneath huge portraits of high-born ladies with painted faces and powdered hair and he has described how, in the dead of night, the horrible pictures came to life. Often, in the room alone, he would shriek with fright as lifeless objects seemed to move and speak. Glazed beer bottles, lined up along the stairs of his Dresden boyhood home, he tells us, he saw as laughing devils that mocked and taunted him as they perpetually changed shapes.

Inevitably, his obsession with the supernatural found expression in music. Wagner has also described how the sounds from the Leipzig orchestra tuning up had thrown him into a state of mystical excitement and how he heard the long-drawn-out sounds of the oboe as a call from the dead to rouse the other instruments. The striking of the violin was a greeting from the spirit world, and he has written that the first violin he ever heard came from the cold stone figure of a violinist by Dresden's Palace of St. Anthony. In dreams, he had seen and spoken to Shakespeare and Beethoven and had awakened on such occasions bathed in tears and sweat.

Even before his sea voyage, Wagner had heard of the Dutch ship that sailed forever, her captain doomed to eternal wandering on the seas for having called upon the devil for help in overcoming unfavorable winds. From his correspondence, it is known that while still in Riga he had read Heinrich Heine's spoof of the tale, involving, as does Wagner's opera, redemption through the love of a woman. It is Heine's work, *The Memoirs of Herr Von Schnabelewopski,* that is usually credited as the source of Wagner's story. True, such redemption is a theme that runs throughout Wagner, but there is other evidence that Wagner drew mainly on Heine's irreverent essay.

In the final scene of Wagner's opera, the taunting Norwegian sailors sing to the eerie crew of the mysterious Dutch visitor:

> Have you no letter, no message to leave,
> we can bring our great-grandfathers here to receive?

In all probability, Wagner was capsulizing Heine's mention in his essay of an English ship bound for Amsterdam, which was hailed on the high seas by a Dutch vessel. The crew of the Dutchman, so Heine's story went, gave a sack of mail to the Englishman, asking that its contents be delivered to the proper parties in Amsterdam. Upon reaching their destination, the English crew was chilled to find that many of the addressees had been dead for over a hundred years.

The *Thetis* remained in Norway for three days. Like every place in which the enigmatic composer set foot, his movements and activities have been the subject of intense scrutiny by persistent Wagnerian researchers. There can be little doubt that, whatever the ultimate inspiration for the opera, there was much in his Norwegian visit that influenced the final story at least in some details.

"Sandwike here, How well I know the bay." This line is sung by Daland, the crusty Norwegian sea captain, in the very beginning of the opera. The name is not fictional. According to Wagner's autobiog-

The home in Sandwike, Norway, where Wagner is believed to have sought shelter from a storm and stayed for two days in July 1839. It and the surrounding area may be the model for the setting of his *Flying Dutchman*. (Aust-Agder-Arv, 1967–68 edition. Aust-Agder-Museums: Arendal, Norway. Used by permission of Aust-Agder-Arkivet, Arendal, Norway.)

raphy, the *Thetis* sought shelter in the storm at Sandwike "a few miles away from the much larger town of Arendal." It happens that there are two small villages named Sandwike very near Arendal. Which Sandwike hosted Wagner was the cause of some controversy in Norway. The question was finally put to rest with the discovery in 1935 by a Viennese opera singer of the list of vessels calling at the port of Boroy during July 1839 and including, on July 29, the *Thetis*. Boroy is a tiny island containing the northernmost of the two Sandwikes. The discovery in 1947 of the original pilot's log for the same period confirmed the arrival of the "Thetus [*sic*] Capt. R. Wulff on a voyage from Koenigsberg to London," along with three other vessels seeking shelter from the storm.

According to Wagner's autobiography, he, Minna, and Robber stayed two nights at the house of a certain ship's captain who was away at sea. Which was the house? That, too, was a matter of interest to the Norwegians.

In 1839, there were but eight houses in all Sandwike, of which only two were the large, so-called captains' houses owned by sea captains. The most likely of the two, according to the old-timers there, speaking, no doubt, from hearsay, was that of a Captain Jens Jensen, whose then forty-nine-year-old wife, Martha, was described as an active woman "never lacking room in her house or her heart." Eventually, the persistent Wagnerians found shipping invoices proving that, during the last part of the month, her husband had indeed been at sea in his own sloop.

The final direct evidence to an otherwise circumstantial case was provided by the discovery of summaries by one of Martha's grandchildren of stories that the grandchild's mother, Martha's daughter-in-law, had passed down to her. These included a reference to the fact that Martha had as houseguests the Wagners who "were well received and went for long walks with their dog."

It may all be unimportant, except for the fact that the Jensen living room, by at least one account, was not at all unlike Wagner's second-scene description of Daland's house. Imaginative eyewitness accounts aside, what could be a more likely model than the home that harbored him for two of his only three nights ashore?

Built in 1762, the house had fourteen windows facing the bay and, when torn down in 1885, provided enough lumber for three new houses. Intriguingly, both the description and photograph reveal, in the nearby granite walls that border the sea, a protruding cliff such as that depicted in some productions from which Senta, in the final moments of the opera, flings herself into the bay.

As a final curiosity, a few miles from Sandwike there was an estate called Daland.

On the first of August, the *Thetis* once more set sail for London. It soon met with storms in the North Sea that dwarfed the one they had encountered in the Baltic. The terrified Minna begged her husband to tie her to him so that they might drown together. The superstitious sailors blamed their misfortunes on their stowaway passengers, and the young couple also had to endure the accusing glances and curses of the crew. One of their two black trunks was washed overboard.

They spent eight days in London, finally arriving in Paris in late September, where they spent two miserable years. Near starvation, they survived mainly on credit and by begging and borrowing from friends. Relying on Möller's offer of help, Wagner wrote his elderly friend in Königsberg, but heard nothing from him. Years later, while living in Dresden, he was visited by Möller, who, in no uncertain terms, told the composer that he had heard of humiliating and derogatory remarks Wagner was said to have uttered about him. Wagner protests his innocence; we have no memoirs from Möller, so that is all we know of the matter. Interestingly, in his autobiography, Wagner laments losing "the chance of such assistance in our great need," but expresses no regrets about the loss of the friendship.

He lost another friend in those trying times. Robber disappeared. Several months later, while returning a borrowed metronome, Wagner spotted the dog, like a ghost in the early-morning fog. But upon his approach the dog alternately ran, then stopped and eyed his former master, who followed him "like a maniac." Finally, says Wagner, Robber disappeared near the Church of St. Roch, leaving him, still carrying the bulky metronome, dripping with perspiration and quite breathless. Wagner, assuring us that the dog had been well fed despite his and Minna's own meager rations, insists that his shaggy companion had been stolen. We have no memoirs from Robber either.

With blind and misplaced confidence in his imminent success, in April 1840, Wagner rented more spacious quarters at 25 rue du Helder, where he sketched the seaman's chorus and "Senta's Ballad." Later that year, his profligate ways caught up with him and he spent almost six weeks in a debtors' prison, a small matter also not mentioned in his autobiography.

The following summer, in a house rented in Meudon, just outside the Paris gates, and out of the legal reach of his creditors, he wrote the entire text and completed the composition of his *Flying Dutchman*. He had written the text for all of his previous operas, and would continue the practice for all of his future ones. This was his fourth completed opera, but the first that remains in the standard repertory. It was not produced in Paris. The Paris Opéra had a "list" of composers and took their works in their order on the list. Wagner was facing a four-year wait.

But it saw the light of day in 1843 in Dresden, where he was then serving as conductor of the Dresden Opera. He retained that position until forced to flee in 1849 for participating in a civil uprising. That very year, as it happened, and undoubtedly unknown to him, the *Thetis* went down at sea, presumably with the loss of all her crew.

8

THE OPERA
DIRECTOR AND THE
DRESDEN UPRISING

LOHENGRIN

THE PLOT: Telramund and Ortrud, his wife, accuse one of the late Duke's heirs, Elsa, of murdering her own brother. Should Elsa not succeed to the crown, it would fall to Telramund. To represent her in trial by combat, she calls on a knight, seen in her dreams. He appears, and she agrees to his condition, never to ask his name. Telramund is defeated, but he and Ortrud sow doubt in Elsa's mind, and following their wedding, she asks the knight his name. He reveals that he is Lohengrin of Montsalvat, but must return as the vow is broken. Ortrud reveals the swan as the lost brother who would have been freed had Elsa kept her vow.

The scarred and blackened tower of the Church of the Holy Cross rises high above central Dresden. Like many of its unreconstructed neighboring buildings, it bears silent witness to the devastating allied firebomb raid of February 1945. The raid was the most terrible, but not the only occasion on which that church, or the city itself, had been the target of hostile fire. It had happened before, almost a century earlier.

For four days in early May 1849, blue-coated Prussian troops with spiked helmets fought civilian revolutionaries in the streets of Dresden, then the capital city of the German kingdom of Saxony. The fires of revolution were igniting all over Europe, and the

Street fighting in Dresden, May 1849. A contemporary lithograph. Wagner's participation in this uprising may have been caused by pique over the refusal of the Saxon king to order a performance of *Lohengrin*. It resulted in twelve years of exile from his native land. (Taylor, Ronald. *Richard Wagner.* New York: Taplinger Publishing Co., 1979.)

troops had been offered by King Frederick William IV of Prussia to any German prince or monarch who needed them to suppress uprisings.

Throughout much of the fighting, Prussian riflemen kept up a steady fire on the church tower. They knew that it was manned with observers and that it afforded a commanding view, not only of the city, but of the surrounding countryside and the movement of the troops. One of the lookouts, an undersized Saxon civilian with a protruding chin and receding forehead, tied penciled notes to small stones and threw them to his comrades in the streets below. He was the disgruntled conductor of the Dresden Opera, Richard Wagner.

It was Wagner's bitterness at what he perceived as the pettiness of the politically appointed opera management that drove him into the revolutionary camp. The final push came from their refusal to perform his newest opera, *Lohengrin.*

That refusal had been a stunning blow. The Lohengrin myth had seized hold of him eight years previously, while living, and almost starving, in Paris. An artist friend had given him a volume dealing with the *Tannhäuser* subject, and appended to it happened to be a critical study of the Lohengrin legend. In Wagner's own words, his exposure to Lohengrin opened a new world for him.

In 1845, four years after his first encounter with Lohengrin, his luck had seemingly changed and he was serving as conductor of the Dresden Opera. In the spring of that year, shortly after the composition of *Tannhäuser,* he and his wife, Minna, journeyed to the Bohemian spa of Marienbad in the hills of what is today the Czech Republic.

He tried to follow the advice of the resident physician to avoid exciting his overly frayed nerves. However, his growing obsession with the anonymous Lohengrin epic, which he took with him everywhere, was uncontrollable. Unable to wait out the prescribed hour of his noon baths, he would leave prematurely and dash to his room to work on a prose sketch for his intended opera. His enthusiasm robbed him of sleep. Finally, he gave up thoughts of rest and returned to Dresden.

In November, shortly following the *Tannhäuser* premiere, he completed the text of *Lohengrin* and, as was his custom, read it aloud to a small select circle of friends. One, Robert Schumann, the composer, wondered how music was to be written with so few opportunities for the traditional arias and duets. Another friend thought it offensive to effect Elsa's punishment through Lohengrin's departure. Ferdinand Hiller, a minor and all-but-forgotten conductor and composer, earned immortality of a sort by telling a friend named Meissner, "What a pity that Wagner means to set it to music himself. His musical gifts are not equal to that."

The following summer, while staying in a peasant's home in Gross Graupen, a tiny village south of Dresden, Wagner did a hasty musical sketch of the entire work. On his return to Dresden, he began composing the third act, the only instance in which he began the composition of any opera out of chronological sequence. He saved for last the difficult and psychologically complex second act, which he completed in August 1847. The orchestral scoring was completed in April 1848, and a production was planned by the Dresden Opera for the following season.

Unfortunately, however, the completion of the work and his plans for a production coincided with a culminating crisis in German political affairs.

It had been brewing for a long time. Uprisings in Vienna and Berlin, in February and March 1848, forced limited concessions from the key German states of Austria and Prussia, and promises of reform. It was growing disappointment over the next fourteen months in the failure to realize those promises that led to the Dresden revolt.

In the meantime, Wagner was having his own troubles. In the fall of 1847, the Prussian king rejected his request for a command performance of the still uncompleted *Lohengrin*. Berlin would have been a much more prestigious beginning for his opera than Dresden. Early the next year, he strained the Saxon king's generosity once too often in seeking help with his wretched finances. He received less than he asked for, and a curt, unsolicited note reprimanding him on his profligacy. Two months later came an unceremonious rejection of his gratuitous plan for the reorganization of the German theater. The central point of the plan involved greater participation of artists and writers in management.

Wagner was never one to take life's disappointments lying down. Like Beethoven, he preferred to seize fate by the throat. Interestingly, his earliest mention of revolution came in a letter to a Berlin friend bitterly complaining of the Prussian king's refusal to order a *Lohengrin* production. Throughout 1848 came a series of politically provocative poems and newspaper articles whose anonymity fooled no one.

Then, at the end of that year, came the Dresden Opera's cancellation of *Lohengrin*. The probable reasons: too ambitious an undertaking for such unsettled times, and too good an opportunity to teach the impertinent conductor a lesson.

His breach with the German theater was now beyond salvation. A year later he was to write his sister Klara a revealing letter in explanation of his revolutionary activities. You never considered, he wrote, how I felt when I could not get *Lohengrin* produced for two years, "even in Dresden." Following the cancellation, his words and articles became increasingly rabid, his actions more audacious.

Only a month before the uprising, he authored and published, once again without his signature, a lengthy, incendiary article: "I will destroy every illusion that has power over men . . . I will destroy every trace of this insane order of things . . . I am the revolution." He attended meetings of a revolutionary group in a house rented to a mysterious Dr. Schwartz, who was, in fact, Mikhail Bakunin, a black-bearded Russian firebrand and zealot. Bakunin had a habit of showing up in various cities right before the outbreak of hostilities. A few weeks before the uprising, Wagner and one August Roekel, the publisher of a revolutionary newspaper, surreptitiously ordered 1,500 grenades from a brass founder. During Roekel's temporary absence from the city, Wagner personally oversaw the publication of his seditious journal.

On the fourth of May, the fighting began; streets were torn up and paving stones piled on hastily constructed barricades. Wagner arranged for the printing and personally distributed to Saxon troops placards urging them to desert in favor of the revolutionaries. That he was not arrested and shot is a minor miracle.

On the fifth, the thunder of cannons echoed throughout the city, and late that evening the first Prussians arrived. They had none of the reticence of the Saxon troops in making war on the civilian population. Insurgents were hurled into the streets by the dozens by Prussian soldiers who searched them out from the upper floors of buildings. Others were systematically shot upon capture.

Early the next morning, Wagner was asked by the insurgent leaders to ascend the church tower as an observer. He lightened his task with a nonstop flow of animated abstract discussions on an endless variety of erudite subjects. On one of his descents, he exclaimed to a friend that the view was splendid and the "combination of the bells and the cannons intoxicating."

To protect themselves from Prussian fire, Wagner and a co-occupant used some handy straw mattresses. Wagner was later reported to have boasted that the bullet that could lay him out had not yet been cast. Despite this bit of bravado, there remains the distinct possibility that devotees of Wagner's operas have reason to be grateful for the presence of a few straw mattresses.

The next morning, for her safety, he took his unappeasably angry wife westward to Chemnitz, to stay with his sister. Minna cared nothing for revolution and wanted only to be left in peace. It was on this second trip out of the city, to encourage reinforcements, that he received news that the revolt had been crushed. He was picked up in an elegant coach bearing fleeing revolutionaries, one of whom later wrote: "All the din, the shouting, and the rattling of arms was drowned out by the flaming talk of Wagner."

Through luck, he had separated from his companions before they were betrayed by an informer and were captured. They were tried and sentenced to death, a sentence later commuted to life imprisonment.

A few days later a "wanted" poster for his arrest and bearing his description was widely circulated. With a borrowed passport, he made his way to Switzerland, where he was joined six weeks later by his angry and unforgiving wife: "What kind of future do I have? What can you offer me?" It was the beginning of the end of the marriage.

Once settled in Zurich, his thoughts soon turned again to *Lohengrin*. In April 1850, he wrote to his close friend, Franz Liszt, the conductor of the Weimer Court Theatre, that he was overwhelmed by an immense desire to have the work performed, and that he would entrust it to no one but Liszt. Who else would have touched it at the time is difficult to imagine. Liszt, who was already enchanted by the score, agreed. He was soon bombarded with the most detailed instructions from the exiled composer: music, casting, scenery, acting, costumes, and decorations. "Give the opera as it is, cut nothing," he wrote. "Let me for once do as I like."

His desire to attend the premiere could hardly be contained. Could Liszt not suggest some way by which he might be smuggled over the border to Weimar and back again to Zurich? Liszt's reply painted in a few chilling words the prevailing hostility toward him: Your return to Germany, he tells Wagner, is an "absolute impossibility." "But your *Lohengrin*," he says, "will be given in all of its magnificence."

The premiere took place on August 28 at the Court Theatre in Weimar. The orchestra numbered only thirty-eight, with only twenty-one strings. The chorus was similarly lacking, and the second act processional march was played without a procession. Nonetheless, Liszt's praise was ecstatic: "It is a sublime work from one end to the other. The tears rose from my heart in more than one place."

Over the next decade, the opera took firm hold in the leading houses of Germany. In 1859, even Dresden yielded. It was heard by scores of thousands of Germans, but not by Wagner. He once toyed with the idea of going to Paris and engaging an orchestra to perform the opera solely for himself and his friends. Despite repeated rebuffs, he sought amnesty from the German states, not the least reason for which was his agonizing desire to see *Lohengrin*.

In 1859, amnesty finally came from all the German states except Saxony. By this time he was immersed in other problems, including the production of his recently completed *Tristan und Isolde*. After failing in several cities to have it performed, he turned to Vienna.

In producing *Tristan,* he was to fail in Vienna also, but on at least one occasion he did find surcease from his troubles there. On May 15, 1861, shortly after arriving, he attended an opera performance at the famed Kärntnertor Theatre. His entrance into the hall was the occasion of a massive demonstration of affection and respect that brought tears to his eyes. A few moments later, almost eleven years after its Weimar premiere, Richard Wagner finally heard *Lohengrin*.

9

TRIBOULET AND FRANCIS I

RIGOLETTO

THE PLOT: *Rigoletto, the hunchback jester to the Duke, mocks the husbands and fathers of the Duke's conquests until his own daughter, Gilda, is abducted by courtiers and brought to the Duke. Fearing a curse uttered by a wronged father, and seeking vengeance, Rigoletto hires an assassin to kill the Duke. At the urging of his sister, infatuated with the Duke, the assassin agrees to kill the next person coming to his inn, and to deliver to Rigoletto that body in a sack instead of the Duke's. From outside the inn, Gilda, also enamored of the Duke, hears this, knocks on the door, is stabbed, and dies as she is found by her father in the assassin's sack.*

For most of the first half of the sixteenth century, France was ruled by a multitalented king known to history as Francis I. He was a true man of the Renaissance: skilled in military and political affairs, a tough negotiator with the papacy and with foreign sovereigns, yet a patron of the arts and host to Leonardo da Vinci in the artist's old age. He was, unfortunately, also well known on two other counts. One was his cruel and relentless persecution of Protestants. The other was his keen eye for the ladies. He was renowned for his sexual prowess, which, combined with his royal prerogatives, left no one's wife or daughter safe.

His biographies tell of his liaison, at sixteen years of age and still

known as the Duke of Valois, with a young woman who caught his
fancy at a wedding celebration. As a result of her parents' insistence,
she was already wedded to an elderly lawyer. The affair began when
the young duke, disguised as a commoner, entered her home in the
absence of the husband. There was no intermediary, but the stealthy
entry was otherwise not too dissimilar to that portrayed in the second
act of *Rigoletto*. No abduction, however, was necessary thereafter.
The precocious young duke soon made it a practice to hide in a
nearby monastery until the opportune time. Later, upon leaving the
home of the absent lawyer, he would stop there again in order to
pray.

As king, he had a court jester whose name was Triboulet. All we
know about Triboulet is that he was from the town of Blois, located
on the River Loire about halfway between Orléans and Tours. Much
of the king's childhood had been spent at the château at Blois, and he
frequently returned, both to reside for varying periods of time and to
conduct hunting forays in the nearby forests. Presumably he made the
acquaintance of Triboulet there, and must have tagged the man as a
likely candidate for the job of court jester. Whoever Triboulet was, he
could never have guessed that his presence at court would, three hundred years later, command the attention of two of the great creative
talents of history, precipitate battles with the censors of two nations,
and immortalize the institution of court jester.

His road to posthumous fame started when someone in the town
of Blois, probably in the very early nineteenth century, saw fit to state
in a published history of that community that, among its other claims
to fame, Blois was the birthplace of the court fool for the renowned
Francis I. Hopefully, Blois has since found more to boast about.

One copy of the history found its way to the shelves of a white
stone-walled home located between two orchards in the village of
Sologne, just a few miles from Blois. The home was on 1,800 acres of
grounds, an estate known as La Militière, owned by a retired French
general, Joseph-Léopold-Sigisbert Hugo. Owing to his distinguished
career in the service of Napoleon Bonaparte, he still, in 1825, had
enough clout with the court of Charles X to reserve places on the mail
carriage from Paris for his son Victor and Victor's wife and their
young daughter.

Victor was enchanted with the town and with La Militière, with its "ivy rioting over the walls," as he described it to a friend. He was then twenty-three, and a struggling, but very promising, writer. Browsing through his father's books, his eye fell on the reference to Triboulet. About Francis I, he already knew, and those who have read Victor Hugo will not doubt that it was neither Francis the sovereign ruler nor Francis the military tactician who came to his mind, but Francis the philanderer, Francis the rake.

When the wheels first began to turn we do not know. But seven years later, when he began to write the play that had taken shape from that bare reference to Triboulet, Victor Hugo had already written several successful dramas. He was not one to change names to protect anyone. Triboulet, and, more to the point, Francis I, were identified by name. There is no reason to suppose that Triboulet was a hunchback, but, in a stroke of genius, Hugo made him one. Some scholars have claimed to see in Triboulet the progenitor of the hunchback of Notre Dame.

The play, *Le Roi s'amuse,* often translated as *The King's Diversion,* received its first performance on November 22, 1832; it was also the last performance for fifty years. But, apparently, it was an exciting evening. The foundation for the excitement was already being laid some months before the play's opening.

In the July revolution of 1830, fighting at the barricades resulted in the installation of King Louis-Philippe I, sometimes called the Citizen King, sometimes the Bourgeoisie Monarch. In the fall of 1832, the crown still lay uneasily on his head. His government was much too insecure to endure the sarcasms of a brilliant writer. The situation had not been helped at all by an abortive insurrection that broke out on June 5 of that year, even as Hugo was working on the drama, and obliging him once to dodge bullets himself.

The premiere was to be in the Théâtre-Français. Any questions about the suitability of a theatrical work for public performance was a matter for determination by the Ministry of Public Works. Hugo won a preliminary battle with that office when he assured the minister that he made no allusions whatever to Louis-Philippe; that he painted a portrait of Francis I, and that it was Francis I whom he intended to paint; that he could understand someone finding a resemblance between that monarch and certain others of France's past kings, but that it was impossible to draw a comparison between him and Louis-

Victor Hugo in 1829, etching by Achille Deveria. A year later Hugo was obliged to dodge bullets during a civil uprising in Paris as he worked on *Le Roi s'amuse*, the play on which Verdi's *Rigoletto* is based. (Used by permission of Bibliothèque Nationale de France.)

Philippe. Was this not, however, an attack on the institution of royalty itself? Above the interest of royalty, insisted Hugo, was the interest of history. Asked if there were any means of softening the details, Hugo replied that there were not. Remarkably, the play was allowed to go on.

There was latent tension between the audience members in the pit and those in the boxes. It was exacerbated all the more by the news that made its way through the theater just as the play commenced that there had been an attempt on the life of the king. At the end of the first act it was the pit, and applause, that prevailed. But thanks to the excessively awkward manner in which the heroine, Blanche (Gilda in *Rigoletto*), was carried from the stage by the courtiers, heels over head, hisses prevailed in that act with cries of "immorality" from the boxes. The third act was the denouement of the play, and of Hugo's supporters in the pit. First came shouts of protest from the boxes at seeing the king appear in his dressing gown. But the coup de grace was the enraged cry of Triboulet at the king's courtiers as they barred his way to his daughter. He calls them by name, some of the most respected names of French aristocracy, and cries, "Your mothers slept with their lackeys, and you are bastards." It was greeted by a roar of disapproval from much of the audience, which was then in no mood to show sympathy for the mechanical difficulties with the staging that had developed in the last act. The play ended in a general melee in which the plaudits were drowned out in a storm of hisses.

The next morning Hugo received a note from the theater stage manager. He had just been ordered by the minister to suspend further performances of the play. Hugo was indignant and genuinely astonished. He immediately had the play published with a lengthy author's preface, making his case to the public against the "brutal act . . . revolting to honest men."

What, he asked, was the motive for such an "odious, unjustifiable" act. Immorality? "Ho, there, my masters!" Hugo went through a scene-by-scene analysis of his play, raising and refuting any possible claim of immorality. His conclusion: a singular fear on the part of the new government "of all that advances, of all that stirs, of all that protests, of all who think." "Two years ago," said Hugo, "we feared for order, now we tremble for liberty." Although he was unable to sue the minister, barricaded behind his official immunity, he brought suit against the Théâtre Français. The commercial court declared the case to be outside its competence.

The reactions of contemporary critics and writers are an odd mixture. One of them, writing from the vantage point of several decades later, suggested that Hugo's astonishment should have been even greater at having been allowed to perform the play at all. They appear unanimous in their belief that political reasons, not public morality, lay behind the government action. Many combined their comments with criticisms of the merits of the play, which most of them found wanting. Some thought the government action was more foolish than malicious, and that it would have been better to trust to the judgment of the public and wait for the play to fail.

Today when we hear that an opera is based on another literary work there is a tendency to assume that the original has been much reworked, and that the similarities must be slight. Often, that is the case. Many times, however, it is not. The similarity between *Le Roi s'amuse* and *Rigoletto,* in both general structure and most details, is almost startling. To anyone familiar with the opera it is no simple matter to form an opinion of the play, as it is almost impossible to read it without intrusion by the melodies of *Rigoletto.* The total effect is powerful, and it is difficult to allocate credit as between the printed words and the pervasive music. For a judgment on the merits of the play itself we may have to rely on those few who saw it, and Hugo scholars who have read it.

Despite the largely negative criticisms, a few commentators found it very moving and effective. And, almost twenty years later, one of Hugo's contemporaries was overwhelmed, and almost driven to ecstacies, by it. But in his case, even though the music had not yet been written, he may indeed have heard it, or the bare outlines of it, as he read the play. That one, of course, was Giuseppe Verdi, then thirty-seven years old. He had already written fifteen operas, but not yet any of the greatest works for which he is most widely known. Of these he was about to write his first.

Verdi was not much given to ecstacies. It was not in his nature. His friend and librettist, Francesco Piave, who had already written three librettos for the composer and was about to work on a fourth, must have been rather taken aback to receive Verdi's letter of April 28,

1850, written from his home in Busseto. If the composer had ever written with such unrestrained enthusiasm over any other proposed subject, the document must be lost. No other such effusiveness appears among his collected correspondence. The first few paragraphs contained his usual negative or noncommittal comments about various subjects and their suitability as opera plots.

Then this: "There would be another subject that, if the police would allow it, would be one of the greatest creations of the modern theater . . . The subject is great, immense, and there is a character who is one of the greatest creations that the theater of all countries and all ages can boast. The subject is *Le Roi s'amuse* and the character I speak of would be Triboulet." When would this opera be written? "As soon as you receive this letter, start moving: run throughout the city, and find an influential person who can obtain permission to do *Le Roi s'amuse*. Don't sleep. Stir yourself. Hurry."

The city that Verdi referred to was Venice, then under Austrian domination. Verdi had signed a contract with the Teatro la Fenice there for an opera to be staged in February 1851. Ten days after his letter to Piave, his enthusiasm has not subsided in the slightest. He writes again on May 8: "Oh, *Le Roi s'amuse* is the greatest subject and perhaps the greatest drama of modern times. Triboulet is a character worthy of Shakespeare!! This is a subject that cannot fail." So once again he tells Piave, "Arouse the interest of the Presidenza, turn Venice upside down, and make the censorship allow this subject."

Piave, on what basis we do not know, assured Verdi that it would be done, and, with Verdi giving instructions by mail, prepared the libretto. The opera is to be called *La Maledizione, The Curse*. Verdi's most emphatic instruction to his librettist: "The whole subject lives in that curse." Verdi began composing in the spring, satisfied with Piave's assurances about the approval of the Austrian authorities. On August 5, the subject was formally submitted to them by Piave and Verdi, who had come to Venice for that purpose. When approval was not immediately forthcoming, Verdi returned to Busseto to continue with the composition.

By August 24 he is getting uneasy and writes to C. D. Marzari, the president of the Teatro la Fenice. If approval is not obtained, there is no time for Verdi to immerse himself in another opera, and the contract should be canceled. Blame for the potential problem is placed on Piave, on whose assurances Verdi has placed such reliance. By November he is obviously getting concerned about what changes may be required. He writes to Piave, telling him what he can and cannot change or remove. The sack with the body must stay. The scene where the king enters the bedroom of the daughter can go. Don't be led to make changes that alter the characters or the situations, he warns Piave.

On the first of December the ax fell. The chief of police informed the president of the Teatro la Fenice that the military governor of Venice "deplores the fact that the poet Piave and the celebrated Maestro Verdi were unable to choose a field wherein to display their talents other than that repulsively immoral and obscenely vulgar . . . *La maledizione.*" The performance was prohibited and the theater president enjoined from any further insistence on it. In Verdi's own words, the decree was so unexpected that "I nearly went out of my mind." Piave, he tells Marzari, had assured him since May that the opera would be approved. "Piave has a serious responsibility: all the responsibility!" A new work, now by winter, said Verdi, is impossible.

Whatever assurances Piave thought he had, whatever had gone wrong, he must have been frantic to salvage the situation. With Marzari, he reworked the libretto, hoping to please both the general director of public order and Verdi. Whether it would have pleased the general director we do not know. A copy was sent first to Verdi. Unintentionally, Piave and Marzari were waving a red flag at an already angry bull.

In a note to Marzari dated December 14, Verdi says that he has not read the new libretto thoroughly, but has seen enough to know that it now lacks character and importance and has become cold. No copy of the reworked libretto survives, but it is obvious from Verdi's response that the monarch, who in the original libretto had already been transformed into the duke of a French province, was now turned into a respectable gentleman, and that Triboletto (Triboulet has now been Italianized) is no longer a hunchback. In this letter to Marzari, dated December 14, Verdi's frustration comes pouring forth:

> The old man's curse, so awesome and sublime in the original, here becomes ridiculous because the motive that drives him to curse no longer has the same importance . . . Without this curse, what pur-

pose, what meaning does the drama have? . . . The Duke must absolutely be a libertine; without that there can be no justification for Triboletto's fear of his daughter's leaving her refuge . . . Why does the Duke go to a remote tavern alone . . . without an amorous rendezvous?—I don't understand why the sack was removed: What did the sack matter to the police? . . . Who is the composer here?

And there the matter stood. Piave made peace offerings, but Verdi's notes to him are cold and sharp. The controversy seemed deadlocked and hopeless, the pliable Piave caught between two unmovable blocks of granite.

Enter the voice of reason. One Carlo Martello suggested to Piave that if the scene were changed from France to Italy, with whom Austria was not on friendly terms anyway, especially to a minor Italian principality, and the names changed accordingly, then the changes in substance required would be much less serious. He also suggested a change in the opera's name from *La Maledizione,* which religious persons would find offensive, to the name of the jester.

It was done. And it worked. Verdi and the secretary to the presidenza signed an agreement on December 30 in Verdi's home in Busseto. The monarch would be the Duke of Mantua, a tiny Italian province. The already Italianized Triboletto became Rigoletto, presumably for its easier roll from the tongue.

This Martello, judging by his intercession here, must have been a peacemaker, one of much human understanding and a true devotee of the arts. Perhaps. But he was also a commissary of the police, the one, by coincidence, who had signed the original order of prohibition against the opera. He was also known for his ruthless pursuit and cruel punishment of Italian patriots. From all accounts he could have been a good prototype for Baron Scarpia in Puccini's *Tosca.* Characters in opera are so much simpler than those in real life.

The opera premiered on March 11, 1851, at the Teatro la Fenice. It was an unqualified success. It was also the first of Verdi's great masterpieces, and remains one of the most popular in the entire opera repertory.

In both the Hugo play and the Verdi opera, the monarchs, Francis I and the Duke of Mantua, are depicted as shameless debauchers, libertines without consciences. They cause suffering and are never called to account. Evil triumphs absolutely. In *Le Roi s'amuse*, as Triboulet places his foot on the sack and gloats over his supposed vengeance, we hear the cynical words of the still living Francis I: "Changeful woman!—Constant never! He's a fool who trusts her ever!" In *Rigoletto*, the refrain from the lilting "La Donna è mobile" tells Rigoletto that the Duke still lives, and tells both Rigoletto and the audience that the Duke continues his wanton ways.

There is some evidence, however, that real life may have exacted a price. Francis I, the real one, died at the age of fifty-two after a long and painful illness. The carefully recorded symptoms included massive infections, a foul stench that emanated from his wasting body, and an uncontrollable stammering. His contemporaries called it the plague. Our own contemporaries, those who claim to know about such things, call it syphilis.

Alphonsine "Marie" Duplessis, "The lady of the camelias" (1824–1847), by Vienot. The tragically short-lived love of the younger Alexander Dumas, she ultimately gained immortality as Violetta in Verdi's *La Traviata*. Maurois, Andre. *The Titans: A Three-Generation Biography of the Dumas.* Harper & Row, Publishers, 1957.)

10

ALEXANDRE DUMAS AND THE LADY OF THE CAMELLIAS

LA TRAVIATA

THE PLOT: *Violetta, a wealthy courtesan afflicted with consumption, is persuaded by Alfredo to live with him in the country. Alfredo's father visits her and demands that she leave his son, as the scandal of her illicit relationship with Alfredo is spoiling his daughter's prospects for a happy marriage. She makes the sacrifice, telling Alfredo in a note that she no longer loves him. The angry Alfredo publicly insults her, but as she lies dying of consumption, he returns. He tells her that he has learned the truth and loves her still as she dies in his arms.*

There really was a Lady of the Camellias. That is the name of the play, *La Dame aux Camélias,* on which *La Traviata* is based; the play, one could almost say, that Verdi set to music. The play and the opera are that much alike. The differences, for our purposes, are trivial.

The author of the play was Alexandre Dumas, the son, not the more famous father. Much to the annoyance of the elder Dumas, father and son became known as Dumas, père and Dumas, fils. It was père who soared to international literary fame with *The Count of Monte Cristo, The Three Musketeers,* and a prodigious lifetime output of over three hundred volumes. The success of Dumas, fils was much more modest. It began, not with the play, but with a novel, *La*

Dame aux Camélias, which, several years later, was turned into the play.

The real lady of the camellias died in Paris on February 3, 1847. In May, Dumas, fils took a room at the Hotel du Cheval Blanc, reread her many letters to him, and wrote his novel. Dumas, fils is the real-life Armand Duvals of his novel and play, and the Alfredo Germont of *La Traviata.*

The novel was a great success. Its heroine, Marguerite Gautier, was portrayed as the tragic, noble, yet pathetic figure of the fallen woman we know from the opera. Options for single women without means were apparently very limited then, and contemporary accounts tell of a multitude of young women rescued from poverty and drudgery by wealthy, famous, or influential men. Unless such tales are much overblown, there must have been a huge readership ready to identify with her. The story of the novel, and of the play and the opera, is indeed very moving. The true story, however, if not quite so melodramatic, has the ring of—what else? Truth.

Dumas, fils was twenty, quite tall, handsome, an impeccable dresser, and very ingratiating. One September night in 1844, in the company of a wealthy friend of similar bent, he went to the Théâtre des Variétés. Their eyes were not on the stage; they were searching the boxes occupied by finely gowned and jewel-bedecked young ladies, seeking out pairs of eyes that might also be wandering, longing for companionship more lively and romantic than that of their rich, middle-aged rescuers. Seated in one of the front boxes was a woman the same age as Dumas, fils, but already well known for her great beauty, aura of refinement, and a talent for squandering money that was now legendary.

Years later, Dumas, fils painted a word portrait of her. The passion still exudes from his description of her tall and slender figure, small waist, swanlike neck, and the rivers of diamonds and bracelets. A Dresden figurine he called her, and found in her expression the exotic look of the Orient.

She was to become the Marguerite Gautier of the novel and the play, the Violetta Valery of *La Traviata*; her real name was Alphonsine Plessis, but she now called herself Marie Duplessis. Coming from a family of farmworkers, it seemed, perhaps, more fitting to her new station in life. Her father, thought by the villagers to be a witch doctor, deserted his family when she was quite young. It is reputed that she was later sold by her mother to gypsies who placed her with a dressmaker in Paris.

In short order, the exotic beauty was comfortably ensconced on the rue de l'Arcade in a furnished apartment paid for by a restaurateur. He was soon replaced by a duke, an elegant young man about town and a member of the aristocratic Jockey Club, and Marie was soon the chief subject of conversation at the Théâtre des Italiens and at the Opéra. Her various apartments were usually filled with flowers of all types, except roses, whose strong scent she claimed made her dizzy. Her favorites were the almost odorless camellias, which her adoring protectors showered upon her. A biographer of Dumas, père describes her as "imprisoned in a fortress of camellias."

By 1844 she was reputedly the most elegant woman in Paris, not alone for her physical beauty, or her expensive jewelry or dress, but equally for the air of culture and refinement she carried. That she should have exuded such a quality is not surprising, however deep or shallow it may have been; she had been trained by masters, namely, a host of the most brilliant and sophisticated men of that sophisticated city. She was reasonably well read in the classics, many of which were in her generously stocked library, and she quickly exhibited a talent for the piano and a love of poetry. After those who carp and moralize have done their worst, there must still have remained a genuine intelligence and much sensitivity.

Marie's companion in her box at the theater that September night was a very elderly man, a former ambassador to Russia, the Comte de Stackelberg. She left the theater alone before the end of the performance. Through the good fortune of meeting a mutual acquaintance, a woman who lived next to Marie's apartment on the boulevard de la Madeleine, and through various machinations, the two young men and the neighbor were soon in Marie's apartment with Marie and the elderly count. However, Marie soon managed to treat Stackelberg with sufficient rudeness that he left. Her mood quickly turned exuberant.

Supper was served, and there was drinking and laughter. Dumas was fascinated by the disinterested, callous behavior of the young woman toward her benefactor, but pained and alarmed to see the feverish flush in her cheeks that accompanied the excessive drinking and the increasing laughter. Finally, seized with a fit of coughing, she hurried from the room. Dumas followed and found her lying face-down on a couch; there was blood in a nearby bowl. The likelihood that this delicate creature was living with a hovering presentiment of death, yet hastening the process by her excesses, gripped him like ice.

Dumas was deeply moved, and his obviously genuine fear for her touched the young woman. She described herself to him as a "gloomy mistress, nerve-ridden, sick and melancholy, who spits blood and spends a hundred thousand francs a year." That was all right for a wealthy old fool, she protested, but every young lover she ever had had left her. Her words did not discourage Dumas; she undoubtedly knew they would not. They became lovers.

So far, so good. With some changes here and there, the real story is reasonably similar to the novel, the play, and the opera. But any similarities after these opening scenes are a good deal less pointed. If there was any self-sacrifice or change in behavior by her, evidence of it is hard to come by. Whether, in the solitude of their intimate hours together, he attempted to reform her, or to extract an oath of faithfulness, we do not know, and Dumas, fils never tells us. If he did, he failed. That he was truly enamored of her is a safe assumption from all that he wrote and from all that can be documented of his behavior during the next eleven months.

Dumas, fils was not wealthy at this time of his young life. He lived off the generosity of Dumas, père, and père was himself in dire straits. Dumas, fils borrowed from whomever he could, but it was not sufficient to appease the pleasure-hungry Marie, who, every day, sent him her wish list. It always included, at a minimum, dinner, the theater, and a bouquet of camellias. So, inevitably, there were other lovers; inevitably, there were also lies, and Dumas, fils knew it. There was still the old count, and there was a younger man, Édouard Perregaux, the grandson of a famous financier. The three were juggled with skillful dexterity: an invitation to one, an apology to another, and a request for favors, such as theater tickets, from a third. "Lies keep the teeth white," she once explained to a friend. Dumas, fils began to drift away. She sent a note, an outwardly tender, but half-hearted, attempt to mollify him.

On "30th August, Midnight" 1845, he sent her his farewell. "I am neither rich enough to love you as I would wish, nor poor enough to be loved by you as you would . . . You have too much heart not to understand the reasons for this letter, and too much intelligence not to forgive me. A thousand memories."

So the middle of the play, and of the opera, do not track real life. But what about the finale? The real-life last act? Some of it was as we see it on the stage, but much of what is on the stage is pure embellishment. There was dissipation and a tragically early death. But there was no final duet.

In October 1846, fourteen months after his last farewell, Dumas, fils, traveling through Spain and Portugal with Dumas, père, his memory still filled with thoughts of Marie, wrote to her from Madrid. He has heard that she was ill, he tells her. He was headed for Algiers, and a note to him there assuring him of her forgiveness would allow for such a happier return to France; her cure, an even happier one. He never received an answer.

In 1845, in addition to Stackelberg and Perregaux, she had been introduced to Franz Liszt, the great pianist, composer, and lover. Liszt, who once claimed that he had no liking for the Manon Lescauts of the world, admitted that he was captivated by this one: "She had a great deal of heart." But he declined anything permanent, as he did her suggestion for a trip to the Orient together. In 1846 she journeyed to London with Perregaux and participated in a civil ceremony of marriage with him, incomplete in formalities and unrecognized by the law of either France or England.

She was, by now, ravaged by tuberculosis, the galloping consumption, a condition she tried to hide with heroic efforts and increasing adornment with precious jewelry. But she was soon confined to her apartment on the boulevard de la Madeleine. Evenings she would often lean with her elbows on the windowsill and watch the passing parade of fashionable society en route to dinner or to the theater. As her body degenerated, so did her source of income. Her treasured jewels were sold, one at a time. During her final days she refused to see even the faithful Édouard Perregaux.

She died on February 3, 1847, at the height of the Mardi Gras season. Two days later her body was taken by hearse to the Montmartre cemetery. Perregaux was one of only two friends to walk bare-headed behind the hearse amid a throng of curiosity seekers. It was he who bought her permanent resting place. Her tomb was surmounted by a sculptured bouquet of camellias in a glass.

Dumas, fils knew nothing of any of this until his return to France. Marie's furniture and other "rich objects," as the announcements advertised it, were auctioned off at her apartment. He attended and bought her gold chain as a memento. The proceeds of the auction more than covered her debts. In accordance with Marie's will, the balance went to a niece in Normandy on the condition that she never go to Paris. Jules Janin, a contemporary writer, said of Marie's death that it "produced a certain sensation and was talked about for three days, which is a long time in this town so full of refined passions and endless partying."

So, this was Marie. Janin summed her up thus: "It was the dearest and most charming occupation of her life to enhance her own beautys." If she was not quite the model that we might have expected for Marguerite and Violetta, we may be sure that Dumas, fils never forgot her.

In the opera, Violetta is, of course, the most important person in the life of Alfredo Germont. Second, as we know from the opera, is his father, Georgio Germont, that noble, respectable, high-minded, religious, God-fearing gentleman from Provence. This father, it will be recalled, persuades Violetta to renounce her love for Alfredo so that Alfredo's sister, "pure as an angel," may marry her "beloved and loving fiancé," a marriage to which her beloved presumably would not consent were he to learn of this profane liaison of his prospective brother-in-law. As for Violetta's own happiness, says the elder Germont, why, she will find that in heaven. His promise, he says, is inspired by God. How Verdi himself detested such hypocrisy is all too clear from his letters. In the novel and the play, this father of Armand is named Georges Duval.

If Dumas, fils has modeled the life of Marguerite, at least to a fair degree, after Marie, is Dumas, père the model for Georges Duval, and Georgio Germont?

Not a chance. Père once wrote to his son: "One never says no to pleasure." Never could he be accused of failing to live according to the advice he gave. Oblivious to consequences, impervious to empathy for any pain he might have caused, his contempt of women honed to a fine edge, charming, gregarious, witty, a master at repartee, he left in his wake a series of conquests that would have been the envy of the most prolific of the legendary womanizers of history. The names of the best known of a plethora of renowned actresses could be, and have been, mentioned. To us, of more importance is one of his very first dalliances, that with a seamstress, Catherine Labay, his neighbor and eight years his senior. In July 1824 she bore his son, Alexandre.

Seven years later Dumas, père sought custody of his son after executing an official act of acknowledgment. Labay, through an oversight, had failed to register such an acknowledgment at her son's birth, and Dumas, père preceded her correction of that oversight by five weeks. The boy was old enough to remember the legal battle that continued for many months and that ended with his placement by the authorities in a boarding school. Alexandre Dumas, fils, remained close to his father throughout his life, but he later wrote of the torment caused him by the ordeal his mother endured on account of his father, and at the age of forty-two told a friend that he had never forgiven his father for it.

That Dumas, fils never matched the callousness of his father, or his great facility for moving blithely from affair to affair with nary a backward glance, was not at all the fault of Dumas, père. For a brief while it looked as though Dumas, père might succeed in molding his son in his own image. But in this, at least, Dumas, père failed. Dumas, fils brooded and suffered. He seems to have been haunted first by memories of the grief of his abandoned mother, and later by those of the tormented Marie. And it is said that the thought of adultery filled him with disgust.

From where, then, comes the character of the sanctimonious Georges Duval, and Giorgio Germont? It has been suggested that it is really the mother of Dumas, fils who is portrayed, the luckless Catherine Labay. More likely, the fictional character is the deliberate antithesis of this aspect of his father's own character, which undoubtedly repulsed the sensitive Dumas, fils. Whatever the source for this character, if any at all, Dumas, père gloried in his son's success. When first told by fils that he planned a stage adaptation for *La Dame aux Camélias*, père demurred; it would not succeed on the stage. After

Verdi as a young man. Though he gained fame early on, *Rigoletto,* which he wrote at the age of thirty-seven, was the first of his operas for which he is best known today. (Conati, Marcello. *Encounters with Verdi.* Ithaca, N.Y.: Cornell University Press, 1984.)

Giuseppina Strepponi Verdi. She married the composer in August 1859, after the couple had lived together for twelve years. (Painting in the Villa Sant'Agata, Busseto, Italy.)

reading the adaptation, however, in tears, he embraced his son and promised that it would be produced.

It took a while. The censors would not permit it. It was too scandalous a proposition for the stage, though much more sedate than the novel. But in December 1851, following a coup d'état, came the installation of a friend of fils as a minister of the crown, and approval for production of the play. It opened on February 2, 1852, and shocked, scandalized, and delighted the Parisian public. One of the city's best-known critics, Théophile Gautier, wrote: "At last Marie Duplessis has the statue which we asked for her. The poet has taken over the task of the sculptor." Père was informed of his son's success by telegram in Belgium, where he had been obliged to flee the previous month with creditors hot on his trail.

It is known that Giuseppe Verdi was in Paris in February 1852 with his constant companion, Giuseppina Strepponi. According to one of his contemporary biographers, Arthur Pougin, he attended a performance that month of *La Dame aux Camélias,* was "struck with enthusiasm for it, and at once formed the project of making an opera of it." The circumstances, and the chronology of the opera's creation, seem to corroborate him. It seems all but inevitable that the play would have intrigued him. That even in the midst of rehearsing for *Il Trovatore* he became absorbed in *La Traviata,* at times working simultaneously on both operas, is hardly surprising. A number of aspects of *The Lady of the Camellias,* to a dead certainty, must have hit in Verdi many vulnerable spots.

One of them, in fact, must have hit a raw nerve; namely, his own unconventional romance with Giuseppina. The play of Dumas, fils caused many expressions of shock and moral outrage among the more genteel elements of Parisian society and was banned for a number of years in London. Such a reaction could have been no surprise to Verdi, but must have opened many wounds. He and Giuseppina had experienced much the same shocked response to their open and unlicensed cohabitation, beginning in the town of Busetto in northern Italy, where Giuseppina was openly shunned for two and a half years. Then, less than nine months before the premiere of the Dumas play, Verdi and the former diva scandalized the little nearby village of

Sant'-Agata by moving together into a home there that Verdi had built for them.

Just twelve days before the first performance of *La Dame aux Camélias,* Verdi wrote a letter to Antonio Barezzi, the father of his long-deceased wife. It was in response to one he had just received from Barezzi. The two men had been on terms of the closest friendship, and they so remained, all of which makes Verdi's letter of January 21 the more pointed. We do not have Barezzi's letter, but whatever the older man said provoked, in part, this from the sensitive composer:

> I have nothing to hide. In my house there lives a lady, free and independent, who like me, prefers a solitary life . . . Neither I nor she is obliged to account to anyone for our actions . . . and even if it is a bad thing, who has the right to ostracize us . . . she has every right, both because of her conduct and her character to that consideration she habitually shows to others . . . my nature rebels against mere conformity . . . you . . . must not let yourself be influenced, must not absorb the ideas of a community which . . . is now complaining and gossiping about me and my business.

We can only imagine the impact his first exposure, both to the play and to public reaction, must have made on him just twelve days after writing such a letter.

Nor could the death of the beautiful young heroine have left him unmoved. His own wife had died from illness in 1840. Together, two years before that, they had suffered the loss of their seven-month-old son; the following year, the death of their seventeen-month-old daughter. In the Dumas play, Marguerite sells her jewels to pay the expenses of the country retreat she and Armand enjoy. In the early days of Verdi's marriage, he became ill and was unable to pay the rent. As he recalled forty years later, his wife sold her jewels and paid the rent with the proceeds. At the time of her death, Verdi's wife was twenty-seven. Her name was Margherita.

Finally, at the play Verdi would have heard Armand imploring the ailing Marguerite, "We will live quietly away from this wild Paris, and the friends who are now killing you. We will seek amidst the woods and fields, health and strength for you, and we shall find them."

Fifteen years after the premiere of the play, Giuseppina, now Verdi's wife for eight years, wrote a letter to a friend describing how it was that she and Verdi came to leave Paris in 1848 and first live together in the country, just outside the city:

> I asked Verdi with some insistence to leave Paris and to take, beneath the pavilion of the open sky, those salutary baths of air and light that give as much vigour to the body as calm and serenity to the mind.

In 1851 they moved to Sant'-Agata, and according to Giuseppina, "We began our infinite pleasure, planting a garden, which at the beginning, was called Peppina's garden."

Could Verdi possibly have heard the words of Armand without recalling that initial venture with Giuseppina into country life, or their first days together in Sant'-Agata just a few months before?

On May 4 he signed a contract with the Teatro la Fenice in Venice for a new opera, which he said he would probably call *La Traviata, The Lost One,* despite the fact that he did not receive a copy of the text of the play until the following October. His librettist was Francesco Piave, whom we last saw working on Verdi's *Rigoletto. La Traviata* was first performed on March 6, 1853, and was a total fiasco. The reasons were said to include poor casting, such as an overly endowed soprano who brought down the house with laughter upon announcing that she was dying from consumption, and other problems equally as unimportant to the history of this musical masterpiece. On May 6 of the following year it was revived at the San Benedetto Theater, also in Venice. It was a tremendous success, and, despite some sniffing that it was an outrageous attack on marriage, it has been impervious to critical carping, of which there seems less and less each decade.

Dumas, fils may yet, through the magic of *La Traviata,* outlast père. The liaison between Dumas, fils and Marie Duplessis, which lasted but eleven months, has brought immortality to them both.

Richard Wagner in Paris, two years after completing *Tristan and Isolde*. (Kapp, Julius. *Richard Wagner, Sein Leben, Sein Werk, Seine Welt.* Berlin-Schöneberg: Max Hesses Verlag, 1933.)

11

WAGNER AND
FRAU WESENDONCK

TRISTAN AND ISOLDE

THE PLOT: *Tristan brings the Irish princess Isolde as bride to his uncle, King of Cornwall. She is outraged to be so treated by Tristan now, as she once saved Tristan's life when she could have killed him as her enemy. She plans to poison him and herself, but is thwarted when her maid substitutes a love potion for the poison. The veneer of Isolde's bitterness and Tristan's loyalty to the king evaporate, and they express their intense love. Discovered together in a nocturnal tryst, Tristan allows himself to be mortally wounded, and is taken to his boyhood home in France. Isolde follows to heal him again, but arrives as he dies.*

*J*n the center of the manicured Rieterpark in Zurich's Enge District is a stately structure known as the Villa Wesendonck. Today it houses the Rietberg Museum and its famed collection of Oriental art. If the walls could talk, they might tell an interesting tale of the building's first owner, his refined and talented wife, and of their unhappy, quarrelsome tenants in a small cottage that once stood nearby.

The owner was a wealthy Rhinelander named Otto Wesendonck, partner in a New York silk-trading firm. In 1851, at the age of thirty-six, he settled in Zurich with his twenty-two-year-old wife, Mathilde.

Two years later, they chose as a site for their permanent residence the "Green Hill" in Enge, then a rural suburb.

Zurich was alive at the time with political refugees from the unsuccessful German revolution of 1848–49, one of whom, as we have seen, was the restless, driven, fiery-eyed composer and former conductor of the Dresden Opera, Richard Wagner.

Wagner's years in Zurich were not happy ones. His letters from 1852 on speak increasingly of his loneliness, the biggest factor in which was undoubtedly the growing tension between himself and his embittered wife, Minna. They were temperamentally incompatible, and Minna was unable to understand the paths his staggering artistic growth had been taking. By his reckless intrusion into an armed uprising, he had shattered the normal middle-class respectability she had briefly enjoyed in Dresden and she did not mean for him to forget it. Worse, he was surviving by accepting gratuities from friends, a practice she detested.

One of the generous friends was Otto Wesendonck, whom Wagner met in February 1852. At the same time, Wagner also met, and soon became deeply enamored of, Otto's wife, Mathilde. His growing romantic interest in her over the next six years precipitated, or at least paralleled, a philosophical preoccupation with the nature of love itself, evidence of which abounds in his letters. The most interesting of these is a communication to his friend Franz Liszt in Weimar in late 1854: "As I have never in my life felt the real bliss of love, I must erect a monument to the most beautiful of all my dreams . . . I have in my head 'Tristan and Isolde'."

What he had in his head was the germinating outline of one of the most awesome monuments of sound ever sculpted. His story is based on the legend of "Tristram and Iseult," a series of episodes involving the two lovers, and dating back to early Celtic antiquity. Beginning in the early twelfth century there were at least five written versions, the best known of which is *Tristan and Isolde* by Gottfried von Strassburg.

Wagner bound the essence of the stories into a single unified tale filled with painful longing, philosophical implications, and symbolism. His poem deals with love and death, both of which are the subjects of yearning by the two lovers. This love/death is cast in opposition to the world of reality in the metaphor of night and day, darkness and light. He set it to tightly knit musical themes, the entirety of which seems carved, like a monolith, from solid rock. From the opening phrase of the prelude, the themes grow ceaselessly out of each other until the benedictionlike finale known as the "Liebestod," or love/death, which resolves at last the three acts of otherwise never-ending tension.

In February 1857, Wesendonck's magnificent home neared completion coincidentally with the growing absorption of his wife and Wagner with each other, and with the blossoming concept of *Tristan and Isolde* in Wagner's wildly excited imagination. At Mathilde's urging, Wesendonck bought a small piece of adjoining land with an existing cottage, and placed it, at a nominal rent, at Wagner's disposal for life. At the end of April, the composer and his wife took possession of the small dwelling, which Wagner soon termed the "Asyl." There, in comparative quiet and security, he continued work on *Siegfried,* the third of the *Ring* dramas. In late August the Wesendoncks moved into their completed mansion on the Green Hill, and Wagner and Mathilde were now separated by only a few yards of garden.

In August 1856, he had written to his co-revolutionary August Roekel, languishing in Waldheim prison, that so possessed had he become of the *Tristan* subject that only with some effort could he force it into the background to continue with the *Ring.* But the following June, two months after moving into his Asyl, he can no longer resist *Tristan.* He writes under a bar in the second-act draft of *Siegfried,* "When shall we see each other again?" On the following day, he writes Liszt, "I have led my young Siegfried into a beautiful forest solitude. There I left him under a linden tree and, with tears from the depth of my heart, said farewell to him." At the end of August, he began his poem of *Tristan,* the creation of which, says Wagner in his autobiography, was "written in plain letters in my book of fate."

Turning to more mundane matters, he noted laconically that Otto had become rather uneasy "at the way I made myself at home in his house." Just how much he did make himself at home during his almost daily visits to Mathilde is one of the few remaining secrets of Wagner's life.

Only a day or two before commencing his *Tristan* poem, the Wagners had visitors: Hans von Bülow, the pianist and conductor, and his nineteen-year-old bride of a few weeks, Cosima, the daughter

The Wesendonck Home on the "Green Hill" in Zurich, and Wagner's "Asyl," site of a blossoming love relationship between the composer and his benefactor's wife. (Kapp, Julius. *Richard Wagner, Sein Leben, Sein Werk, Seine Welt.* Berlin-Schöneberg: Max Hesses Verlag, 1933.)

of Franz Liszt. In eight years, von Bülow was to become the first conductor of *Tristan and Isolde;* Cosima was destined to become, at about the same time, Wagner's lover, and five years later, his second wife. As each act of the poem was completed during the next three weeks, Wagner read it aloud to a small, select group, including the interesting combination of Minna, Mathilde, and Cosima.

In early October, he began the composition sketch of the first act. At the end of November, he interrupted work on *Tristan* to set to music five poems written by Mathilde, one of a very few occasions on which he wrote music to words written by anyone other than himself. He completed that project the first of May 1858. By then, Wagner's personal Asyl had been transformed into a personal hell.

On April 7, he had sent a lengthy note to Mathilde rolled inside a penciled sketch of the instrumentation of the *Tristan* prelude. The servant to whom the papers were entrusted was relieved of his package by Minna while crossing the garden between the two houses. Biographers may argue over the significance of the effusive language in which the otherwise harmless note is couched, but to Minna it left no doubt at all. She burst immediately into her husband's room, and leveled at him a withering verbal assault.

"She gave a vulgar interpretation to my words," complained Wagner in later years. She also provoked an ugly confrontation with Mathilde, spread her tearful lamentations indiscriminately among her Zurich friends, and precipitated an atmosphere of unbearable tension among the four principals.

Wagner finally prevailed on Minna to take an extended rest at the health resort at Brestenberg on Lake Hallwyler, from which she returned in mid-July. During her absence, he completed the composition draft of the second act. A month after her return, he gave up the hopeless struggle for peace, took leave of his wife and the Wesendoncks, and moved to Venice with a recently acquired Erard piano to complete the orchestral scoring of the second act. His last days in Zurich he later described as a "veritable hell." To his sister Klara, he wrote of "unheard of scenes and tortures." Following Wagner's departure, Minna left for Dresden, but first refueled local gossip by advertising in the local papers that her personal effects would be sold cheaply owing to a sudden departure. To a Berlin acquaintance she later expressed her determination to avoid a first performance of "that fateful *Tristan* which I cannot bear for its origin." Mathilde was described to the same acquaintance as "that cold woman spoiled by happiness."

Wagner spent eight months in Venice in one of the dilapidated Giustiniani palaces on the Grand Canal. His letters to Mathilde exude the sights and sounds of Venice and his own enchantment with the second-act music that flowed from his pen. The letters to Minna, with some exceptions, alternate between angry retorts and descriptions of his daily routine, financial affairs, and clinical details of his ailments. But his genuine concern for her welfare was unmistakable.

After completing the second act, he left Venice. The Venetian authorities had thus far resisted attempts by the Saxon government to expel the former revolutionary, but Wagner did not want to risk an interruption while working on Act III. Nor did he want to endure the heat of a Venetian summer. So in March 1859 he went to Lucerne for six months, where he composed the music for that last act, which seemed to him to assume a life of its own. He appeared at times awed by it, and wondered if it could ever be realized in performance. He also, to Minna's consternation, made peace with the Wesendoncks, who made the short drive from Zurich to celebrate the completion of the opera with him over champagne.

There followed six years of frustrated attempts to stage *Tristan,* which ended with the accession to the Bavarian throne of the nineteen-year-old Wagner idolater, King Ludwig II. In June 1865 it was produced in Munich in the midst of a real-life drama that paralleled that of the opera. Whatever doubts there may be about Wagner's relationship with Mathilde in Zurich, about his relationship with Cosima von Bülow, whose husband conducted the premiere, there were none. It created a scandal that rocked polite society in the Bavarian capital, and made the episode on the Green Hill appear, in comparison, a teapot tempest.

Thus, Mathilde was not the last love of his life by any means. Nor was she the first extramarital distraction. Did she inspire *Tristan and Isolde,* as some of Wagner's many biographers maintain? Or was she the most available and convenient symbol of the Irish princess in his mind, as claimed by others? Much in Wagner's life proves his need to live out the stories of his works, at least while he was writing them. But there is this to be said on behalf of the former proposition. This opera is unique, not only for its powerfully unified structure, but for its place in Wagner's life story.

When, in the spring of 1849, Wagner fled to Switzerland, he had already conceived in embryo form almost the entire balance of his life's work: "Siegfried's Death," which later grew into the four operas of his *The Ring of the Nibelung; Die Meistersinger, Parsifal*—everything except *Tristan and Isolde.* It alone, among his mature works, seems to have come alive spontaneously, to have taken root in the wild.

So, do we owe *Tristan and Isolde* to Mathilde? Or does Mathilde owe her brief sojourn with the composer to *Tristan*? There is evidence for either proposition. But none of it is so powerful as the internal evidence of the music itself. The final shape of the work may well have been influenced by his love for this lady. But the work itself, or something very much like it, seems to have been, like a force of nature, inevitable.

12

THREE MEN AND
AN OPERA

FAUST

THE PLOT: *Faust, an aged philosopher, despairs of finding wisdom in books, and is about to take poison. Mephistopheles appears, and offers him his youth and a young maiden, Marguerite, in return for his soul. The sight of Marguerite is irresistible, and Faust accepts. Aided by the wiles of Mephistopheles, Faust successfully courts Marguerite. Months later, Marguerite, now with child, is imprisoned for her illicit love. Faust goes to her and urges her to escape with him, but he himself is dragged off to the underworld. The delirious Marguerite dies, and is borne to heaven by angels.*

The original idea for an opera based on Goethe's *Faust*, with music by Charles Gounod, was that of Leon Carvalho, the manager of the Théâtre Lyrique in Paris, or of the librettist, Jules Barbier, or of Gounod himself, depending on whose memoirs one chooses to believe. Each of them claimed credit for the idea, and the prompt and positive response to it by the other two.

Barbier claims that he first offered to collaborate with Giacomo Meyerbeer, who indignantly refused, feeling that the Goethe poem was sacred and should not be touched.

Gounod's autobiography tells us that as a man in his early twenties in Rome, his favorite amusement was reading Goethe's *Faust*, and

Charles Gounod, the composer of *Faust*. Through poor business acumen the vast profits from that popular opera went mostly to publishers. (Prod'homme, J. G., and A. Dandelot. *Gounod: Sa Vie et ses Oeuvres*. Paris: Librairie Ch. Delagrave, 1911.)

that during a nocturnal stroll on the isle of Capri, he envisioned a Walpurgisnacht scene as depicted in the poem. At the age of thirty-two he saw a performance of *Faust and Marguerite,* a stage play by Michel Carré.

By then both the legend itself and its use as a subject for musical composition were hoary with age and use. The consensus of opinion, though not unanimous, is that it began with the publication in 1587 of a collection of stories about a German scholar and alchemist, a Dr. Johann Faustus, who died about 1540. The book was popular throughout Europe, and the legend was kept alive by Christopher Marlowe's *The Tragical History of Dr. Faustus* in 1588. Troups of English actors took the play to Germany, where the story was picked up with renewed vigor in puppet plays, all revolving around Faust's pact with the devil.

Goethe's monumental dramatic poem was begun about 1774 when the poet was not yet twenty-five years of age. It is divided into two parts, the first of which was published in 1808; the complete work in 1833, a year after Goethe's death. During the time he spent writing it, over twenty-eight authors published works based on the legend, but it is the Goethe epic that eclipsed the others and captured the attention of the literary world. When Gounod began his opera it had already been the subject of compositions by Spohr, Berlioz, and Boito. Even Beethoven had once considered and outlined a plan for it, and as a young man in Paris, Richard Wagner had composed a "Faust Overture."

The episode on which the story of the Gounod opera is based is contained in its entirety in the first part of Goethe's poem, and it is entirely original with him. The philosophical and religious character of the poem, developed mostly in part two, was neither in Carré's play nor Gounod's opera.

Barbier and Gounod agreed to enlist the aid of Carré in preparing the libretto. The playwright agreed very reluctantly, having no confidence in the project, and his contribution was minimal, though his share of the paltry profits equaled those of Barbier and Gounod.

The opera had originally been scheduled for November 1857, but Carvalho, the theater manager, halted work on it upon hearing that the prestigious Théâtre St. Martin was about to stage a melodrama based on the legendary theme. But the play folded after a short run, and Carvalho once more asked Gounod and Barbier to move forward with the opera.

There followed more than the usual problems with casting, rehearsals, and revisions. Carvalho's wife, Madame Ugalde, insisted on and was given the role of Marguerite. She seemed, by all accounts, to share with her husband a determination to alter to suit her own tastes any opera in which she participated. According to one biographer, "Her bad taste was monumental; her will implacable. She loaded the melodic lines with arabesques and trills. No aria was safe from her greedy hands." Meanwhile, Gounod and Barbier were fighting to prevent Carvalho's tampering with the scenes, the church scene having been displaced from after that of Valentine's return to before, then after, then before, and finally after, where it had started.

The censor almost called a halt to the whole shoving match by threatening to remove the church scene as offensive to the papal state. Relations between the papacy and France had been strained, and the censor feared political repercussions. Biographers differ as to whether it was Gounod or Carvalho who pulled the coup, but one of them invited the apostolic nuncio to Paris, Monseigneur de Segur, to a rehearsal at which the censor was present; then, in the presence of the censor, the monseigneur was asked his opinion of that scene. He is reported to have replied: "I should like all theater to have scenes like that. Suppress the cathedral scene? Who on earth asked you to do that?"

The censor left and was heard from no more. Nor had anyone informed him that the monseigneur was a close friend of Gounod's, or that the monseigneur was totally blind.

If opening night was not a brilliant success, neither was it a failure. The opera had a run of fifty-seven performances at the Lyrique that season. Meyerbeer, according to Madame Ugalde, was at seven or eight of them. Despite his refusal to compose the music himself, Hector Berlioz praised it unstintingly. From its original form as an opéra comique, that is, with spoken dialogue, it was turned into grand opera by the addition of recitative for an 1860 Strasburg performance. It was played throughout Europe, and its popularity in Hamburg saved the opera company there from bankruptcy. In 1863 it began a forty-four-year run at London's Covent Garden, and in 1890 George Bernard Shaw, not to be outdone by anybody, claimed to have seen it there ninety times within the prior fifteen years. It reached New York in 1864, and in 1883 was selected for its first performance by the newly created Metropolitan Opera Company.

For all of that, Gounod earned very little money. He was, alas, no businessman. Despite praise from the critics and artists, public response was not immediate, and publishers were hesitant. Publication of the text and score, at the time the prime means of revenue for composers and librettists, was about to be undertaken by Gounod, Barbier, and Carré themselves, but was finally contracted for in France with a small firm owned by Antoine de Choudens. The ten thousand francs he paid was divided equally among the three of them. Thirty years later, Choudens had earned over three million francs on his investment.

The situation in England was even worse. The London publisher neglected to secure the copyright, and the three Frenchmen earned nothing from the sale of copies that were freely pirated in England and her extensive colonies. The German rights were sold for one thousand francs, again divided three ways.

Choudens, however, was all business; he cared not a whit for the music. He is reputed to have threatened to punish his young children when they misbehaved by forcing them to attend a performance of *Faust*. His spirit, or a mirror image of it, still lives in the wealthy Texan who reportedly made a huge gift to an opera company in that state with the sole condition that he never be requested to attend any opera performance.

13

THE PARIS OPÉRA
AND THE JOCKEYS

TANNHÄUSER

THE PLOT: *Tannhäuser returns to earth after a sojourn in the sensuous realm of Venus. He meets his friends, the minstrel knights, and joins their contest of song. The subject is "love," and in the heat of the contest he inadvertently reveals his period of revelry with Venus. Through the pleas of Elizabeth, niece of the Landgrave, he is spared punishment and joins pilgrims en route to Rome to seek absolution. But he alone is deemed unworthy of redemption by the Pope. Bitterly he plans to return to Venus when he hears that Elizabeth has died and will seek his redemption in heaven. With a prayer on his lips, he joins her in death.*

Opera was serious business in those days, and as much so in France as anywhere. The first French performance of *Tannhäuser*, sixteen years after its Dresden premiere, took place at Paris's glittering Opéra by direct order of no less a person than Emperor Napoléon III. No cost had been spared. The cast, personally selected by Wagner, had been through more than 160 rehearsals. The staging, according to the virtuoso pianist and conductor, Hans von Bülow, defied description, but was described by him nonetheless as "a thing of marvelous beauty." It was still four years before he would lose his wife, Cosima, to Wagner, by whose music he was, and would always remain, entranced.

The first performance, on March 13, 1861, was attended by

The Paris Opera, from an 1844 engraving. One of the most prestigious opera houses of the mid-nineteenth century, it was steeped in politics, bureaucratic red tape, and possible corruption. Verdi suffered failure here; Wagner, a debacle. (*Verdi: A Documentary Study*. London: Thames and Hudson.)

the upper echelon of Parisian society and the full court, including the Empress Eugénie and the emperor himself. To the casual observer, the opera should have been a brilliant success. For the overture, the bacchanal, and the first scene, it was. Then all hell broke loose.

Following the opening, high-tension Venusberg scene, as the soothing offstage melody of the shepherd boy's gentle soprano wafted through the hall, a shrill whistle pierced the stillness of the audience. It was a signal for a chorus of loud whistling, shouting, and laughter. This was a well-planned attack by members of the Paris Jockey Club, who had turned out in force. They were immediately challenged, and far outnumbered, by the balance of the audience who had come to hear the opera.

The battle lasted throughout the performance, which somehow

staggered and stumbled in fits and starts to the end. It did so amid alternate outbursts of laughter, hissing, and whistling by the Jockeys, applause by the other spectators, and shouted threats and insults between the two groups. It continued through the second performance on the eighteenth, the opera often being interrupted for fifteen minutes at a time, and through a third on the twenty-fourth. On the street the hawkers, never ones to miss a bet, were peddling "Wagner whistles."

After the third performance, the management reluctantly permitted Wagner to withdraw the opera rather than require him to submit it to further savaging. This despite the fact that many believed the opera supporters were carrying the day, that their superior numbers would prevail, and that with time the Jockeys would tire of the game and fade away.

What was the Jockey Club? Who were their members, and what was their problem? Let Minna tell it. Minna, Wagner's estranged wife, had come to Paris to join her husband during the rehearsals and performances of his *Tannhäuser,* a futile attempt at a reconciliation. Minna, always unsophisticated, unpretentious, and uncomplicated, wrote the following month to her illegitimate daughter, Natalie, whom Minna had borne long before her first fateful meeting with Wagner:

> The so-called Jockey Club are the rich frivolous gentlemen who have their mistresses in the ballet, nearly all employed without any salary, with whom they amuse themselves after the ballet, behind the scenes, and this in the most indecent manner.

Minna had it right. This clique of wealthy young aristocrats liked to dine leisurely each evening, then arrive at the Opéra in time for the second act, during which they would see their sweethearts perform or they would know the reason why not. So it is that many operas that premiered or were later performed in Paris, then an opera capital of the world, have second-act ballets. But there was no ballet in the second act of *Tannhäuser* and Wagner refused to insert one, pointing out that, dramatically speaking, it would have been nonsense. This was not sufficient excuse for the Jockey Club, and Wagner's stubbornness was answered by their violent disruption of the opera.

Minna also mentioned in her letter the ugly subject of politics:

"The Emperor was there all three times, but he could do nothing, they are Legitimists."

Minna had it right again. Legitimists were the powerful, aristocratic opposition to the emperor. They counted among their friends the Prince of Wales, an admirer of attractive young female stage performers. He enjoyed accompanying his Jockey friends as they made their rounds of the dressing rooms. André Maurois, biographer of Alexandre Dumas, has painted a vivid word picture of the Jockeys and their "wavy whiskers and curly hair, square monocles set in the eye, towering stove pipe hats on their heads."

Napoleon III had ruffled their feathers by ordering *Tannhäuser* performed in the first place. The Opéra was steeped in politics, and the performance of an opera by this German composer was not, by their lights, politically correct. How, then, did it happen that *Tannhäuser* was performed? Because Wagner, bless his much-maligned soul, could do politics with the best of them. He had been in exile from Germany with a price on his head since his precipitous flight from Dresden in 1849. But he was not without friends in high places.

One of his influential friends was the ambassador from his native Saxony, Baron von Seebach, who missed no opportunity to plug for his compatriot at the French court. A second friend at court was Count Hatzfield, attaché to the Prussian Embassy, who made a direct appeal to Empress Eugénie. But the prime moving force was Princess Pauline Metternich, granddaughter of Klemens Metternich, former Austrian chief minister.

Pauline had married Klemens's son, Richard, her uncle, and hence was now also the famous statesman's daughter-in-law. Richard also happened to be the Austrian ambassador to Paris, and she took full advantage of that fact to push the production of *Tannhäuser*. Because of her efforts on Wagner's behalf, it is tempting to think of her as a grande dame, a gracious lady of culture and refinement.

Alas, the descriptions that have come down to us paint no such portrait. She is credited by Ernest Newman, still the greatest among Wagner's small army of biographers, as having distinguished herself "even in that milieu of extravagance and vulgarity by the freedom of her tongue and the pert audacity of her behavior." She is described by biographer Martin Gregor-Dellin as "an exceedingly silly and excitable woman," and by a contemporary, and ungallant, though obviously direct sort of fellow, Count Horace de Viel Castel, thus: "She drinks, she smokes, she swears, she is ugly as sin, and she tells stories."

What a pity! But in this imperfect world we must judge everything in balance, and Wagner needed help from anywhere it might be forthcoming. More damaging from Wagner's viewpoint was the fact that for political reasons Pauline was despised by many French legitimists and aristocrats, including members of the Jockey Club.

Wagner had come to Paris in the fall of 1859 from his refuge in Switzerland, not to perform *Tannhäuser* but to find a forum for his newly completed *Tristan and Isolde. Tristan* was a difficult and thoroughly perplexing work to musicians of the day, written in a new and strange musical language. Several companies in his native Germany had attempted, then finally abandoned, the project. Wagner ultimately realized that his personal presence would be necessary at rehearsals to instruct and explain to the artists, by his own example, how to sing, conduct, and act this complex new work. The door was closed to his personal presence in Germany, so he looked to Paris, the city in which he and Minna had spent two miserable years of failure, frustration, and poverty over twenty years earlier.

Whether his personal presence was always such a unique advantage may be called into question by accounts of his audition before Leon Carvalho, director of Paris's Théâtre Lyrique. Wagner meant to impress upon Carvalho the beauties of *Tannhäuser,* and to that end sang the second-act finale, accompanying himself on the piano. According to a witness to the scene, Wagner played "with his hands, his wrists, his elbows, he smashed the peddles, he ground the keys." According to Carvalho himself:

> He howled, he threw himself about, he hit all kinds of wrong notes and to crown it all, he sang in German! And his eyes! The eyes of a madman! I did not dare to cross him; he frightened me.

Wagner was indeed like that at times, and there is no reason to suspect the slightest embellishment or exaggeration on the part of Carvalho.

Wagner's plan was to give a series of concerts to raise money to support himself and Minna and to acquaint the Parisian public with his music. This was to be followed, as a further introduction, by performances of *Tannhäuser,* all leading hopefully to a performance of *Tristan.* Specially for these Paris *Tannhäuser* performances, he completely rewrote the Venusberg scene and added a bacchanal.

Three concerts in January and February 1860 were well received but were economically a monumental disaster even in a life filled with such disasters. He never mastered the French language, he sought no advice with regard to the contract he signed, and the impresarios with whom he dealt offered none. From the concert receipts Wagner was obliged to pay all expenses, including orchestra and theater, and wound up with an 11,000-franc deficit.

He rebounded from this reverse by rushing headlong into another, namely, a series of three concerts in Brussels. Once more the impetuous composer found that the large, enthusiastic audiences that attended the first two concerts did not translate to profits, owing to various contract clauses he understood as little as he did those in Paris. After realizing that his receipts would not cover his traveling expenses, he canceled the third concert and returned to Paris. Many years later, in speaking to a friend about this debacle, he confided, "We can't count on any country in which French is spoken. Take my word for that."

By his Paris landlord he was swindled even more flagrantly. Upon his arrival in that city, he leased a home on the rue Newton for three years. The landlord required payment in advance for the final two years. He must have known, as Wagner did not, that all buildings on the rue Newton would soon fall prey to a massive renovation of the city. Under the direction of a renowned architect, Georges-Eugène Haussmann, Paris was about to be transformed into the city of circles and boulevards we know today.

In February 1860, rumors of the impending demolition reached Wagner. His inquiries to the landlord were met with the disingenuous suggestion that Wagner sue him and that he would in turn sue the city. When the futile lawsuit ran its course, Wagner recouped nothing. French law at the time placed such risks on the tenant, and Wagner moved with Minna to much more modest quarters on the rue D'Aumale.

In mid-March, in the midst of these troubles, came the emperor's order to produce *Tannhäuser.* Wagner was elated, but there followed a deluge of new complications and reverses that dwarfed those he had thus far experienced in Paris.

There was trouble with his lead role. The cast he selected was all French or Italian except for the role of Tannhäuser. For that role he chose Albert Niemann, a heldentenor of heroic build and voice. Wagner purposely chose a German, noting that the typical French tenor was ill-suited to the role. This German tenor, engaged by the Opéra at 6,000 francs per month for nine months, was to cause Wagner more grief than the rest of the cast combined, more, probably, than the entire Jockey Club.

Niemann was delayed in arriving in Paris for reasons that may tell something of his temperament. For assaulting the conductor during a backstage brawl at the Hannover opera between acts of *Lohengrin,* he was sentenced to four weeks in prison. But he was not lacking in a sense of humor. He passed his time in confinement by singing through the window of his cell the prison scene from *Il Trovatore.*

Niemann's nature was such that he declined all advice from anyone, composers included, on how to interpret any role. He could see the opera only as a vehicle in which to display his vocal virtuosity, and it was obvious that this role frightened him. Wagner begged him to look at the inner dramatic content, promising that, so interpreted, the dreaded phrases were not difficult. The intensity of the face-to-face sessions between singer and composer can be surmised from the bitter nature of their correspondence. Insultingly intransigent letters from the tenor were answered by the composer with surprising restraint, but Wagner's frustration and disappointment with his tenor simmer between the lines.

Sometime in late 1860, Niemann got wind that a cabal of journalists was determined to wreck both *Tannhäuser* and Wagner. Many circumstances indicate that such a conspiracy may not have been entirely imaginary, and may have included Wagner's enemy, the composer Giacomo Meyerbeer, who was rumored, rightly or wrongly, to be adept at buying favor with the press. There were also increasingly visible signs of coming physical sabotage by the Jockey Club. When Niemann realized that a catastrophe might be in the offing, he fell into a moodiness bordering on depression and became more and more difficult and obstinate. He demanded cuts of phrases he considered too difficult, noting, almost on the eve of the first performance,

"I shall be very happy, indeed, if I escape . . . with my voice intact."

There were problems with translators. It was a rule of the Opéra that any opera performed there had to be in French. So Wagner selected two translators to render his verses into French. He was dissatisfied with one, Lindau, and the theater manager, Alphonse Royer, was dissatisfied with both and foisted a third on him. None of the three showed much enthusiasm for the job. Lindow brought suit for additional compensation for "author's rights" but was thrown out of court. Wagner's other selected translator refused to have his name appear on the program, and the manager's appointee refused to have his name stand alone. So no one was credited with the translation.

There were also problems with Wagner's health. In mid-October, he suffered, for several weeks, an episode of what was termed typhoid fever, experiencing among other symptoms a temporary blindness and hallucinations. Those close to him were greatly alarmed and few doubted that the nervous tension involved in the mountains of problems with *Tannhäuser* was a major factor.

Despite these obstacles, as the often-postponed performance date approached, Wagner succeeded in welding together what promised to be a coherent, sensitive rendering of his opera. The musicians, in particular, had come a long way since the early days when they had bristled under his direction and had pointedly informed him that they were French musicians, not Prussian soldiers.

But, due to another rule of the Opéra, his efforts went for nothing. Every new work had to be conducted by the house conductor. In this case he happened to be one Pierre Louis Felipe Dietsch, by all accounts a pitiful incompetent. According to von Bülow, Dietsch was "an old man, destitute of intelligence and memory, utterly uneducable and lacking in ear." Dietsch first entered the scene to conduct the full rehearsals beginning in mid-February, barely a month before the first public performance. Almost immediately the entire fabric began to unravel. After the second such rehearsal Wagner sent a letter to Royer demanding that he be permitted to conduct the remaining rehearsals plus the first three performances. The demand went as far as one of the emperor's ministers, by whom it was politely rejected as contrary to the inviolable rule of the Opéra.

That the second act should have a ballet was not a rule of the Opéra but it was a tradition, the violation of which was the coup de grace to the Paris *Tannhäuser*. From every quarter Wagner was beseeched, urged, begged, or threatened. Vainly he offered compromises: a first-act bacchanal, which he intended to add anyway and had already written, or perhaps a ballet to be held after the performance. Nothing would appease the Jockey Club but a second-act ballet.

With incredible naiveté he expressed the assurance that once these young men had seen the opera they would understand that such an insertion would be a dramatic anomaly and an artistic impossibility. Whoever suggested to him that these gentlemen had the slightest interest in the dramatic integrity of this or any other opera remains a mystery.

So at that first performance on March 19 all was not what it seemed to be to the casual observer, and the smoldering volcano erupted. Niemann, panic-stricken at the thought of damage to his career, gave little thought to the composer, to the opera, or to the cast. After the first performance he wrote to a Berlin friend that the "opera called *Tannhäuser*" was "hissed, hooted and finally laughed off the stage." But "the *player* of Tannhäuser, God be praised, saved his artistic honor." After the second performance he could make no such pretense. He went down with the rest of them. He was hissed and booed by the Jockey Club in his third-act Rome narrative and gave a mute gesture that one onlooker took to mean "I can't help it if the opera is no good."

Though Wagner said little about Niemann, it was clear to those close to the composer that he was deeply hurt. On the eve of the third performance he wrote to Joseph Tichatschek, his aging original Tannhäuser from Dresden, about "the miserable coward who runs around howling that he ruins his voice with my *Tannhäuser*." Five years later, in a letter to King Ludwig of Bavaria, though acknowledging his vocal qualities, he referred to Niemann as a "crude effect snatcher whom I detest from the bottom of my soul." Wagner's request to Royer to withdraw the opera after that second performance was refused.

Neither Wagner, Minna, the emperor, Empress Eugénie, nor most of Wagner's friends attended the third performance. It was on a Sunday, as requested by Wagner in the hope that the Jockeys would not be present. They were present in force. The police were also present, not to ensure a peaceful performance, but to protect the aristocratic

Jockeys from an irate audience. Pierre Baudelaire, the French poet, and a staunch Wagner admirer, later wrote: "Ten obstinate people armed with shrill whistles can . . . cut through the voice of an orchestra as powerful as that of the Opéra." Cut through it they did. As Wagner later received first-hand accounts of the catastrophe, he was outwardly calm, but his companions noted that his hands shook. Royer reluctantly permitted him to withdraw the opera. Niemann's compensation for his nine-month effort was 54,000 francs; Wagner's, for the entire venture, 750.

So it ended. His many enemies rejoiced. His many friends were enraged. Many thought it might have been salvaged. But Wagner had no further heart for the struggle. The overriding passion of his life at this time was not *Tannhäuser.* That was a mere means to an end. The goal was *Tristan,* and however this battle might end, a *Tristan* in Paris was now beyond hope. Shortly before the first performance, von Bülow wrote that Wagner "would gladly give himself up to the executioner the next day if only he could have conducted a good performance of his *Tristan* the night before."

While in Paris he received the long-sought amnesty from all of the German states except his native Saxony. He returned to Germany later in 1861, where he continued his search for a haven for *Tristan.* In his later utterances, rarely did he mention this unhappy episode in Paris. He almost seemed to have put it all behind him.

But it is possible that he may have tried to exact a small measure of revenge. Ten years later, France and Prussia were at war and the battle raged on French soil. General Helmuth Moltke laid siege to Paris, causing its beleaguered citizens severe deprivations and hardships. Wagner wrote a poem in dramatic form entitled "A Capitulation." It was one of the few he wrote that he never set, nor intended to set, to music. Whether or not it is as malicious as some biographers claim, it does indeed mercilessly satirize the suffering of the unfortunate Parisians. What was the motivation? Misplaced wartime jingoism? Revenge for his first two-year residence in Paris as a frustrated, starving young man? Or for this *Tannhäuser* fiasco of his middle age? It all makes for interesting speculation. But most likely even Wagner never knew.

14

AN EXCESS OF CORPSES

LA FORZA DEL DESTINO

THE PLOT: *Leonora is about to elope with Don Alvaro, when her father, who opposes this union, is accidentally killed by Alvaro. Leonora's brother, Don Carlo, swears vengeance. Leonora finds refuge from Don Carlo in a cave by a convent. Alvaro, living in a monastery, is discovered by Carlo, who insists on dueling with him. The spot selected for the duel is near the cave where Leonora hides. Carlo is mortally wounded, and when Alvaro goes to seek the friar to take his confession, Leonora comes on the scene and embraces her brother, who stabs her to death.*

*G*enius works in strange ways. Verdi undoubtedly read hundreds of plays in his endless search for suitable material. Just as likely, he dismissed most of them without a second thought. But something in a convoluted plot by Spanish playwright Angel de Saavedra, otherwise known as the Duke of Rivas, apparently lighted a creative spark.

It was 1861, and he was living in Turin with Giuseppina Strepponi, who was now his wife, attending, as a newly elected deputy, a meeting of the Italian parliament. But he was more concerned about a subject for an opera he agreed to write for the director of the Imperial Theatre in St. Petersburg. According to Giuseppina, Verdi scratched his head and mentioned to her a certain play he had once read and liked but could not find again. Soon they were searching in every bookshop and secondhand store in Turin, without result. According to Giuseppina, Verdi seized by the "scruff of the neck" a certain person who was headed for Milan, gave instructions, and a copy of the play was finally located by him in that city. The play was *Don Alvaro*, subtitled *La Fuerza del Sino* (in English, *The Power of Fate*). It was to be the source material for *La Forza del Destino,* and Verdi was to lavish on this curious drama much brilliantly colorful music.

To many it was surprising that Verdi was planning to write another opera at all. Just two years previously at a dinner party in Rome, he astonished the assembled guests by announcing in no uncertain terms that he would no longer compose. He was forty-six and had written twenty-one operas, eighteen since the 1842 premiere of his *Nabucco*. He had referred to that period since *Nabucco* as his "sixteen years in the galley," claiming that during it he had never enjoyed a moment of peace.

As if to underscore his seriousness he had a fling with politics, marked by his election to the parliament of the newly unified Nation of Italy. He ran at the urging of one whom he revered as the "father of our country," Count Camillo de Cavour, who later served as parliamentary president.

The retirement was not idle talk. In his remaining forty-two years of life he composed but five operas, arguably his five greatest, each after much coaxing, and most for a special occasion. The occasion for the first of the five, *La Forza del Destino,* was the request for an opera to be premiered at the Imperial Theatre in St. Petersburg. The request was buttressed by the assurance of the director's emissary that "the public here adores you," and the urging of Giuseppina, who was enthralled by the prospect of a visit to Russia.

Verdi's tentative choice of a subject, Victor Hugo's *Ruy Blas*, was rejected at first by the Russian authorities as politically unacceptable. Later they softened and assured Verdi of their agreement to any conditions "apart from insisting that Tsar Alexander declare a Republic in Russia." By this time, however, Verdi had cooled to the *Ruy Blas* subject.

After locating Saavedra's play, Verdi chose once again as his librettist Francesco Piave, whom we saw allied with Verdi in *Traviata* and *Rigoletto* and, as per custom, Verdi did the initial prose draft and division into acts and scenes. Though drastically changing much of the structure of the play, they kept intact, in that initial rendering, the final scene, full of murder and, as it originally stood, Alvaro's suicide upon the death of his beloved Leonora, a grisly finale even by operatic standards.

The premiere on November 10, 1862, was a brilliant success with audience and critics alike. With unusual perception regarding works of new musical style, a St. Petersburg journalist deemed it superior to Verdi's earlier works and praised the innovations it contained. The only dark note in the coverage concerned the plot: "too sad, too grim, too long." Verdi was personally awarded the Commander's Cross by Tsar Alexander, who attended the fourth performance.

In February 1863 came performances in Rome and Madrid. The censor in Rome insisted on changing the title to *Don Alvaro* and on many alterations in the story, which he gratuitously, but with deadly accuracy, termed wretched. The reception in Rome was good; less so in Madrid, where much of the audience, including the author, Saavedra, looked upon it as a desecration of a Spanish masterpiece.

But dissatisfaction with the story, especially with the gory ending, persisted. A few months later, Verdi wrote Piave: "Our first problem is the finale. We've got to get rid of all those corpses." Until it could be reworked, Verdi banned all performances in Italy, though not elsewhere.

Unfortunately, he did not follow through for some time due to the press of other matters but not, most probably, due to any obligation as a parliamentary deputy. To call him fiercely independent in the discharge of those duties would not be precisely correct. In fact, he always voted exactly like his idol Cavour. In that way, said Verdi, he could be "quite certain of not making any mistakes." By February 1865 he had had enough of politics. He wrote to Piave that he had no desire or taste, no aptitude or talent, for it. The 450 deputies, said Verdi, are really only 449, for Verdi as a deputy doesn't exist. He did not offer himself for reelection.

Meanwhile, his concern for *Forza* had not diminished. "Tell me," he had written his publisher Tito Ricordi, Giovanni's son, in December 1864, "have you no poet, no literary friend who is capable of finding me a denouement for that opera?" But he rejected Ricordi's every suggestion, as well as those from the play's author, Saavedra, and Arrigo Boito, the composer and poet who would later author the librettos for his *Otello* and *Falstaff*. In the end, with a performance scheduled for Milan's La Scala in early 1869, with Piave paralyzed by a stroke, he turned to Antonio Ghislanzoni, later his librettist for *Aida*.

The reworking of both the drama and the music was extensive. The body count of the final scene was reduced by one with the cancellation of Alvaro's suicide, which is replaced by his decision to live and be redeemed. The idea was Verdi's, and it provides the occasion for the stirring trio that concludes the opera. Whether it amounts to an improvement dramatically is a matter of opinion. The opinion of author Gualtiero Bartalini is apparently not entirely positive. In a delightful little book published in 1981, titled *Opera Psychotherapy*, he spoofs in verse some of the more outrageous opera plots. To the story of *Forza* he devotes some of his best efforts, including this gem of a preface:

> The strong arm of coincidence is stretched beyond repair;
> There's blood and thunder, cold revenge, and cloaks and daggers
>   everywhere.
> If without doubt you figure out what this frenetic play's about,
> You'll be at home with Sherlock Holmes, and even Sigmund Freud,
>   no doubt.

Verdi vowed not to attend the Milan performance. He had boycotted La Scala for twenty-four years, motivated by pique with that company over its switching of the sequence of acts in one of his early operas. But he did attend and was outraged when the vengeful Milanese booed him after the first act, their own retort to the twenty-four-year snub.

The critics were not kind either, but their unkindest cut was the charge that he was now imitating Wagner. "Imagine," he wrote, "after 35 years in the theatre to be called an imitator!!!!!!" The exclamation points are Verdi's, all seven of them. The charge was entirely unjustified, but would, also without justification, be repeated after each of his next and last four masterpieces.

15
VERDI AT THE OPÉRA

DON CARLOS

THE PLOT: Don Carlos, son of Spain's Philip II, and Elizabeth, Philip's wife, are in love. Carlos and his friend Rodrigo both support the struggle of the Flemish against Spain, but when Carlos confronts the King with drawn sword, Rodrigo disarms him. Nonetheless, the Grand Inquisitor demands that the King punish Rodrigo as well as his son for their disloyalty, and the King has Rodrigo slain. Carlos meets Elizabeth near the tomb of Emperor Charles V only to say farewell to her, but their embrace is seen by the jealous King, who moves to slay Carlos. Suddenly, the ghost of Charles V appears and leads Carlos into the tomb.

*I*n 1867 the city of Paris celebrated France's contribution to the industrial age with a gala event known as the Universal Exhibition. To house it, a gigantic edifice of iron and glass was constructed near the École Militaire. Scores of nations participated. Among the crowned heads attending were those of Belgium, Spain, Russia, Prussia, Turkey, and Japan; before it was over, 30 million visitors had gawked at 52,000 exhibits.

Today, such a grand extravaganza would require the presence of one or more popular entertainers of international fame. In nineteenth-century Europe, it required a new opera, one specially written for the occasion, to be performed in Paris's most opulent house, the Opéra,

A contemporary lithograph of the Paris Exposition of 1867. It was in celebration of this event that Verdi was commissioned to write *Don Carlos*. (The Violett Collection, Paris. *Verdi: A Documentary Study*. London: Thames and Hudson.)

and written by a world-renowned composer. The French government turned to Verdi.

Why Verdi accepted, or how Émile Perrin, the manager of the Opéra, was able to persuade him, is worth pondering even today. True, Paris was the opera capital of the world and the Opéra was its high temple. Budding artists and composers dreamed of, and connived at, reaching its stage. But according to too many reports to ignore, it was a miasma of bureaucratic wrangling and stultifying inaction, and the way to success often lay through flattery, political influence, or bribery. The leading French composer of the day, Hector Berlioz, had none of his works performed there; he could not stomach the intrigue. Many French masterpieces, including Bizet's *Carmen*, Massenet's *Manon*, and Debussy's *Pelléas et Mélisande* were all first performed at other Parisian houses.

Verdi's own prior experiences there had been nothing to cele-brate. *Jerusalem,* a French version of his *I Lombardi,* had been a de-pressing episode. In 1850 he had rejected a request to compose an opera for that house, expressing disgust with Paris as a major factor. He tried again in 1855, but the production of his *Les Vêpres sicili-ennes,* written specially for Paris, was a bitter disappointment.

Yet in mid-1865, he was again at the Opéra, this time to oversee a production of his revised *Macbeth.* Once more, the experience was disheartening, but by the end of August, before returning to his home in Sant'-Agata in northern Italy, he had signed a contract to write a new opera for the planned 1867 exhibition. Before he was through, he would have much cause to, and undoubtedly did, regret it. Several Shakespearian plays were considered and bypassed in favor of Fried-rich Schiller's *Don Karlos.* Per the rules of the Opéra, it would be in French, hence it was titled *Don Carlos.*

Performance at the Opéra was moribund with rules; two particu-lar ones were to prove quite vexatious. The performance was not to run past midnight, as the last departures of the suburban trains were at 12:35 A.M. Nor could the curtain time be moved forward because that would conflict with the dining habits of the patrons. A further requirement, not official but ignored by composers at their peril, was the one imposed by the Jockey Club, that group of young aristocrats who six years earlier had wrecked *Tannhäuser* for Wagner's refusal to insert a second-act ballet. For the same reasons they required it then, a ballet was demanded now.

The recasting of Schiller's play and the composition of the libretto in French was initiated by Joseph Méry, who had authored a play used by Verdi for one of his earlier operas. Owing to the illness of Méry, who died in 1866, the work was completed by Camille du Locle, son-in-law of the Opéra's director. The opera was cast in five acts. Verdi went to Paris to compose the first act, then in March 1866, returned to his home in Sant'-Agata to continue. He never felt more comfortable than when in Sant'-Agata in the midst of the neighboring farmers of whom he counted himself one. By mid-May, he had com-pleted Act II, by early June, Act III. Then, international politics and war raised their ugly heads and interrupted his idyllic life.

On June 19, Italy, seeking recovery of Venice from Austria, joined Prussia in its recently declared war against that state. This caused tensions with the French, who considered themselves allies of Austria. In addition to the prospect of rehearsals in a potentially hostile atmosphere in Paris, Verdi felt immediately and personally threatened by his nearness to possible combat in Italy. Even before its outbreak, he had written to his Paris publisher, Léon Escudier, that he would not be surprised one morning to see a cannonball roll into his room. By early June, only several days before the declaration of war, he wrote to a former comrade from the Italian legislature that he would leave at the first cannon shot, and that he would run a thousand miles to avoid an appearance by the Austrians "if only to avoid seeing their ugly faces."

The Italian troops must have shared his sentiments. They were quickly routed by a smaller Austrian force at the Battle of Custozza on June 24. The Austrians gained little from it, however, as ten days later they were crushed by the Prussians at Koenigrätz and were forced to sue for peace. Rumors soon became rife that Venice was to be ceded by Prussia to France as a reward for remaining neutral.

Verdi first heard these rumors in Genoa where, as promised, he had fled the combat zone with his wife, Giuseppina. He was incensed. He vented his outrage in a letter to Escudier in which he expressed the hope that France would refuse to accept the city. He explained that it would be impossible to come to Paris now that it was rejoicing over such an insult to Italy; that he could not compose and that he was "sick unto death." A few weeks later, however, he wrote that Perrin had refused to permit him to break his contract and that he was leaving for Paris despite the intense discomfort it would cause him. He stayed but one day in Paris, then went with Giuseppina to a spa in the Pyrenees, where he completed the composition. Under the terms of the Peace of Prague in mid-August, Venice was ceded to Italy, not to France, and we hear no more about it in Verdi's letters.

The rehearsals, which began that fall, were plagued with strikes, postponements, illnesses, imagined illnesses, a little malice, and much indifference. In December, Giuseppina wrote a friend touring America of her exasperation with the army of Opéra personnel who would argue for hours on end over "such silly questions" as whether this or that performer should gesture by raising a little finger or the whole hand. She referred caustically to the "tortoises of the Opéra" and the agony to her husband caused by the "machinery of marble and lead!" There were numerous revisions and cuts, some initiated by Verdi, others forced on him by the time constraints of the theater rules. Some of the deleted pages have been discovered in recent years and restored in modern performances.

The premiere came on March 11. That night, Verdi left for Genoa where, the following day, he wrote a terse note to a friend: "Last night, *Don Carlos* was not a success!" The audience reception has been described as "polite, but without enthusiasm." It is possible that the Parisian audience took its cue from Napoleon III's Spanish empress Eugénie. In a show of displeasure, she turned her back, according to one report, on the scene between the Inquisitor and the King, or, according to another report, on the plea of the Marquis of Posa for liberty for Flanders. Perhaps both reports were correct. Either one of such gestures, obviously politically motivated, could have dampened the enthusiasm of her loyal, politically correct subjects.

After forty-three performances, *Don Carlos* was withdrawn from the Opéra's repertory and was not performed again in Paris until 1963. Verdi was deeply depressed and went into a long stretch of melancholy. But to his delight, several months later it was applauded by wildly enthusiastic audiences, first at London's Covent Garden, then in Bologna. "What will they say at the Opéra," wrote the exultant Verdi, "when they hear that it took only forty days to stage an opera in London, whereas they always need four months." And in Bologna he boasted, "Here they have been rehearsing for less than a month and obtained great effects." However, the following year, the opera failed in Bordeaux and Brussels.

Critical opinion has remained divided on the merits of this opera. Verdi himself never seemed to have been completely satisfied with it. The pattern of cuts, revisions, and additions continued. Thoroughly revised, it was performed for the first time in Italian translation (hence as *Don Carlo*) at Milan's La Scala in 1884.

Repeated listenings leave little doubt that *Don Carlo* contains many passages as deeply moving and as dramatically intense as anything Verdi wrote. They also leave little doubt that it does not have the unity of style or consistency of musical inspiration that the composer exhibited in many of his best works. Some critics explain this by claiming that Verdi was in a "transitional phase"; that he was moving to a different, more complex style than that of his so-called "middle period," but one that he had not yet mastered.

They can believe such nonsense if they wish, but there is evidence that Verdi had other ideas about the source of the problem, ideas that apparently deepened and jelled after many months' reflection. Two and one-half years after the Paris premiere, Verdi wrote to du Locle one of the most revealing letters that the normally restrained composer ever penned. It was in response to entreaties by du Locle, now a director of the Opéra, for another new work for his house. Verdi let him have it with both barrels:

> In your opera houses there are too many wise men! . . . Everyone wants to pass judgment according to his own ideas, his own tastes and what is worse, according to a system. Everyone wants to give an opinion, express a doubt and, [the composer] ends up by correcting, adjusting—or to put it better—spoiling his own work. . . . I simply cannot again crawl under the candine yoke of your theatres . . . the artists must sing not in their fashion but mine . . . everything must be under my control and one will alone must prevail—mine! . . . My ideas on art are quite different from yours. I believe in inspiration; you believe in construction . . . I am not prepared to give way in spineless fashion and deny my profoundest convictions.

And then, perhaps the source of this outpouring:

> I should be most upset if I were to write an opera for you, my dear du Locle, which you might have to withdraw after some dozen performances, as Perrin did with *Don Carlo*.

Verdi had had it with the Paris Opéra. And, as is clear from his next and last three operas, he was through once and for all with any compromise of his own artistic instincts.

16

A CASE FOR INCEST

THE VALKYRIE

THE PLOT: *Siegmund is sheltered in a hut by Sieglinde. They learn that they are the separated twin children of the god Wotan. Sieglinde's husband, Hunding, is Siegmund's enemy, and he and Sieglinde flee, armed with a sword left by Wotan for his son in time of need. In combat, Siegmund is killed when Wotan reluctantly, and at the insistence of Fricka, Goddess of Marriage, helps the wronged Hunding. Brünhilde, the Valkyrie goddess, sends Sieglinde, with the shattered sword, to the forest to bear the child of Siegmund that she is carrying. For having defied him by attempting to help Siegmund in the combat, Wotan strips Brünhilde of her godhood, and puts her in a sleep, to be awakened and claimed by a mortal man, but surrounds her by fire that only a hero can pass.*

"*U*nnecessary . . . immoral and unspeakably degrading . . . so revolting, indecent and impure that it ought never to have been tolerated on the English stage."

This cry of outrage was penned by the music critic for London's *The Era* following the performance of *The Valkyrie* in the course of that city's 1882 premiere of Richard Wagner's entire *The Ring of the Nibelung.*

The Valkyrie, second of the *Ring* operas, was first seen as part of the entire tetralogy in Wagner's new Festival Theater in Bayreuth in

Scene from Act I of the first production of Wagner's *The Valkyrie*, Munich, 1870. The element of incest shocked some Victorian-age critics. (Mander, Raymond, and Joseph Mitchenson. *The Wagner Companion*. New York: Hawthorne Books, 1977.)

1876. But it had been performed alone in Munich in 1870, on the order of King Ludwig II of Bavaria. The impatient king, having paid for the rights to the opera with money from the Bavarian treasury, would wait no longer for the completion of the remaining works. Wagner's attempts to stop the performance caused the most serious rift of all in the stormy, up-and-down relationship between the two.

The Valkyrie quickly became the most popular of the four operas. The *Ring* was performed in subsequent years throughout Europe, and, to the acute distress of *The Era*'s critic, in 1882 arrived in London. The cause of his unhappiness with *The Valkyrie* was the first-act love scene between Siegmund and Sieglinde. They fall in love simultaneously with their discovery that they are long-separated twins, then flee the house of Sieglinde's husband to consummate their love. As for the composer, the critic felt that he had "lost all sense of decency and respect for the dignity of human nature."

One may sympathize with the critic's anguish, but hardly with the visitation of the sins of the parents on the innocent offspring. The following evening, he claimed to see in Siegfried only a reminder of the "horrible and revolting character of the previous drama." Whether the episode is as revolting and degrading as the critic complains is a matter of opinion, but in calling it "unnecessary" he unwittingly opens the door to some rather interesting inquiry.

Did Wagner make these lovers brother and sister for shock effect or audience titillation? No doubt this critic thought so. But had he seen in its pristine form the source from which it was taken, there would not have been words enough in the English language to express his horror. Like practically all other parts of the *Ring*, this one did not come full-blown from the composer's imagination—depraved or otherwise. It, like most of the rest of the cycle, was taken and recast from the myths and sagas of ancient northern lands. This particular saga contains not only incest but revenge, murder, and cruelty, not the least of which must be laid at the door of the incestuous sister, Signy.

This opera comes from the *Volsunga Saga,* lore that grew over many long Icelandic winter evenings when the household, gathered together at spinning or weaving, would listen to one of their members tell anew some old story of adventure. Only after generations had rounded and polished the sagas were they first written down, by an unknown scribe, probably between 1140 and 1220 A.D. It was not at all unusual for Wagner to condense his source material mercilessly, extracting only what was vital to his own vast, but tightly knit, work, often changing names, incidents, and time sequences in the process.

Some of the changes for the first act of *The Valkyrie,* involving the conception of Siegfried, the hero of Wagner's *Ring* cycle, were quite drastic. The model for Siegfried was one Sigurd, the hero of the *Volsunga Saga.* Most of the adventures and most of the character of

Wagner's *Siegfried* come from Sigurd. In the *Saga,* it is Sigurd who slays a dragon and awakens Brünhilde, as does Siegfried in the opera. And, as *The Era*'s critic might have pointed out, the union of Sigurd's parents was not incestuous. His parents in the source material were Sigmund (named Siegmund in Wagner's opera) and Hjordis. They were not brother and sister, and they were properly married.

In the *Saga,* Sigmund does indeed commit incest with his sister, named Signy, compared to whom both Electra and Lady Macbeth are warm and sympathetic characters. The offspring of this union was Sinfjotli. But this was before Sigmund's marriage to Hjordis. The only important aspect of Sinfjotli that Wagner used in the creation of his Siegfried was the incestuous birth. Everything else seems to be patterned after Sinfjotli's legitimate half-brother, Sigurd.

Why did Wagner use this element of incest? And since he did, why did he discard almost all other aspects of that earlier, incestuous episode, transforming the sister, Signy of the *Saga,* a ruthless, blood-chilling character, to Sieglinde, the most human and gentle portrayal in the *Ring?*

The likely answers to both questions are spread clearly upon the record. The second question is the easier one, and the answer is that Wagner did not seem able to draw an ugly portrait of anyone's sister. He could draw villains, blood-curdling villains, even villainous wives, but he could not depict a villainous sister. The entire subject of the brother-sister relationship was almost sacred to him. We see it in his operas and in his autobiography.

His three earliest operas, as well as his better-known *Lohengrin,* include brother-sister relationships, the sisters being always depicted in an admirable, appealing, and often heroic mold. In two of these early operas the stories center around them, and in both he did violence to his source materials in rearranging them to do so. These stories, as he recast them, show more than a little of the influence of his own young life. Wagner's autobiography leaves us with a definite impression that, as a child and young adult, his every whim was catered to and that he was, as we might say today, "spoiled rotten"; not by his twice-widowed mother, but by his four sisters.

In his autobiography we hear little of his mother, even less of his two older brothers. But of his three older sisters, as well as of his half-sister, his only younger sibling, he speaks often and with a depth of feeling that seems reserved especially for them. It is clear that he was the recipient of their constant admiration, encouragement, and doting attention, which may have contributed much to the supreme confidence with which he fashioned, then forced on a skeptical world, his own unique art form.

Each played her own role in his young life. But it was for Rosalie, the oldest, ten years his senior, that he reserved the most special place in his affections. He described the relationship between them as one which, in its "purity and sincerity could vie with the noblest form of friendship between men and women." In terms of adoration, almost of awe, he described how she, only seventeen years of age, rallied their large family upon the death of their stepfather and took to the stage to support them. Sixteen years later he saw her for the last time while on a short visit to his Leipzig home from his employment in Magdeburg. Less than a year later he was devastated to hear of her death. She died in childbirth, as does Sieglinde in giving birth to Siegfried, an invention of the composer not to be found in the *Saga*.

Shortly after his last meeting with Rosalie, he penned his comic opera, *The Ban on Love,* based, with changes, on Shakespeare's *Measure for Measure*. The major change was in the role of Isabella, sister of the condemned Claudio. In Shakespeare she is a minor character of no particular distinction or impact on the course of events. In Wagner's opera she is pivotal and is endowed with dignity, wit, and ingenuity. His next, and first successful opera, *Rienzi,* was based on a contemporary novel of Sir Bulwer-Lytton. In Bulwer-Lytton's novel, the thirteenth-century tribune, Rienzi, has a loving wife, Nina, who chooses to die with her husband in a conflagration ignited by an angry mob. A minor character in the novel is Rienzi's sister, Irene. Wagner's Rienzi has neither wife nor sweetheart. But his sister Irene is as fully devoted to him as is Bulwer-Lytton's Nina, and it is she, the sister, who chooses to die with Rienzi in the flames.

Only six years later Wagner cast the plot of his *Ring* and picked and chose from the ancient myths those characters and incidents he would use and those he would discard. Assuming that he did not want to depict Sigmund's sister as the icy, merciless character she is portrayed as being in the *Saga,* why did he decide to use the incest element at all? Was he, as a modern psychiatrist might say, acting out a repressed, subconscious wish?

In all greater likelihood Wagner used this material, not because of his personal history, but in spite of it. Because of his own life history he changed it dramatically. But his decision to use it in the first place was probably sparked more by an unerring dramatic instinct, and by reasons much more compelling than personal history or subconscious desires: namely, a powerful dramatic force in the portrayal of the incestuous parentage of a great mythical hero. It is a force silently lurking in the background of the *Ring,* but poetically explicit in the *Saga.* Obvious though it may be, it is driven home with a shattering impact in the grisly tale, much abbreviated here, that Wagner read and used.

King Volsung, so the *Saga* goes, had ten sons, including Sigmund, and one daughter, Signy. Signy was betrothed by her father to King Siggeir (Wagner's Hunding). The wedding was held in King Volsung's hall, which had been built around a huge oak tree. During the wedding feast a stranger entered. He had but one eye and wore a broadbrimmed hat. Unknown to the guests, he was the god Odin (Wagner's Wotan). In his hand was a sword, which he drove into a tree trunk. Then he announced that whoever should draw the sword from the tree would have the finest weapon he could ever hold. With that, he left.

One after another the men tugged at the sword in vain. But in a dramatic burst of strength, Sigmund pulled it from the tree. King Siggeir offered to buy it at three times its weight in gold, but Sigmund disdainfully refused. King Siggeir, silently harboring a fierce anger and vowing revenge, left the next morning with his bride and his retinue. Months later he got his revenge. While guests in Siggeir's home, and ignoring the warnings of Signy, King Volsung and nine of his sons were treacherously murdered. Only Sigmund, with the surreptitious help of his sister, Signy, escaped and hid in the forest.

Thereafter Signy, living with her hated husband, and Sigmund, living alone in the forest, shared the same solitary obsession—revenge for the slaughter of their kin. She bore two sons by Siggeir, and when the eldest was ten years old, she put him to the test. She sewed a glove onto his hand through skin and flesh, a test he failed by crying out in pain. She sent him to her brother in the forest, and on her demand, the youth, deemed of no use in the quest for revenge, was slain by

Sigmund. The second son failed in a similar fashion and met the same fate on the orders of the iron-willed Signy. Very little do we see of this lady in Wagner's sensitive Sieglinde.

Now she turned to other resources to find a hero worthy of their purposes. She changed shapes with a sorceress and, as a stranger, went to the shelter of her brother, seeking temporary refuge. According to the *Saga,* "His eyes were often on her and a fair and goodly woman she seemed to him." She stayed three nights, then returned to King Siggeir.

The child born to Signy from this union was Sinfjotli. When he was ten he was put to the same test, but with far different results. He cried out neither when the glove was sewn to his flesh, nor when, as Signy tore it from his hand, his skin came off with it. He was sent to live in the forest with Sigmund, who was unaware that the youth was his own son.

When Sinfjotli grew to manhood, he and Sigmund went to the hall of King Siggeir, seeking at last to requite the long-harbored passion for revenge. They were discovered in their hiding place by two young children of Signy and King Siggeir. On Signy's merciless instruction they were killed by Sinfjotli, who threw their lifeless bodies at the feet of their father. Sinfjotli and Sigmund were overpowered and bound and buried alive.

But with Signy's help Sinfjotli freed himself and Sigmund. The two men set fire to the hall, and when the king demanded, "Who kindled this fire?" Sigmund answered that it was he with his sister's son, and that the Volsungs still lived. To which Signy adds, following a recitation of the entire bloody history, that she, in the guise of a sorceress had gone to Sigmund, stunning the king to learn that she is Sinfjotli's mother, surprising Sigmund to learn that he is the father.

It is then that she makes dramatically explicit to Sigmund what in the *Ring* exists only in silent omnipresence. "Now behold," she says to Sigmund, "Sinfjotli is the son of thee and me. And therefore has he so great hardihood and fierceness in that he is the son of Volsung's son and the son of Volsung's daughter." It is in these, her last words, that vindication of Wagner's artistic instincts can be found: Siegfried as the son of Wotan's son, and as the son of Wotan's daughter.

Whereupon, in true Wagnerian fashion, she kisses Sigmund, her brother and lover, and Sinfjotli, her son and nephew, and walks into the fire to die with King Siggeir, her husband and enemy.

Was this incest element necessary to Wagner's *The Valkyrie* and to the *Ring*? Yes. There is a dramatic logic here, as there was in Signy's calculated union with her brother. It is a logic that has outlasted the chagrin of *The Era*'s critic and, probably, of much of Victorian Europe. It might also be observed that had Wagner truly been interested in shock effect and audience titillation, what a wealth of material he passed up!

17

THE FORGOTTEN MAN

AIDA

THE PLOT: *Radames is selected to lead the Egyptians against the invading Ethiopians. He is loved by Amneris, the Egyptian princess, but he is in love with Aida, the Ethiopian princess, now a slave girl in Egypt. Aida's father is captured and, urged by him, Aida wrings from Radames the secret positions of Egyptian troops. Amneris overhears this, and Radames is convicted of treason and condemned to be buried alive. After he is sealed in the tomb, Aida reveals herself, having come to join him in death. They embrace as Amneris, above, chants a prayer.*

$\mathcal{T}$hirty-two-hundred years ago, in a series of battles fought near the mouth of the Nile River, Ramses III, King of Egypt, led his armies to victory over invaders from North Africa and the Aegean. If the world ever forgets his glorious triumph it will not be his fault. To guard against such a calamity he constructed a magnificent temple on the Nile, filled with sculptures and paintings depicting scenes from the great battles. The site of this memorial is Thebes, about 350 miles south of his once-proud capital of Memphis, now only a ruin near present-day Cairo. Ramses III also happens to be the grandson of Seti I, mentioned elsewhere in these pages in connection with Mozart's *Magic Flute*.

The temple still stands. Among its more interesting aspects are the pictures that cover the inner walls of the galleries and the hieroglyphic inscriptions that explain them. There are battle scenes, but for those viewers whose thoughts turn to *Aida*, there are scenes of greater interest: the victorious king viewing prisoners led before him by his generals, one thousand prisoners from one battle, according to the inscription, and three thousand slain; the king offering his prisoners to the gods of the city; and the king hearing entreaties by prisoners to spare their lives so that they may celebrate his great courage.

For a description of one of the most intriguing of these panels, from the perspective of our opera at least, let us hear directly from the "father of Egyptology," Jean-François Champollion. It was he who, in 1822, deciphered the Egyptian hieroglyphics through the study of the famed Rosetta Stone and the obelisk from Philae. In a picture on the upper register of one of the walls of Ramses's temple, says Champollion, the king is carried in a richly decorated shrine borne by twelve military chiefs, heads adorned with ostrich feathers, the throne with golden images of the sphinx and the lion. He then describes the fanfare that precedes it:

> A band of music, wherein may be distinguished the flute, the trumpet, the drum and chorus singers, forms the head of the procession; then come the relatives and favorites of the King, among whom may be noticed several high priests; and lastly, the eldest son of Ramses, second in command of the army, burns incense in his father's face.

What makes this description of particular interest, apart from the image it evokes of "The Triumphal March" from *Aida,* is the fact that it, like the descriptions of many other panels, is reported to us in a book by one François-Auguste-Ferdinande Mariette, *Monuments of Upper Egypt,* first published in 1869.

And who was Mariette? He was the author of *Aida.* It was from his fertile imagination, and from his alone, that the story of *Aida* was conceived. He alone sketched the story that persuaded a bitter and reticent Giuseppe Verdi to once more compose an opera. That sketch was full and complete, and is paralleled to a remarkable degree, down to the smallest details, in the final libretto of *Aida.*

Mariette was not a professional writer. Like Champollion before him, he was a renowned archaeologist and Egyptologist. His work was first financed by the French government, later by the viceroy of Egypt, Ismail Pasha, often known by the honorary title khedive. According to descriptions that have come down to us, Mariette was a huge man, tall and broad-chested, forbidding and imperious in black spectacles and red fez, but in manner very modest and courteous.

It was Mariette who uncovered from the sands of Egypt many of its ancient treasures, then established the Museum of Egyptian Antiquities in which to house them. At the Paris Universal Exhibition of 1867, he arranged a display that revealed for the first time in centuries the full splendor of the art of that ancient land. And it was he who uncovered the colossus of the sphinx. At the age of thirty-seven he had been awarded the title bey, and later that of pasha, terms reserved for persons of great distinction, and entitling him thereafter to be known as Mariette Bey, or Mariette Pasha. From France, Italy, and Prussia he received decorations of high honor, and in 1887, six years after his death, his researches were praised as the most vast and important ever made in Egypt.

That such a man was entrusted with the task of advising on the authenticity of the details of staging and costuming for scenes of ancient Egypt is understandable. How it came about that he authored the story of the opera, much less so. Yet, despite periodic attempts to prove otherwise, any fair reading of the history leaves little doubt: The author of the story of *Aida* is Mariette Bey. Opera programs often state that *Aida* is based on a story by Mariette, and he otherwise rates an incidental mention here, a reference there, a footnote somewhere else. None of it tells the full story.

That story begins in March 1867, immediately following the premiere of Verdi's *Don Carlos* at the Opéra in Paris. The librettist for that work, it will be recalled, was Camille du Locle, a somewhat haughty, but amiable, producer of grand opera. The failure of *Don Carlos* permanently embittered Verdi against the Opéra, and the vexatious interference by its personnel with his artistic judgment. He blamed them for spoiling the integrity of his opera, and was resolute in his determination that it would never happen again.

His friendship with du Locle continued, but despite the entreaties of his former librettist, now a director of the Opéra, Verdi would not hear of writing again for that house. But du Locle, filled with admiration for Verdi, was filled also with visions of financial benefits that

Drawing of Camille du Locle, Bibliothèque de l'Opera, Paris. Du Locle, opera producer and theater manager, was a friend and admirer of Verdi. Verdi was a friend, but not necessarily an admirer of du Locle. (*Verdi: A Documentary Study*. London: Thames and Hudson. By permission of the Bibliothèque Nationale de France.)

Bronze bust of Auguste Mariette, Musée Municipal, Boulogne sur-Mer. He was the unpaid and barely acknowledged author of the story of Aida. Verdi gave Mariette's son short shrift when he sought compensation for his father's work. (*Verdi: A Documentary Study*. London: Thames and Hudson. By permission of the Collection du Château-Musée de Boulogne-sur Mer, France.)

another venture with him could bring. If Verdi would not write for the Opéra, then perhaps for some other house. But no story seemed to please the composer. Suggestion after suggestion was rejected.

In 1868, the year after the *Don Carlos* fiasco, du Locle traveled to Egypt. His guide was the same expert in Egyptian antiquities who had accompanied the Empress Eugénie and other notables who visited that nation: Auguste Mariette. Whether that is the first time the two men met is not known. What is known is that Mariette had written a short story in 1866, never published, which he entitled "La Fiancée du Nil." It was *Aida* in embryo form.

Du Locle was consumed during this period with his determination to find a story suitable for Verdi, and he undoubtedly mentioned it to Mariette. And just as likely, the idea of an opera based on his story of ancient Egypt, to be premiered in Cairo, caught fire in the imaginative mind of the archaeologist. Later events leave little doubt of this.

Crucial to such a project was the consent of the khedive, the Paris-educated viceroy. Fortunately, he was the epitome of the enlightened despot. He brought modernization and reform to Egypt and, more to the point of our story, harbored a love for Italian music in general, and that of Giuseppe Verdi in particular. He is said to have remarked once, "My country is no longer in Africa; I have made it part of Europe." The opening of the Suez Canal, on November 17, 1869, was preceded by many festivities, including the inauguration, on November 1, of the new Cairo Theater. The viceroy requested that Verdi write a hymn for the opening, a request the composer refused, explaining that it was not his custom to write "occasional" pieces. The theater opened instead with a performance of the maestro's *Rigoletto*.

Soon thereafter Mariette must have sold the khedive on the idea of an opera on an Egyptian theme, to be premiered in Cairo, as in December 1869, the proposal was communicated to Verdi through du Locle, probably the last few days of that month when du Locle visited him in Genoa.

Quite apart from the khedive's love for Italian opera, the theme and setting of Mariette's story may well have had immediate appeal for him. In 1861, before his assumption of the office of viceroy, he had led an army of 14,000 men to suppress an insurgence of slaves in the Sudan, and both before and during his reign there had been recurring hostilities with the Ethiopians. It is, of course, the Ethiopians who are the invaders of Egypt in Mariette's sketch and in the opera.

But Verdi, prone to seasickness, was not interested in an opera for Cairo, and even less so in the sea voyage it would require.

Du Locle was not alone in his frustrations. By early 1870, Tito Ricordi, Verdi's publisher, was bombarding not only the composer but also his wife, Giuseppina, with his entreaties. "Art needs Verdi," he wrote her, "I turn to you, Signora Peppina, so that you may help and advise me in this." Honestly, if obliquely, he acknowledged that he, too, needed Verdi. Verdi's almost lackadaisical response: "It is not the labor of composition that burdens me; it is the difficulty of finding a subject to my liking."

From Ricordi he requested two plays that had apparently piqued his interest. The plays would be sent, assured Ricordi, but "In the meantime I commend myself to God and the devil . . . that they may let us find the long-awaited plot." From du Locle, Verdi requested a translation of a comedy by a Spanish writer, López de Ayala. Du Locle promptly obtained and forwarded it to Verdi. Du Locle must also have renewed the proposal of Mariette, probably in late March or early April 1870 during a visit by Verdi to Paris. And Verdi must have again refused, a rejection communicated by du Locle to Mariette, for on April 27 Mariette writes to du Locle that he had "expected M. Verdi's refusal, which will rather annoy the Viceroy."

But that letter to du Locle also contained something else: Mariette's outline of the story of *Aida,* which he states that the viceroy fully approves of. Nothing will be spared, he assures du Locle; everything will be "as splendid as one can imagine," and everything will be authentic. The viceroy wants a purely ancient and Egyptian opera. And, he cautions, don't be alarmed by the title *Aida;* it is an Egyptian name. Before that sketch was received by du Locle in Paris, then by Verdi in Milan, and Verdi's answer received by du Locle and Mariette, more than a month would pass, and many more impatient letters would be circulated.

The very next day, April 28, Mariette again writes to du Locle. He has told the viceroy of Verdi's prior refusal, and his highness is indeed annoyed and chagrined as Mariette had predicted. The viceroy, says Mariette, alluding to Verdi's antipathy to sea travel, is willing to hold rehearsals in Paris, Milan, or anywhere. But if Verdi should not accept, "we are thinking of Gounod and even Wagner. If the latter should accept, he could do something grandiose."

On May 7, the impetuous du Locle has obviously still not received Mariette's April 27 letter with the sketch, but writes to Verdi assuring him that there is indeed an outline in existence, "which is not absurd," even containing "some beautiful dramatic situations"; that the viceroy is willing to agree to any terms, and pleading with the composer to consider it favorably. On May 10 he writes again, tongue in cheek presumably, suggesting that Verdi ask for one of the biggest pyramids as a bonus, and that his highness may be willing to give it to him. Finally, on May 14 du Locle has received the Mariette sketch and immediately sends it on to Verdi with a short note.

The note points out that only four copies of the sketch have been made, and that one of them is enclosed. The sketch was a booklet of twenty-three pages. Verdi and his wife later made an exact translation of the French into Italian that required both sides of seven legal-sized sheets of paper. Hence the words "sketch" or "outline" hardly convey a sense of the detailed nature of the story. Du Locle also suggested that Verdi name his terms, and enclosed Mariette's letter of April 28 mentioning Gounod and Wagner as possible alternatives. On May 19 Mariette writes du Locle that the viceroy is "burning with desire" to get the project started. "If Verdi cannot do it, get M. Gounod; if necessary, see Wagner."

Finally, on May 26, the ice melted. Verdi had read both the play of the Spaniard, Ayala, and the story outline of *Aida*. The Spanish drama, said Verdi to du Locle, is done by the hand of a master, but "one neither laughs or cries. It's cold and doesn't seem to be made for music." Then his verdict on *Aida*:

> I have read the Egyptian outline. It is well done; it offers a splendid mise-en-scene, and there are two or three situations which, if not very new, are certainly very beautiful. But who did it? There is a very expert hand in it, one accustomed to writing and one who knows the theater very well.

Answered du Locle: "The Egyptian libretto is the work of the viceroy and Mariette Bey, the famous archaeologist. None else has put a hand to it." On what information, if any, or for what motivation du Locle named the viceroy as a coauthor is not known. It has been suggested that it was intended to impress Verdi. In any event, no one believed it, including Verdi. He so stated in a letter to Ricordi a month later, and in December 1870 told his publisher that he was removing the khedive's name from certain unspecified documents as "I am not sure he actually did the outline which was written by such a sure hand."

The rest, as is often said, is history. Except that history has had very little to say about Mariette's role to this point, and virtually nothing after it. He spent much of his time in Paris over the next year, making several voyages there to give his advice on costumes, scenery, and stage direction in ceremonial scenes, all on the orders of the khedive, but willingly. Only twice do we hear from his letters complaints about his all but unrecognized and totally uncompensated role.

In June 1870, on the eve of his first departure for Paris, he wrote his brother Eduard that the trip did not enchant him. He had labored at the 1867 Exhibition for no remuneration, all of which went to others. Would the same thing happen again? True, he was not writing the music, said Mariette, "but the outline is mine; that is, I have put all the scenes in order, and the opera has essentially come out of my bag." It is he, continued Mariette, who goes to Paris to have "the sets executed, the costumes manufactured, to lend everything the local color that must be ancient Egyptian." Verdi was making 150,000 francs for the Cairo production alone, he wrote his brother; du Locle would certainly be handsomely rewarded with royalties for his rendition in French verse of Mariette's story. He himself, he said, might well receive nothing.

Lengthy and detailed correspondence between the principals corroborates every line of Mariette's letter, including Verdi's fee. Nonetheless, we hear no more such anguished outpourings until a year later when he wrote to Paul Drahnet, general manager of the viceroy's opera house in Cairo. He had heard an ill-founded rumor that the opera's premiere would be changed to Milan because of complications caused by the Franco-Prussian War, which now raged in all its fury. Said Mariette:

> I would find in this procedure something indecent with regard to me, something that would be difficult for me to explain. *Aïda* is, in

effect, a product of my work. I am the one who convinced the Viceroy to order its presentation; *Aïda,* in a word, is a creation of my brain, and it seems to me that before disposing of it so completely, one should at least have the courtesy of writing to me about it.

The premiere, after numerous delays caused by the war and particularly the Prussian siege of Paris, took place at the Cairo Opera House on Christmas Eve 1871. It is one of the great success stories of operatic history. Although Antonio Ghislanzoni is credited with the Italian libretto, much, if not most of it, is the work of Verdi himself. Verdi was very tactful, but in improving and rewriting Ghislanzoni's verses, Verdi's bearing toward him is that of a master to an apprentice.

There have been scholarly theories about other possible authors of the story, supported by guesswork and speculation but not by the slightest evidence. Fanciful suggestions about sources from which Mariette may have gleaned the idea for *Aida* seem equally as whimsical. It has also been bandied about that Mariette based his sketch on an actual historical event described in some ancient Egyptian writing. If such a writing exists, someone has kept it well hidden. Without something more than has heretofore been offered, we are compelled to conclude without reservation that *Aida* is the brainchild of Auguste Mariette.

He is in good company. Verdi wrote only two more operas, both based on plays by Shakespeare. His previous opera had been an adaptation from a play by Schiller. In the operatic repertory there are very few story lines created specially for the opera, and none for Verdi except *Aida.*

Financially strapped and wracked with diabetes, Mariette died in Paris in 1881 at the age of sixty. He received nothing for his story. There is evidence in his correspondence that the khedive deemed it inappropriate for him to ask for compensation, and neither Verdi nor anyone else offered it. Ten years later, one of his sons apparently felt that the injustice might be righted. There is a letter to Verdi from du Locle, begging the maestro to excuse him for the annoyance, but advising that a complaint had been received from Mariette's son "who demands an explanation."

Verdi's answer does him no credit:

Ricordi, in fact, has spoken to me about this claim of Mariette's son. That's a bolt from the blue! You know how things went: I think you will recall that you yourself gave me four little printed pages, without the name of the author, telling me that the Khedive would like the opera to be on that subject, since it was Egyptian; and I supposed that the author of those little pages was the Khedive himself. As for Mariette Bey, I knew only that he was responsible for the costumes etc. That's all. I can't tell you anything else, and I don't understand what claims this Mariette can have.

Did the "four little pages" result from confusion in Verdi's mind of the number of pages (twenty-three) with the number of copies of the story that Mariette had printed (four), as mentioned in du Locle's transmittal letter? Considering that he and Giuseppina must have spent many hours of painstaking work in translating the text, that would seem passing strange. Assuming the most charitable view of that point, however, what do we make of the rest of this somewhat myopic version of events? Could the seventy-eight-year-old maestro have had a lapse of memory about Mariette's seminal role? Perhaps. But he seemed to have remembered everything else.

18

BIZET AND
LA MOGADOR

CARMEN

THE PLOT: *Carmen, arrested for fighting, charms Don José, the soldier assigned to guard her, and he allows her to escape. His commanding officer, also enamoured of Carmen, is threatened by her gyspy band following an argument with José, obliging José to desert from his unit and join the gypsies. But Carmen soon finds a new interest: Escamillo, a swaggering bullfighter. Desperately jealous, José confronts her before the bullring where Escamillo is fighting. She ignores both his pleas and his threats, and as she tries to enter the arena, José stabs her to death.*

Moderation is no part of my nature . . . I feel with a passion that devours me . . . I have always been capricious and proud. No one, among women whose tendency it is to say "yes," derives more pleasure than I do from saying "no." So the men to whom I have given the most are those who asked least of me.

*T*hese words come from the *Mémoires* of Céleste Vénard. By marriage, she was the Comtesse Lionel de Chabrillan, but was more often known as La Mogador. She once worked in a dance hall and found herself obliged to fight off swarms of men determined to dance with her. Her amused and delighted employer compared her to the beleaguered Moroccan city of Mogador, then under attack by French forces. The name stuck.

130

Georges Bizet. The deeply depressed composer died at the age of thirty-six, within three months of the production of *Carmen*, never knowing the acclaim to be accorded both him and his opera. (Curtiss, Minna. *Bizet and His World*. New York: Alfred A. Knopf, 1958.)

Céleste Vénard, La Mogador, the captivating actress, author, and temptress, briefly a friend of Bizet, may well have been the real-life model for his *Carmen*. (Curtiss, Minna. *Bizet and His World*. New York: Alfred A. Knopf, 1958.)

If the words from her *Mémoires* sound a bit like those of the sensuously melodic "Habañera," sung by the title role in Georges Bizet's *Carmen*, it may not be entirely coincidental. More likely than not, the comtesse was the real-life model for the operatic character. She claimed her relationship with Bizet was entirely platonic, and so it may have been. She showed no hesitancy in laying before the public many of her other relationships that were not. But there is no doubt that Bizet came under her spell, and was fascinated by the wildly romantic La Mogador. Neither do we know whether he ever read her *Mémoires* with its intriguing paragraph so similar to the words of his Carmen. But in the many hours they spent together we can assume that she uttered similar thoughts, or that Bizet sensed them.

It was 1865, five years after the publication of the *Mémoires;* she was forty-one, he was twenty-seven, when they met on the train from Paris en route to the little village of Le Vésinet, about twelve miles distant. She had just purchased an estate there, next to Bizet's home. Bizet was unmarried, and, before his first encounter with Céleste, there is little evidence of growth in emotional maturity or worldly knowledge beyond that exhibited by him about seven years earlier while a student in Rome.

"I deplore, without understanding them," he had written his parents, "all the transports of the thing known as love. I don't agree with anyone about it, and I am glad of it." For his cousin, who rejected the daughter of a military officer to marry a servant girl pregnant with his child, Bizet had "the most profound contempt." Concerning the delights enjoyed by some of his comrades during visits to Paris, he says: "I know that disease, but I will have none of it." In yet another letter home, he declares that he "would willingly risk my life for a friend, but would think myself an idiot if I lost a hair of my head on account of a woman."

Clearly, he was not ready for La Mogador. She was, by any standard one chooses, a most unusual woman. To her credit is a prolific literary output, much of it before her meeting with Bizet: novels, plays, operetta librettos, and poems, in addition to the *Mémoires*. Only in recent times was a second volume of memoirs discovered, a volume that tells us much of the details of her relationship with Bizet, but perhaps neglects to tell us much more.

She had a good deal to write about. Born in the Paris slums, she had never known her father. He was apparently one of a long series of her mother's lovers. Céleste was only thirteen when one of them turned his attentions to her, to which she reacted by running away. She was arrested and imprisoned, and upon release found that she was registered by the police as a prostitute. At sixteen she was ensconced in a bordello. There she made the acquaintance of a writer, a former lover of George Sand, Alfred de Musset, one of the better patrons of the house. In her *Mémoires* she treats him with a disdain bordering on contempt.

She was next employed at the dance hall where she earned her nickname, having been hired as the partner of the proprietor to assist in popularizing a dance, new at the time, called the polka. The nickname stands as enduring testimony to her success.

She became an equestrian and was a brilliant rider at the Hippodrome in Paris. The male admirers, no fewer in number, and now of a higher social strata, dazzled her. A duke supplied her with her own carriage and horses. Inexorably, she was drawn into the midst of the glittering musical world of that musical capital, courtesy, to a large extent, of Alphonse Royer. He was director for several years of the Opéra, and librettist and translator for several of the operas of Donizetti. She also became the object of a fierce obsession by a precocious protégé of the brilliant concert pianist and composer, Franz Liszt. The young musician was Jewish, which was not to the liking of La Mogador, and under her spell he gave up his religion and neglected his career, finally entering the priesthood.

An accident cut short her riding career, but not her prodigious attraction for men. She became the mistress of "a young sprig of a nobleman," as a Dumas biographer called him, who had gambled away his fortune. He was Lionel, Comte de Moreton de Chabrillan. Apparently he did not ask for much as, for once, the affections were returned. To help her penniless lover she became an actress at the Variétés. There she attracted the attention of Thomas Couture, a famed painter, and the younger Alexandre Dumas, who wrote a part specially for her in one of his plays. Couture fell hopelessly in love with her. He made a drawing of her face, and a cast of her hand, which reposed for many years in a Paris museum.

It was to help pay the count's debts that she turned to writing. She started with her memoirs, deterred not at all by the fact that she herself was barely able to read. She enlisted the help of one of her former lovers, and the volume was, not too surprisingly, a popular success.

It did not help. Chabrillan soon bankrupted his mistress as well as himself, and left for Australia. Through family influence he was appointed as French consul in Melbourne. He then returned to Paris, and the two were married, but not before he removed Céleste's name from the official list of prostitutes. The couple lived together in Australia for two years, after which she returned to Paris with a completed novel, *Plon-Plon*. Her husband died in Australia in 1858.

In 1859, at a time when young Bizet was still a student in Rome, she introduced herself to Alexandre Dumas, père, showed him the novel, asked for his help in revisions, and suggested that they sign as coauthors and share the profits. He declined, but, predictably, took a personal interest in her career, or perhaps in her. What he did was probably better than signing the manuscript. In his own newspaper he praised it, and other critics took their cue from him. Her deceased husband's family nonetheless requested that she not use their family name, and she complied.

She became director of a well-known theater, then was forced to abandon it in the face of relentless critics who took pleasure in reminding the public of her colorful past. More receptive were the audiences of a large theater in a poorer section of the city, where she was employed as the manager. Her biggest success was a dramatic adaptation of one of her own novels, *Les Voleurs d'Or*. Enthusiasm mounted when, despite her attempts to remain incognito, she was identified as the author of the story. The author of the stage drama itself, however was never identified to those audiences. He was Alexandre Dumas, père. She accompanied the play on tour and earned enough that upon returning to Paris she could purchase an acre and a half at Le Vésinet.

So it was that she met Bizet. She claims that at the time he was very sad and "living on hope." The sadness apparently soon melted, and he confided to his new neighbor that he expected to be bored a good deal less once she settled into her home. It seems that he was. At his suggestion she purchased a piano, giving him a key to her spacious home in order to compose at his pleasure. But he preferred to play when she was there, acknowledging to Céleste that her presence inspired him. He would improvise for hours at a time while she contented herself with admiring the beauty of his hands.

Bizet often entertained a few intimate friends in the evening in his more modest quarters. They were all men, except for Céleste, and she tells us that she was honored to be included. She, too, entertained friends at times, mostly a bohemian lot, in whose presence Bizet felt less than honored. They included a pianist who pounded rather than played, and a female beer hall singer whose great popularity impressed him as little as her talents. To cap it all, Céleste's mother was living with her, and she hated both the piano and Bizet. On one occasion she threw a dish at him from the second floor as he tapped on Céleste's window on his way home from the railroad station. He generally preferred to visit when Céleste was home alone. Understandably, not everyone is persuaded by her claim that the relationship was innocent.

Céleste was now singing for a living. She appeared every evening at a café, and sang, among other numbers, "Ay Chiquita" by a composer named Sebastián Yradier. Bizet must have liked his music. There is a copy of this song in his music library, and the theme of another song by Yradier, "El Arregilito," which Bizet, according to his biographers and musicologists, "borrowed" for *Carmen*'s "Habañera."

How much of the real-life Céleste Mogador do we see in the fiery, sensuous woman who dominates Bizet's opera, and how much of the fictional character Carmen from the novel of that name, published in 1846 by the French writer Prosper Mérimée? The story of the opera is based on the novel. Mérimée's title character is skillfully drawn, and it does indeed require much skill to make a sympathetic character out of the ruthless, cold-blooded gypsy girl we see in his pages. Aside from Don José, she has another lover, a "rom," as he is called by gypsies, a common-law husband in modern vernacular. But unlike Escamillo of the opera, he is no swashbuckling hero, no idol of the gypsies or anyone else. He is, in short, no prize. He is killed by Don José, who then becomes Carmen's rom. When she herself faces death at the hands of Don José, it is not because of jealousy—there is no other lover now—but because of her refusal to run off with him to America. We admire her independence. But a femme fatale she is not.

The fierce pride, the haughty air, the skilled use of her sexuality to manipulate her admirers—little of it do we see in Mérimée's work. The only hint of it comes from his Don José, who tells the story's narrator: "I did not care for the look of her at first, and I went on with my work: but she, like women and cats who do not come when they are called, and come when they are not called, stopped before me."

From Mérimée's Carmen herself we hear nothing of that nature. She does not say, like La Mogador, "The men to whom I have given the most are those who asked least of me." Nor does she speak like Bizet's Carmen, who addresses love, a "willful wild bird," in language such as this:

> Threats and Prayers alike unheeding;
> Oft ardent homage thou'lt refuse,
> Whilst he who doth coldly slight thee
> Thou for thy master oft thou'lt choose.
>
> Would you seize him? he gets free!
> Care not for him—then he'll prove
> Thy slave instead of master—Love!

These are the words of Bizet, not of his librettists, Henri Meilhac and Ludovic Halévy. They were a prolific pair of writers for whom at the time this opera was far from the most important project in their lives. They were more interested in the one-hundredth performance of a now long-forgotten piece called *La Boule*.

It was early 1873 when Bizet began work on *Carmen*, eight years after his meeting with Céleste. In June 1869 he had married Geneviève Halévy, the daughter of a once well-known composer, and the cousin of the *Carmen* co-librettist. Sometime before his marriage, Céleste fades from the pages of his biographies. We can assume that she also faded from his life, as their relationship seems to have been a cause of some resentment against him by the Halévys.

Except for his brief relationship with Céleste, there is nothing in Bizet's background to make him a likely candidate to shock the public with his operatic renderings. But the story of the creation and first staging of *Carmen* is rife with episodes of shock to the public morals. In the vastly different social mores of today, it is difficult to imagine this. But the problems involved are eloquently summarized in the spontaneous expression of outrage from Adolph de Leuven, one of the two directors of the Opéra-Comique, who was approached by Halévy with the proposal for *Carmen*. De Leuven's reaction was swift and unequivocal:

> *Carmen!* Mérimée's *Carmen?* Isn't she killed by her lover? And that background of thieves, gypsies and cigar makers! At the Opéra-Comique, a family theater! The theater where marriages are arranged! Every night five or six boxes are taken for that purpose. You will frighten off our audience. It's impossible.

Not only marriage arrangements, but all sorts of business and social arrangements, as well as light-hearted conversation, took place in the stalls and boxes of the theaters of the day. This was 1873. It would be three more years before Richard Wagner, in his specially built theater in Bayreuth, turned out the lights, faced all seats irremediably forward, and demanded strict attention to the performance, banning even whispered conversation. Operatic performance was still, for many, a pleasant background for the discussion of more important matters.

The Opéra-Comique, with its generally light-hearted fare, was particularly known as a favorite place for arranging marriages, and a sordid stage portrayal was hardly a conducive backdrop to this.

The other director was Camille du Locle, whom we last saw at the Opéra just a few years earlier. He favored the *Carmen* project, and the impasse was resolved by the resignation of de Leuven. But that was not the end of the problem. Du Locle's approval had been anything but wholehearted.

A running battle ensued. On one side was du Locle, supported, in varying degrees, by the two librettists who feared a public outcry. They insisted on toning down the acting, by Carmen in particular, on changes in the text, and, finally, in the story itself. On the other side was the fiercely resisting composer, supported by the principals, Paul Lhérie as Don José and Galli-Marie as Carmen. She was not the first choice for the role. That honor had gone to Marie Roze, who declined after reading the text, due to the "very scabrous side of this character."

Du Locle liked neither the text nor the music, which he, incomprehensibly, deemed incomprehensible. After many rehearsals he decided that the ending must be changed. There had, after all, never been a murder on the stage of the Opéra-Comique, excepting, of course, well-motivated ones. Only the threat of Lhérie and Galli-Marie to withdraw rather than accept any changes forced the director to back down. When a man of the cloth asked for a box for opening night for himself and his family, du Locle invited him to a rehearsal so that he might first decide if the subject matter was acceptable.

Bizet did in fact agree to quite a number of changes. But there were two portions of the text to which he held absolutely fast. One was Carmen's part of the card trio. The other was the "Habañera." He was totally dissatisfied with the words of the "Habañera" prepared by his librettists. According to his friend, the New Orleans–born composer Ernest Guiraud, he rewrote them thirteen times before he was satisfied. On the final version he noted in the margin, "Do not change any of this."

Little wonder. The text fashioned by the librettists is tepid stuff, watery soup compared to Bizet's own poetry, and completely unsuited to the torrid music he composed for it (with the melody he borrowed from Yradier). In the text that Bizet discarded, the librettists had written: "Illusion and fantasy/This is how love begins/And this for life, or for six months or for eight days/one morning on his way, one discovers love, it is there/It comes without anyone doubting, and without anyone doubting it leaves/It takes you, it carries you away/It does with you all that it wants/It is a madness, a dream/and it will last as long as it may."

Halévy and Meilhac were reportedly skillful and successful poets. But they had obviously never met La Mogador.

The premiere came on March 3, 1875. After the first act, Bizet was warmly congratulated by a host of well-wishers. In the second act only Micaëla's aria was applauded. In the last two intermissions there were fewer and fewer felicitations. It seemed that du Locle was right. This was not at all the traditional form of the Opéra-Comique. During the last intermission, to a friend's encouragement Bizet responded grimly, "I sense defeat." The final applause was lukewarm. When one well-meaning companion congratulated him on his success, Bizet snapped, "Success! Don't you see these bourgeois have not understood a word of the work I have written for them?" Following the performance Bizet dejectedly wandered the streets till dawn in the company of Guiraud.

Even before the second performance on the fifth, the reviewers had proclaimed the work a failure. Typical in tone, if somewhat higher pitched than most, were the comments of *Le Siècle*'s Jean-Pierre-Oscar Comettant. Referring to the chorus of women from the cigarette factory, he cried "A plague on these females vomited from hell!" He proclaimed Micaëla to be the only "decent and sympathetic character in the midst of this inferno of ridiculous and uninteresting corruption."

Most of the invectives were hurled at the story. But the music got its share. The French musical world was divided at the time into pro- and anti-Wagner forces. The Wagner haters, and such they were, decried the use of repeated musical motifs and the heavy orchestration. The Wagner idolaters, and such they were, too, thought that Bizet had not gone far enough toward the "music of the future," as Wagner's compositions were called. Thus judged by what it was not, instead of what it was, neither group was pleased. Wagner's own reaction to the work: "At last. Someone with new ideas."

Concerning the critics, however, it is always good to keep a proper perspective, a task for which Ernest Newman is uniquely suited. As he so deftly put it: "The musical press of Paris in the eighteen-seventies included a greater number of stupid and self-sufficient nonentities than have ever exercised the functions of musical criticism in Paris or any other town before or since."

At the second performance, audience reception improved, and some of the reviews were more thoughtful, and more favorable, but the damage had been done. There were forty-five more performances that year, but mostly to half-empty houses. Many of the tickets were given away, and receipts did not even cover expenses.

The reactions of his peers were entirely different. Not only Wagner, but Brahms, Gounod, Debussy, Grieg, and Puccini praised it. Tchaikovsky was so carried away with it that he embarrassed his brother, Modest, who accompanied him to the performance. Five years later, he predicted that it would soon be the most popular opera in the repertory. Saint-Saëns wrote to Bizet that he found it "marvelous."

The reviewers also found it marvelous—but not until the thirty-six-year-old composer died on June 3, 1875, just three months after *Carmen*'s premiere. Eventually even Comettant came around. They did not apologize for their hasty, ill-considered, derogatory language, nor did they attempt to explain it away. They merely ignored it.

Bizet had long suffered from recurrent throat angina. He had also been gripped by a state of depression even before the rehearsals for *Carmen*, a condition that steadily worsened following the premiere. Many writers link, however tenuously, the savage criticism of *Carmen*, the aggravated state of Bizet's depression, and his premature death. The medical cause of death, however, according to Dr. Eugene Gelma of Strasbourg, who studied the matter earlier this century, was "a cardiac complication of acute articular rheumatism."

There is, of course, no medical proof that depression either caused or hastened his death. Had he been able to hear in life some of the posthumous tributes bestowed on him and his *Carmen*, beginning with his funeral, death might still have come at the same time in the same way. That he never lived to hear them is a tragedy nonetheless.

Except for *Carmen*, Bizet would cut a very small figure in the musical landscape today. Other symphonic and operatic works of his are frequently played, but only because of *Carmen* does he stand with the giants. Just how much does he, and do we, owe to the captivating lady who suddenly entered his life, and just as suddenly left it? It is a question worth a passing thought or two, even though it can never be known for certain.

19
A MOST UNUSUAL TRIANGLE

EUGENE ONEGIN

THE PLOT: During a brief visit by Eugene Onegin to her family, the young Tatyana becomes deeply enamored of him and later writes an effusive letter declaring her love. Onegin tells her that it was not appropriate to write in such fashion to a stranger, that he does not wish to marry at all, and suggests she exercise more restraint. He wanders abroad, aimlessly and unhappily. Upon his return, at a chance meeting with Tatyana, he learns that she is happily married to a prince. He now yearns for her, and asks that she share love with him. She acknowledges that she loves him still, but he is shattered when she contemptuously refuses his pleas.

On May 30, 1877, Peter Ilyich Tchaikovsky wrote to his brother Modest that he had tracked down a copy of the poetic novel, *Eugene Onegin,* and read it through "with delight."

He probably read it with a good deal more than delight. More likely, he was transfixed by it, at least by the "letter scene." He may well have rubbed his eyes, and wondered if the line between fact and fiction, between fantasy and reality, was not becoming blurred. There is every reason to believe that, for him, it was.

A scene in the first act of Tchaikovsky's opera, one of the most delicate in the work, depicts the young Tatyana composing a letter,

141

Peter Ilyich Tchaikovsky. The marriage of the highly sensitive, morose composer, probably to stop the growing rumors of his homosexuality, led to tragic consequences. (Bowen, Catherine Drinker, and Barbara Von Meck. *Beloved Friend, the Story of Tchaikowsky and Nadejda Von Meck*. New York: Random House, 1937.)

pouring out her heart to Eugene Onegin, a man she has just met and to whom she has barely spoken. It is taken almost line for line from the novel. But it could almost have been taken from letters Tchaikovsky himself began receiving just a few weeks previously.

In Pushkin's verse, and in the opera, Tatyana tells Onegin that long before she met him she had dreamed of him, and upon seeing him she immediately recognized the man of her dreams. She writes this letter with the greatest trepidation, she says, as one word from him can set her heart afire or leave her desolate.

Tchaikovsky was thirty-seven at the time he read *Onegin* that day in late May, and he was miserably unhappy teaching music at the Moscow Conservatory. For some time he had been seeking a subject for an opera. On May 25, a singer had suggested *Eugene Onegin*. Tchaikovsky did not reply, but on reflection became intrigued and set out in search of Pushkin's novel in verse. In his letter to Modest, he said that after reading it, he spent a sleepless night working out the opera sketch in his mind. How much Tchaikovsky already knew about the novel is not clear, but from his reaction to it at this time, it was probably not a great deal.

About three weeks earlier he had received a letter from a former student at the conservatory, one Antonina Miliukoff, then twenty-eight. It was a declaration of love. The letter has not been found, but it certainly existed, as in one dated May 16, she tells the composer that "For a whole week I was in agony, Peter Ilyich, not knowing whether or not to write you. I see that my letters begin to annoy you."

None of Tchaikovsky's correspondence to her has been saved. The letter of the sixteenth is the first of hers still extant, but the tone of her earlier correspondence can be surmised from the language of that one: "I won't be able to forget you or stop loving you . . . I don't want to look at any man but you . . . It is not the love of a moment but a feeling that has been growing for a long time. I simply cannot, and will not, destroy this feeling now."

She wrote again on the eighteenth, "I stay at home the whole day, wandering from one corner to another like a half-mad person . . . I cannot live without you and so, perhaps I shall soon make an end to myself. Let me look at you and kiss you so I may carry that kiss into the other world." Passionate words, but not a thing do any of her letters say about marriage.

Nonetheless, on July 18 they were married. The moving force in this union was not Antonina, but Tchaikovsky himself. As it happened, the letters arrived at a particularly vulnerable moment in his emotionally turbulent life. He had, for no outwardly discernable reason, become deeply depressed. And the more depressed he became, the more often he spoke of marriage, but his reasons for wanting to marry were not the usual ones.

He was homosexual, as were his brother Modest and the son of their sister, Alexandra Davidov. In 1877, this was not a matter to be openly trumpeted. The secret of Peter and Modest was known only to themselves, to Modest's twin brother, Anatol, and their sister, Alexandra, but not to two other brothers, to their half-sister, or to their father, now eighty-two years of age. It troubled the elderly man very much that his son Peter, at thirty-seven, had never married, and he did not hesitate to say so.

Over the years, Tchaikovsky had occasionally expressed a determination to marry. He seemed to be motivated in part by the belief, prevalent at the time, that marriage was the panacea for all troubles, and in part by the need to stifle the inevitable gossip about him in the Moscow musical world. Both his secret, often referred to in correspondence between Peter and Modest as "It," and his work at the conservatory, grew increasingly oppressive as his creative powers ripened. The signs of depression seem to intensify from early 1875, and with them, so do the expressions of his determination to marry.

In January 1876 he wrote Anatol that he was lonely to the point that if he could not marry he might enter a monastery. In March he claimed to have been constantly unhappy all winter, and six months later, said that,

> From today, I shall make a serious effort to marry, legally, anybody. I am aware that my inclinations are the greatest and most unconquerable obstacle to happiness; I must fight my nature with all my strength . . . I shall do everything possible to marry this year, and if I am not brave enough for that, at any rate, I shall conquer my old habits once and for all.

A month later he wrote to Modest, "I should like to marry, or by some known liaison with a woman, shut the mouths of all despicable gossips."

On May 8, Tchaikovsky wrote to a friend, Ivan Klimenko:

Not a kopek's worth of fun is left in me. Life is terribly empty, tedious and tawdry. My mind turns toward matrimony or indeed any other steady bond . . . teaching . . . I find more irksome every year . . . I am chained to the Conservatory.

Within a few days came the letter from Antonina. The second letter (or perhaps the third) of May 16 contained her address, and he went to see her. Upon a second encounter a few days later, he proposed marriage. He had made at least one inquiry about her at the conservatory, received a negative opinion, but proposed marriage nonetheless. According to Tchaikovsky, and others who knew her, Antonina was an attractive blond-haired woman with a pleasing figure and beautiful complexion. She has, however, been termed "irritatingly stupid" and "subnormal in intelligence" by one biographer, and "besotted and unbalanced" by another. It is claimed by one source that she had a habit of biting her nails to the quick, and that some of her letters are stained with blood from her fingers.

Perhaps all of that is true. From the few letters we have, there does not appear, at that time, much evidence of stupidity or irrationality, but of a highly emotional, perhaps neurotic, woman. Though none of Tchaikovsky's letters to Antonina are extant, some of his letters about her are. One, written after the marriage, was to Nikolay Kashkin, a music teacher and critic who assisted Tchaikovsky in the adaptation of the *Onegin* story. It tells much about the merger of fact with fiction in the composer's hyperactive imagination, and the remarkable ease with which he slipped from one to the other.

Shortly after the first letter from Antonina, he says to Kashkin, he began to write the "letter music" for the *Onegin* opera, yielding to some "spiritual need" to do so, even before having a libretto or a detailed plan of the story. He was so absorbed that he forgot about his own letter from Antonina until he received the second one some time later. He was, he tells Kashkin, completely in sympathy with the fictional Tatyana and indignant with the callous treatment of her by Onegin, whom the composer considered to be cold and base. Consequently, Antonina's second letter made the composer ashamed of himself for not answering the first. This sequence of events, it should be noted, is at odds with known facts and Tchaikovsky's own letters to other parties. He could not have been working on *Onegin* until at least two weeks after her second letter. The confusion, in itself, seems to further highlight the merging of fact and fantasy.

He made pointed mention to Kashkin of Antonina's threat to put an end to herself should the second letter be ignored. "In my mind," says Tchaikovsky, "this all tied up with the idea of Tatyana, and it seemed to me that I myself had acted more basely than Onegin, and I became truly angry with myself for my heartless attitude towards this girl who was in love with me." But he did not mention to Kashkin his determination to marry anybody at all, if only to put a stop to wagging tongues.

An even more interesting letter had been written before the marriage. The wedding was planned for the eighteenth of July. On the fifteenth of that month, with two acts of the opera sketched, he wrote to the "other woman" in his life, a forty-six-year-old wealthy widow, Nadejda Von Meck. The appearance of Antonina created a triangle, but it was not the usual triangle of either fact or fiction.

Von Meck, too, had begun her relationship with Tchaikovsky with letters little more than four months before the first correspondence from Antonina. Her husband had died in early 1876, and in her large Moscow mansion she had become a recluse, or as much of one as the mother of twelve children could be. To the household staff she soon added a full-time violinist who, probably not coincidentally, was a friend and admirer of Tchaikovsky. Sometime, she never said when, she had heard Tchaikovsky's *The Tempest*, and as she later put it: "For several days I was half demented."

In early December, through her violinist, she commissioned from Tchaikovsky a violin and piano arrangement, which he completed quickly. Between then and March 19, five letters passed. On the nineteenth she wrote an effusive note asking for a photograph so that she might "search your face for the thoughts and feelings that inspired you while writing music that sweeps one into a world of emotion,

Nadejda Von Meck. Passionate admirer of Tchaikovsky, she corresponded with him for fourteen years and provided generous financial support, but by agreement between them they never met. (Bowen, Catherine Drinker, and Barbara Von Meck. *Beloved Friend, the Story of Tchaikowsky and Nadejda Von Meck.* New York: Random House: 1937.)

hope and insatiable yearning." Though living in the same city, they corresponded and swapped photographs for fourteen years.

But they never met. Never a spoken word passed between them. A few times she saw him conduct at concerts. On a few occasions their paths crossed by accident, but embarrassed, they each went their separate ways. They did not talk; it would have been a violation of their agreement. This understanding was her idea, and the intensely introverted Tchaikovsky was only too glad to accept. "I can challenge you," she wrote, "as to which of us has more stories about our shyness." She claimed to have severed relations with the world, and that wherever she went, she spoke as little as possible. Said Tchaikovsky: "We both suffer from one and the same illness . . . misanthropy." He had once harbored such a terror of people as to be almost insane from it, but, he claimed, his work saved him.

But between them, in correspondence, the words flowed freely and effusively. On May 12, she says, "I feel so near to you in spirit that I have this impulse to open my soul to you." On the following day, he writes a lengthy letter of his own, a request for a loan of 3,000 rubles, about $1,500 at the time, and a not-inconsiderable sum. She was the only person from whom he would not be embarrassed to ask for money, he says, for which he gives two reasons: "First, you are kind and generous. Second, you are wealthy." Both excellent reasons indeed.

There were various discussions as to how repayment was to be arranged, usually by commissions for compositions, but, not surprisingly, the balances did not decrease, they increased, and by the end of October the advances had evolved into an allowance. Such was the esteem in which she held Tchaikovsky; such was her affection for him, and such was her generosity. It is not difficult to imagine her pain upon hearing of his impending marriage, when he finally wrote her about it on July 15, three days before the wedding.

The first letter from Antonina, he told Von Meck, was written so sincerely and warmly that he answered it. The letter that he answered, of course, was not warm; it was torrid. He emphasized to Von Meck, as he did later to Kashkin, that he always told Antonina that he did not love her, and that he described to her his disagreeable character traits, his irritability, and his unsociability. On first meeting Antonina, he explained to her that he felt only sympathy and gratitude for her love. But from Antonina's next letter, he continues, he found that if he should discontinue all relations after having gone so far, he would drive her to a tragic end. "So I had a difficult alternative—to save my freedom at the price of the girl's ruin—or marry. I could not do otherwise than choose the latter."

So, he said to Von Meck, he is marrying without love because the circumstances permit no other choice. His conscience is clear, he concludes, because "I have not lied or pretended." But he told neither Von Meck nor Antonina about "It," or that he was desperate to marry anybody at all. In his letter to Von Meck, he also said of Antonina that "one of these days, we shall be married." That was literally true, but the statement withheld more than it revealed, namely, that the wedding would be in three days.

Von Meck responded promptly and graciously, wishing him happiness, assuring him of her continued devotion, and asking that he continue to tell her everything about himself. "From my heart, I press your hand. Do not forget one-devoted-with-all-her-soul."

It was two years before she revealed to Tchaikovsky the true depth of feeling evoked by his letter. The catalyst for that revelation was the receipt, in September 1879, of the piano arrangement of his Fourth Symphony, which he dedicated to her. She played it repeatedly, claiming to hear her whole life in it, and to have lain awake for two nights, hearing it again and again in her mind. On the twenty-sixth she wrote him:

> Do you know that when you married it was terribly hard for me, as though something had broken my heart? The thought that you were near the woman was bitter and unbearable . . . I rejoiced when you were unhappy with her . . . I hated that other woman because she did not make you happy, but I would have hated her a hundred times more if you had been happy with her . . . I love you more than anyone and value you above everything in the world . . . forgive my voluntary confession . . . The reason is, the symphony.

As is obvious from this letter, the marriage did not go well. It was, in fact, a disaster of the first magnitude. It was the blackest period of his life, but it ran its course parallel to the composition of *Eugene Onegin,* by all odds his finest opera.

His letters for months after the wedding were filled with despair. Just days after the ceremony, Tchaikovsky, while on his honeymoon in St. Petersburg, wrote Anatol of the "ghastly spiritual torture" of the wedding, of being choked with sobs when the train started, of his yearning to scream. Life might be bearable, he claimed, only because Antonina was not clever, and blindly obeyed him. But it was not bearable at all. On the twenty-third, he wrote that "physically she has become absolutely repulsive to me." It was apparent that she did not believe his confession of homosexuality and felt that all would be well in time.

In August he wrote Von Meck of the panic he experienced after the ceremony. He felt not even friendship for his wife; she was abhorrent to him. The future was a "dreary unbearable comedy." Antonina was not guilty, he admitted; she did not ask for marriage. He did not want to be cruel to her, so he must lead a life of pretense. He feared that music would perish from his life, and thought often of death.

The only benefit to ensue from the marriage was the cessation of rumors about his homosexuality. It apparently stopped the gossip. Otherwise, life in the small Moscow apartment was, for him, a horror. He complained bitterly in his letters about the stifling presence of Antonina in the cramped apartment, and her ceaseless chatter. Even in his own complaints, one can sense her desperate and fruitless attempts to gain his approval. One night in early October, he left the apartment and wandered the streets, seized by the greatest terror of all: For a week he had been unable to compose, and he feared his inspiration had vanished. At a lonely bank of the Moscow River he waded into the icy water up to his waist before reason, and the desire to live, took control. He returned home and told Antonina he had fallen in the water. Only to Kashkin did he ever tell the truth, adding that he was beginning to feel an irrational hatred and contempt for her.

A few days later he suffered a complete breakdown. Only Anatol, among friends or family, saw the symptoms, and he refused to discuss them. For two days, Tchaikovsky was unconscious in a hospital, his life in danger. When the crisis passed, the physician prescribed a complete change of scene. His next letter to Von Meck was from Switzerland, full of self-chastisement for his "cowardice, weakness, and stupidity," and "lack of character . . . blundering and childishness."

In early November came the most revealing letter about Antonina that the distraught composer was to write. He had come to realize that she, despite her gushing declarations, had never loved him. "In her head and heart is absolute emptiness," he wrote Von Meck. Though she claimed to be a good musician, she knew not one note of his compositions, nor had she ever been to the concerts of the Musical Society, where he performed and where she could have easily seen him had she wanted. She is talkative, but everything leads to "the numberless men who have loved her, most of them generals, nephews of famous bankers, well-known actors, or members of the Imperial Family." She had a "strange fury" against every member of her family, most of all, her mother.

The letter also dwelled at length on his impoverished state, and was filled with apologies for asking, but asked nonetheless: "I need money again, and again I can ask no one but you." She responded with the 6,000-ruble yearly allowance. Almost triumphantly he wrote to Modest offering to share the wealth: "Just when you need money,

Modia, I have suddenly become, if not rich, at least comfortably off for quite a long time." It had been done with such tact, he exulted, that he felt little embarrassment.

Such was the background against which *Eugene Onegin* was written. Tchaikovsky never called it an opera. He called it "Lyrical Scenes," from Pushkin's poem. Because it lacked action, he never had much hope for it as a popular repertory piece. To Von Meck he had written in his letter just prior to his marriage that he had chosen it because to him, Pushkin's words were more than mere words. His verses possessed "something that pierces to the depths of one's soul. And that something is music."

After a few weeks in Switzerland, he moved to Vienna. In November, the piano score of *Onegin* was sent to his friends at the conservatory and played for a small audience of severely demanding professors and critics. "The music was marvelous," wrote Kashkin, "it left the hearers breathless." Their enthusiasm was all the greater, no doubt, after the perpetually pessimistic letters from the composer: "Something is broken in me. My wings were clipped, and I shall never fly very high again."

During the three months following his short stay in Switzerland, he was almost always on the move—Vienna, Venice, Milan, San Remo, working on *Onegin* and the Fourth Symphony. On February 13 he sent the completed opera to the conservatory, where, in March 1879, students gave it its first performance. It was attended by the composer. There was much applause from the audience of students and teachers, but Tchaikovsky knew that it was for him, not for the opera. The amateur performance was not adequate, and the opera was inadequately appreciated. Later, professional performances were enthusiastically received, and the work's popularity spread, slowly but persistently. It reached London in 1892, was played in concert in New York in 1908, and in full performance at the Metropolitan in 1920.

After Tchaikovsky's breakdown and flight to Switzerland, he and Antonina never again lived together. Neither were they ever divorced. She knew of his secret, and he lived in deadly fear that, out of spite or malice, she might expose him. She never did, but he did not breathe easily until he heard that she had borne a child and was living with the father. In the 1800s, this, too, was not a matter to be lightly bandied about. That she had her own dark secret gave Tchaikovsky a measure of security. She had a series of children with various lovers and placed them all in orphanages. Her childbearing continued even after her commitment to an insane asylum in St. Petersburg in 1896, where she was still confined at the time of her death in 1917.

We are assured, in a volume coauthored by the widow of one of Von Meck's grandsons, that Tchaikovsky was in no way responsible for Antonina's breakdown, and that it would have occurred in any event. What expertise supported such assurance about a woman they had never met, the authors do not tell us. To a certainty, the experience did her no good. Her love letters resulted, unexpectedly, no doubt, in a personal visit from the highly respected, if not yet renowned, composer, and a proposal of marriage. How her expectations must have soared! As to the trauma to her already precarious self-esteem upon becoming the object of his sudden, and, from her viewpoint, unprovoked contempt, we must draw on our imaginations. She has no biographers.

Von Meck continued both the correspondence and the allowance to Tchaikovsky until 1891, when she suddenly ceased all contact with him. He heard nothing from her, and his letters were returned unopened by a friend with the explanation that she was ill, physically and mentally. To Tchaikovsky, her sudden silence was a devastating blow. There has been much speculation, but the full circumstances of the sudden cessation of this remarkable relationship have never been satisfactorily explained.

It seems safe to say that in the summer of 1877, Tchaikovsky would have written an opera, if not on one subject then on another. Whether it was the letters from Antonina, the music he heard in Pushkin's verses, something else, or mere whim that supplied the greatest impetus to *Onegin* is a matter only for speculation. But it seems a matter of fact that his first response to the flattery of Antonina's letters was gratification, and a hope for peace of mind, however illusory the hope turned out to be. No matter how briefly, her letters were very heartening to him. Echoes of his emotions during those few weeks must certainly exist in the tender lyricism of the letter scene, if nowhere else in his opera.

20

TWIN METEORS

PAGLIACCI AND CAVALLERIA RUSTICANA

THE PLOT OF PAGLIACCI: A troupe of clowns arrives in a village. When Nedda repulses Tonio's advances, he leads Canio, her hus-band, to observe Nedda in the arms of her lover, Silvio. The play performed by the clowns that night parallels life, and before the audience, Canio stabs Nedda, then Silvio, as he tries to save her, Canio declaring: "The comedy is over."

THE PLOT OF CAVALLERIA RUSTICANA: Turriddu returns from the army to find his former love, Lola, wedded to Alfio. He and Santuzza become lovers, but Santuzza, knowing that he has again turned to Lola, tells Alfio, who challenges Turriddu to a duel. San-tuzza sinks to the ground with a scream as she hears that Turriddu has been killed.

*T*he trial was over and the defendant was found guilty of murdering his wife. It was a case that one might hear in any courtroom anywhere, at any time. But it was in Montalto in the province of Calabria, Italy, sometime around 1870. The accused might have been anyone, but he was a *pagliaccio*, a very particular type of clown with a three-hundred-year history, and very popular throughout Italy during the latter part of the nineteenth cen-tury. They were lowly buffoons who wore white- and blue-checked

153

Ruggiero Leoncavallo, composer of *Pagliacci,* the opera twin to Mascagni's *Cavalleria Rusticana.* None of the other operas of either composer ever equaled the success of these two works. (Marek, George R. *Puccini, a Biography.* New York: Simon and Schuster, 1951. Courtesy of George R. Marek estate.)

Pietro Mascagni. He won worldwide fame and a fortune with *Cavalleria Rusticana* at age twenty-seven, but none of his subsequent fifteen operas succeeded. (Marek, George R. *Puccini, a Biography.* New York: Simon and Schuster, 1951. Courtesy of George R. Marek estate.)

suits of coarse mattress cloth with big buttons, blue stockings, short puffed-out breeches, and black caps. This one's name was Alessandro, and the evidence showed that immediately after a performance he had killed his unfaithful wife in a jealous rage.

"Do you feel repentant?" asked the judge. The coarse voice of the *pagliaccio* reverberated in the courtroom: "I repent me of nothing. If I had to do it over again, I'd do it again!" He was sentenced to prison.

One of the spectators in the courtroom was the young son of the judge. The boy's name was Ruggiero Leoncavallo. He often attended court to watch the proceedings, but this case left a lasting impression on him. He was very familiar with the annual Festival of Madonna della Serra, which took place every August 15 at Montalto, with the arrival of the clowns a week before and the raising of their tents in the open fields. He had also observed the villagers arriving from the nearby town of Santo Benedetto for the occasion. It apparently had never occurred to the callow youth that these laughing clowns harbored their own deep passions.

Twenty years later the boy had become a composer, but a very unsuccessful and frustrated one. He wrote one opera shortly after graduating from the music conservatory in Bologna, then could not find the impresario who had promised to produce it. He wandered to places as far afield as Egypt, earning his living by giving piano concerts and teaching music. On returning to Italy, he began work on a complex trilogy of operas, the first part of which he had submitted to Giulio Ricordi, the music publisher. Ricordi had promised to publish it but did nothing.

By 1891, Leoncavallo was impatient and disgusted, but he was also dazzled and perhaps envious of the success of another composer five years his junior, namely Pietro Mascagni. Mascagni's one-act *Cavalleria Rusticana* had catapulted him just a year earlier from obscurity to international fame. This opera was something different under the sun. It involved no gods, no kings or princes, no high-born lords or ladies. There was no philosophy, no introspection, no profound ruminations on the deeper meaning of the action or of life in general. It was peasants and slums, fast action and raw emotion. And it was sweeping the opera houses of all of Europe. It was said by the critics to herald a new movement, one that they termed *verismo*, or "truth."

The scene in the Montalto courtroom came back to him. Leoncavallo shut himself in a room and began work on *Pagliacci*, writing the libretto as well as the music. It was completed in five months and was accepted for both publication and production by Ricordi's rival, Edoard Sonzongo. It was produced in Milan's Teatro dal Verma in May 1892, under the baton of the twenty-five-year-old Arturo Toscanini, two years almost to the day after the first production of *Cavalleria*. It was an immediate success with both audience and critics.

At the beginning of the opera, Tonio steps before the curtain, and in a prologue filled with power and passion explains that what is about to be witnessed is a true story, not merely a play. But he, himself, is part of the opera, and it would, no doubt, be seen as just one more dramatic device were it not that shortly after the premiere, Leoncavallo was forced to defend himself against charges of plagiarism.

He was sued by the French author Catulle Mendès, who claimed that the idea was purloined from his play, *La Femme de Tabarin*. Ironically, Mendès's own play, thirteen years earlier, had precipitated charges of the same nature by one Paul Ferrier, and Mendès, even more ironically, defended himself on the ground that the incident he employed of murder during a play within a play was historical and had been used times without number.

Leoncavallo, however, had even better weapons for defense than that. In an interesting letter to his publisher, he detailed the events he had seen in his father's courtroom and his recollections of seeing the arrival of the clowns in Montalto. Leoncavallo claimed that the clown, Alessandro, after being released from prison, found employment with a baroness in Calabria and that he stood ready to appear in court and tell his story at any trial for plagiarism. Mendès, however, dropped his suit and the action never took place.

Too bad! To anyone who grew up to the sounds of Caruso's "Vesti la Giubba," what a fascinating transcript his testimony and that trial might have provided.

The year after its premiere, Toscanini performed *Pagliacci* and *Cavalleria* as a twin bill at the Costanzi in Rome. The two operas meshed like pieces in a puzzle. They have been bound together as "the opera twins" ever since. This was a marriage made in heaven, and no conductor or manager has been able to tear it asunder. Efforts to separate them, and to perform each separately with one other short

opera or another, have died aborning, causing legitimate wonder as
to whether either of them could have survived without the other.

Mascagni's life paralleled Leoncavallo's almost as much as the stories and styles of the operas. He attended the music conservatory at
Milan, where he shared lodgings with Giacomo Puccini under circumstances not dissimilar to that of the four bohemians in Puccini's *La
Bohème.* Apparently strong-willed, stubborn, and undisciplined,
Mascagni quarreled with the headmaster just as he had with his father, then left to live the life of a vagabond. He carried with him a
copy of Heinrich Heine's *Ratcliff,* his source for a proposed opera.
Finally, he left an engagement paying two dollars a day and settled
down at Cerignola as director of a school for orchestral players. He
married and started a family, slaved over his ponderous *Ratcliff,* and
sent piteous letters to Puccini bemoaning his plight.

In 1888, he went to Naples to see one of Puccini's early operas
and to personally congratulate his friend. The practical Puccini advised him to put aside his proposed *Ratcliff* and to compose a more
accessible work, one easier to produce.

Puccini did not need to draw him any pictures. Mascagni knew
of a competition, now in its seventh year, sponsored by Sonzongo. An
annual prize was offered for the best one-act opera. Mascagni could
not afford to pay a librettist, but he wrote a young friend with a
literary bent in Livorno asking for a one-act libretto. The friend, Giovanni Tozzetti, suggested a well-known short story, namely, "Cavalleria Rusticana." A second writer, Guido Menasci, was called in to assist,
and the two librettists made a present of their work to Mascagni, charg-
ing him nothing, an act of generosity they would later regret.

In a biographical sketch, Mascagni states that he began his opera
at the end; that he had from the first been preoccupied with the finale
and the piercing words, "They have killed neighbor Turriddu." "One
morning," says Mascagni, "as I was trudging along the road to give
my lessons at Canossa, the idea came to me like a stroke of lightning
and I had found my chords."

"We must make a large expenditure today," he told his wife.
Namely, he explained, an alarm clock to awaken him before dawn so
that he might begin work on his opera.

The librettists were unable to keep pace with the composer, jot-

ting down segments on postcards and sending them to him each evening. The music was often written before the words were received,
which then had to be reworked to fit the music.

It was barely completed in time. But before entering it in the competition, Puccini, on behalf of his friend, submitted it to Giulio Ricordi, the House of Ricordi still being the most prestigious in Italy.
The usually astute Ricordi goofed badly with a curt, "I don't believe
in this opera." No one can be right every time. In the Sonzongo competition, it was one of three selected for a full performance at the
Costanzi, from which the winner would be chosen. But from the audience response, there was no doubt about the winner; the announcement was an anticlimax.

The opera was performed in Rome in May 1890. It met with
instant critical and popular acclaim. By 1891, it had been performed
in Paris, Berlin, London, and New York and brought fame and financial rewards beyond Mascagni's wildest dreams. In deep gratitude
to his two librettists, Mascagni presented each of them with a gold
watch—and nothing else. According to Tozzetti, it was the only gold
that either he or Menasci ever saw for their work.

Pagliacci and *Cavalleria* were a double bill, and the fame of the two
composers shot like twin meteors across the sky. Those were heady, but
short-lived, days. Leoncavallo went on to write thirteen more operas;
Mascagni another fifteen. They were all failures. A few seemed to show
some spark and the possibility of life. None of them quite made it. The
popularity of this twin bill, "Cav and Pag," has continued without letup,
but it soon became fashionable for critics to denigrate the stories and
often the music as well. The new movement, *verismo*, which was supposedly ushered in by Mascagni's *Cavalleria*, never happened. *Cavalleria* ushered in only *Pagliacci* and perhaps Puccini's *Tosca*. Otherwise,
neither the composers nor their army of imitators have been able to
repeat the success of these two short works.

While referring to "Cav and Pag" as "filth of the Italian barn-
yard," according to one critic, and "blood and mud of the Neapolitan
slums" according to another, the critics claimed to see much merit in
some of the later operas of the two composers. Mascagni's *Iris*, they
said, was crafted more finely than his *Cavalleria;* Leoncavallo's *La
Bohème* was superior not only to his *Pagliacci,* but even to Puccini's
own *La Bohème*.

The critics should have saved their ink. Operas are not written for critics; they are written for paying customers, and the customers continued to flock to *Cavalleria* and *Pagliacci* and to stay away in droves from all the others. Lamented the depressed Mascagni: "I was crowned before I was king." Commented the aging Giuseppe Verdi: "What a pity! He [Mascagni] is a young man whose feeling for music exceeds his knowledge of it. He could achieve much . . . but . . . I think he has now lost his way." A tour of the United States by Mascagni in 1907, poorly planned and even more poorly executed, ended in lawsuits filled with charges and countercharges.

Leoncavallo died in 1919. Mascagni lived long enough to embrace Mussolini and his black-shirted followers. His last opera, *Nerone,* in 1935, is said to have been in praise of fascism. In 1944, his property was confiscated by the victorious allied armies when he was identified as a supporter of Il Duce. Poverty-stricken, alone, and embittered by the failure of his operas and the crushing defeat of fascism, he died August 2, 1945, in a small room of the Rome hotel where he spent the last year of his life.

FEROCIOUS PANTOMIME

TOSCA

THE PLOT: *Mario helps an escaped political prisoner. Baron Scarpia, chief of police, arrests Mario, then invites Mario's lover, Tosca, to his apartment, supposedly to hear news of him. But in the next room Mario is being tortured, and to save him, Tosca agrees to submit to the lustful Baron. After he orders a supposedly mock execution and signs a safe passage for the lovers, he turns his attention to Tosca, but she stabs him to death. She tells Mario to mimic death when the executioners fire, as the bullets will be blanks. But his execution is real. When soldiers come to arrest her, she leaps over the parapet to her death.*

*J*t is a fall afternoon in Paris, 1894. You are a fly on the wall of the reception room in the fashionable home of a popular French playwright. The playwright himself is present, as are two prominent Italian opera composers. They listen intently as a veteran librettist reads the opera libretto he has prepared, based on a recent play of the host. One of the composers is so moved by some of the verses that he seizes the manuscript from the hands of the librettist and reads the lyrics aloud in a voice trembling with emotion.

The playwright is Victorien Sardou, author of *La Tosca*. With Sarah Bernhardt in the title role, the play, one of seven he wrote spe-

160

Sarah Bernhardt and Julien Sardou, 1903. The famed playwright wrote seven plays specially for the even more renowned actress, including *La Tosca*, the source for Puccini's opera. (Photograph from *The Fabulous Life of Sarah Bernhardt* by Louis Verneuil. Copyright 1942 by Louis Verneuil. Copyright renewed 1970 by Florence Ryan. Reprinted by permission of HarperCollins Publishers, Inc.)

cially for her, has been a smashing success since its Paris premiere seven years earlier. The librettist is Luigi Illica, one of the authors of the text for *La Bohème* by Giacomo Puccini, and this libretto is for an opera, *Tosca*, based on Sardou's play. So the impulsive composer must be Puccini. Right?

Good guess. But the composer is Giuseppe Verdi. He is in town overseeing the French production of his *Otello*, and has dropped in for the reading. He is so impressed that he declares he would like to write the music himself, but at eighty-one feels that he is too old and too tired.

The other composer, however, is a much younger and more vigorous man. At thirty-four, he is already the successful composer of several very popular operas, and he has, in fact, already signed a contract with Giulio Ricordi, third of the line of Ricordis, to publish the music he will write for *Tosca*. So *this* is Puccini, right?

No, this one's name is Alberto Franchetti. Puccini had, indeed, once been quite interested. He had seen *La Tosca* performed in 1889 and had immediately written Ricordi, who was also his own publisher, to try to obtain Sardou's permission to base an opera on his play. Though he had not understood a word of the French dialogue, he was all the more intrigued that he could be so moved by a drama through its pantomime alone. However, Puccini, for whatever reason, apparently cooled to the idea and immersed himself first in *Manon Lescaut*, then in *La Bohème*, and nothing came of it. So in 1893, Ricordi signed the contract with Franchetti.

So why did not Franchetti write the music to *Tosca*? Because, with the blessing and consent of Puccini, his friend and fellow composer, he was snookered out of his contract rights by Ricordi, his friend and publisher, and by Illica, his friend and librettist. When Puccini heard of the profound impression the story had had on Verdi, and more particularly of Franchetti's contract, he was determined to obtain the rights himself, come hell or high water. And Illica and Ricordi were only too glad to help. True, Franchetti had written two highly successful operas, but audience enthusiasm for them in no way matched that for *Manon Lescaut*. Ricordi and Illica knew quite well whose opera would earn greater public response and more money for them.

The scenario by which the hapless Franchetti was finessed out of

Giacomo Puccini. His many love affairs were superficial and short-lived. His true loves seemed to have been the heroines he created in his operas. (Marek, George R. *Puccini, a Biography.* New York: Simon and Schuster, 1951. Courtesy of George R. Marek estate.)

his rights would itself make good grist for some playwright's mill. Illica and Ricordi met with Franchetti and, with consummate skill, went to work on him. After long consideration, they counseled the composer, they had come to the conclusion that Sardou's play was a very poor subject for an opera. The coarseness, the brutality, the overt vulgarity of it all were certain to offend an opera audience. The attempted rape of the heroine was all right for Paris, but far too risqué for the sensibilities of the Italian public and to top it all, the murder of Scarpia by Tosca's own hand would alienate any sympathy for her. And the historical events depicted in the play were entirely unfamiliar and would leave a modern audience cold. By the time they were through, Franchetti could not renounce his composition rights, and obligations, fast enough.

The next day Ricordi signed a contract with Puccini. The precise reaction of Franchetti upon hearing of this turn of events has not been preserved, but we have it on the word of one acquaintance that he never forgave Puccini.

From contemporary accounts of the play, it is little wonder that Puccini, no matter how great the lapse of time, was still determined to write the opera himself. "Bernhardt, knife in hand, over the dying Scarpia, is the nearest thing to great tragedy ever seen in modern times," wrote Clement Scott, an English critic. Nor was Puccini the only one to recognize how little the drama depended on the spoken word, and how much on action. "Ferocious pantomime," one critic called it, not entirely with approval, one that could be expressed "solely through gestures, wringing hands, disheveled hair, knees dragged along the ground, or even by nothing." So clearly visible were Bernhardt's emotions, said another, that the audience could anticipate her spoken words from the preceding pantomime.

What an ideal situation for an opera that would, hopefully, be internationally popular! Puccini's reaction to the play was no doubt similar to that of a journalist at the premiere who called the play "a commodity perfectly suited for export."

The starting point for the work on the libretto for Puccini was the text that Illica had fashioned for Franchetti. Illica worked with one Giuseppe Giacosa, a gifted poet and author. Together, they had furnished the libretto for *La Bohème* and were recalled to service for *Tosca*. They would be used again for *Madame Butterfly*. Illica drew the scenario and developed the plot in detail. Giacosa rendered the text into verse and developed the opportunities for expanded lyricism. There were a number of difficulties, some of which were caused by Giacosa's intense dislike of the drama. Of *Bohème* he had said that it was all poetry with barely a plot; *Tosca,* he said, was all plot but no poetry. In practically every disagreement it was Puccini's judgment that prevailed, a judgment that time would prove almost unerring.

Commencement of the musical composition was delayed until January 1898 because of Puccini's work on *La Bohème*. In April, the composition of *Tosca* was interrupted by his visit to Paris for the French production of that opera. There, for the first time, he met Sardou.

From Puccini's description, Sardou, then over seventy, must have been an intriguing person, but one passionately devoted to the art of the monologue. His own lasted for hours without letup on practically any subject except the matter at hand. However, among the more salient points of the meeting were first, an agreement to certain structural changes in the play, and second, a demand by Sardou for an unheard-of 50,000-franc advance. He finally settled for an also unheard-of 15 percent of the gross box-office receipts.

During a second visit early the following year, Sardou resisted certain unspecified efforts to change the ending of the opera, and Puccini reported to Ricordi: "He wants that woman dead at all costs." In sketching the panorama for the last scene, Sardou depicted the legendary Tiber River between the Castle San Angelo, where the scene is laid, and St. Peter's Cathedral. Puccini tactfully pointed out to the stubborn Frenchman that the river flowed on the other side of the castle, whereupon Sardou, "calm as a fish," said: "Oh, that's nothing," then got a huge map of Rome and talked for a quarter of an hour as to how the geography might be changed.

When Puccini, in a not-infrequent moment of self-doubt, complained that Tosca was different from his previous heroines, Mimi and Manon, and difficult to portray, Sardou's laconic response was that "Women in love all belong to the same family." He catalogued the female roles he had created and curtly added, "They are all the same woman."

The premiere was January 14, 1900, at Rome's Teatro Costanzi. A bomb threat caused considerable tension, and the nervous artists, on hearing a ruckus in the audience, interrupted the first act. It turned out to be only a shouting match between latecomers and resentful patrons who were already seated.

Despite the tension, the opera, by any measure, was, unlike *La Bohème* before it and *Madame Butterfly* after it, an immediate success. The success has continued without abatement. Most of the caustic comments of the critics were directed at the story rather than the music. A writer in one leading Rome journal said that Puccini succeeded in ennobling an action that might otherwise have been perceived as the "most reprehensible vulgarity."

This dichotomy has also persisted to the present. Critics have continued to attempt to distance the piercing lyricism of the music from what they perceive as the baseness of the story. Richard Specht, a

Puccini admirer, in his biography of the composer written thirty-two years after that first *Tosca* performance, admits that, "As a work of art, Tosca is repugnant to me, that the torture scenes nauseate me afresh every time and that in spite of its popular success, it seems to me beyond redemption." But, continued Specht, it wrung from Puccini "his most inspired music," music that made him (Specht) absolutely indifferent to aesthetic considerations.

Perhaps. But there must have been something in the first place about the story of *Tosca* that caused Verdi to snatch the pages of it out of Illica's hand and to read it aloud; that caused Puccini to covet it; and that caused Illica and Ricordi to stoop to chicanery to get it for the best talent available. These practical and experienced men of the theater must have seen something, and it is worth knowing that the theme of *Tosca,* in various settings, in various shapes, has a history and is not new with Sardou. While perhaps not so noble or venerable as the Faust legend, or that of Tristram and Iseult, the story has survived the retelling for hundreds of years. Time and durability are the ultimate validation of any work of art, and the story of *Tosca* has been tested by time.

Mosco Carner, a modern Puccini biographer, has traced the theme of the story through the years. He claims that it has been known since the Middle Ages, and that it forms the content of an old Italian ballad still sung in the province of Emilia-Romagna. He points also to its similarity with Shakespeare's *Measure for Measure* and to the theme of a novel by the nineteenth-century German writer, Paul Heyse. Carner also sees in it a similarity to Victor Hugo's *Angelo Tyran de Padoue,* on which Ponchielli's *La Gioconda* is based.

The story apparently has enough universality that upon the appearance of Sardou's play he was charged several times with plagiarism. Alphonse Daudet claimed that the plot was taken from his *La Saint Aubin*, implying complicity on the part of Sarah Bernhardt. And Maurice Barrymore temporarily enjoined the performance of *Tosca* in English on the grounds that it was plagiarized from his play, *Nadjedza*. But Sardou, calm as usual, denied all such charges, claiming that the idea originated from his reading of an episode occurring during the religious wars in sixteenth-century France.

According to him, a Catholic cleric obtained the privilege of a night with a beautiful Protestant peasant woman with the promise to

save her husband from the execution to which he had been sentenced. The following morning, however, the woman found her husband's body dangling from the gallows.

The critics have continued to reserve their most opprobrious epithets for the story: banal, vulgar, abominable. John Kernan, in his 1952 volume *Opera as Drama,* affixed to it the label "shabby little shocker." But Puccini, Ricordi, and Illica, all wise in the ways of the theater, apparently saw something in this story that is beyond, or beneath, the grasp of the scholars. As Ernest Newman put it, even Puccini's critics had to admit that what he didn't know about the theater was hardly worth knowing.

So, shed no tears for Franchetti. He obviously did not see in this tawdry plot what Puccini, Illica, and Ricordi did or else he would not have been wheedled out of it so easily.

22

FRAU WAGNER AND
THE RELIGIOUS WAR
OF 1903

PARSIFAL

THE PLOT: *Kundry, for having laughed at Christ on the Cross, is doomed eternally to tempt the virtuous. Amfortas, a knight of the Grail, while in her arms was dealt a wound, one that does not heal, by an evil magician. It can be healed only by a "pure fool made wise through pity." When Kundry tries unsuccessfully to seduce Parsifal, an unschooled youth, he understands the reason for Amfortas's fall and his agony. He wins from the magician the holy spear with which he wounded Amfortas, whom Parsifal then heals with its touch. Kundry, freed from her curse, expires.*

A number of quite newsworthy events occurred on Christmas Eve 1903. There was, for one thing, an important development in an international cause célèbre, namely, the infamous case of Captain Alfred Dreyfus, the Jewish French army officer convicted of treason nine years previously. On Christmas Eve the Court of Cassation finally ordered a new trial before a civilian court. For another thing, Great Britain recognized the new Republic of Panama, and American forces took up defensive positions at the site of the planned canal. Then, there was an arrest in an attempted extortion case involving a wealthy trio of intended victims named Carnegie, Rockefeller, and Morgan. On Christmas Day, all of

168

these stories made the front page of the *New York Times*. But none of them rated the lead headline.

The Christmas Day lead headline concerned a performance at the New York Metropolitan Opera House. It read: PARSIFAL A TRIUMPH. It was splashed across the two right-hand columns, followed by the explanatory subheading: "Production Unrivaled in History of Opera in New York—Immense Audience, Deeply Impressed with Wagner's Festival Play, Listens Breathlessly Throughout the Performance."

An opera? And, of all things, *Parsifal*? Perhaps one reason for the extraordinary publicity, but only one, was contained in the first sentence of the story: "For the first time since it was first produced in Bayreuth in 1882, Wagner's *Parsifal* was performed yesterday outside of the Festival Playhouse for which the master composed it."

No matter. For the modern reader the whole thing must still seem passing strange. And those first two front-page columns were only the beginning. The second page was taken up almost entirely with *Parsifal*. There were comparisons, all quite favorable, from a number of notables who had seen productions of the opera in Bayreuth, Germany, in the theater designed specifically for Wagner's operas. One of these notables was an impresario named Oscar Hammerstein, the grandfather of the future composer of musical comedy. For Heinrich Conried, director of the Conried Metropolitan Opera, as it was called then, there were glowing tributes to his energy and resourcefulness in bringing this "historical" event to fruition.

It was customary in those innocent days to devote a few lines to what the gentlemen and their ladies wore to their boxes at the opera. For this performance the subject rated several columns. Even the topmost gallery came in for a share of the attention in a short piece headed "Motley Assemblage in Which Those Who Understood Nothing Were Overawed by the Music."

On page three was an explanation of Wagner's use of musical motifs, together with a complete reproduction of the musical notations of the motifs themselves. There was no need to print the libretto. That had already been done several days earlier, together with a full explanation of the history of the legend and Wagner's sources. Nor did the editors neglect to include a brief, but colorful, account of Wagner's life and struggles.

A similarly high-pitched publicity blitz often greets popular personalities, entertainers, or heads of state. It had happened in times past in European cities for new operas by popular composers like Donizetti, Verdi, or Puccini. But this was New York, this was Wagner! And *Parsifal* had been performed in Bayreuth, with portions heard elsewhere in concert, including New York, for twenty-one years.

A New York German population of about a quarter of a million, mostly recent immigrants, may have been part of the answer. Twenty years after his death, Wagner was still revered among Germans. An attack on the opera by some religious leaders, with the resulting public controversy, may have played a role. But one of the more likely factors to stir public interest was the fierce opposition by Wagner's widow and her unsuccessful legal attempt to block the performance.

Why would his widow have opposed the performance of this opera? Financial reasons? Hardly. She had been offered a tidy sum by the Met, but refused to discuss it. It went deeper. It went back to about fifty-five years before that 1903 performance.

From the beginning *Parsifal* was something special to Wagner. In 1845, while conductor of the Dresden Opera, he had read the poetic rendering of the legend of the grail knight, *Parzifal,* by the medieval author Wolfram von Eschenbach. It made a powerful impression on him, but, as was his custom, he allowed the subject plenty of time to germinate, and did nothing with it at once. Four years later, as a political refugee in Zurich, he was living primarily by begging and borrowing while he worked on his *The Ring of the Nibelung.*

Thanks to his wealthy benefactor and admirer, Otto Wesendonck, in 1857 he and his first wife, Minna, had moved to the small cottage he termed the Asyl. In his autobiography he describes how, on this first Good Friday in the Asyl, he awoke to beautiful spring weather, and that for the first time since reading the Wolfram poem, "Its noble possibilities struck me with overwhelming force, and out of my thoughts about Good Friday, I rapidly conceived a whole drama." He immediately made a rough sketch of the three acts for an opera.

In early 1865, long separated from Minna, impecunious, and driven from city to city by chance and by creditors, at what was undoubtedly the low ebb of his life, came two incredible, almost simultaneous, strokes of good fortune. They enabled him to live in relative financial and emotional security and to successfully complete virtually all of the ambitious projects he had mapped out for himself. One of these strokes of fate was the accession to the Bavarian throne of a young man thoroughly mesmerized by Wagner's music, King Ludwig II, who made it his mission in life to give every possible aid and encouragement to the beleaguered composer.

The other was the entry into his life of Cosima von Bülow. She was the daughter of Franz Liszt and wife of Wagner's friend and admirer, the conductor and pianist Hans von Bülow, whom we last saw at the *Tannhäuser* debacle in Paris. At the age of twenty-seven Cosima made it her self-imposed mission to devote her life entirely to Richard Wagner, who was twenty-four years her senior. In 1868 she abandoned her husband and two young daughters, who later came to join her, and went to live openly with Wagner in Lucerne. In 1870 she entered into marriage with him, determined to see his every ambition fulfilled and to make his life as conducive to the completion of his artistic goals as humanly possible. Certain it is, without Ludwig and Cosima there would have been no *Parsifal*.

By 1878, two of the most far-reaching of Wagner's ambitious projects had been realized. One was the construction of a festival theater, the Festspielhaus, in the Bavarian town of Bayreuth, designed to Wagner's own specifications, with its unique acoustics and unrestricted sight lines. It was accomplished in part through generous loans from the Bavarian treasury, courtesy of King Ludwig. His generosity with his kingdom's money earned for the monarch gratitude, of a sort, from Wagner and fierce resentment from his ministers and the public. The other project was the completion and performance in the Festspielhaus of Wagner's monumental tetralogy, *The Ring of the Nibelung* in 1876. The next major project to be undertaken was the composition of *Parsifal*.

This was the first, and only, opera written with the benefit of the experience of performances in the Festival Theater. Apart from the nature of the drama itself, with its spiritual content and depiction of religious ritual, Wagner was guided in the composition, and in the orchestration, by the sounds he had heard in this unique theater during the *Ring* performances of 1876. The music of *Parsifal*, he told Cosima, was to have the softness and the shimmer of silk. It was to be like "cloud layers that keep separating and combining again."

He began the text of the opera in early 1878. He was a man of the theater, but there was much about the theater that he despised. From the beginning, it was his determination that *Parsifal* never become part of the standard operatic repertory. Production would be limited only to Bayreuth, and the audience only to patrons, that is, those who were supporting him financially. Cosima noted in her diary on September 23 of that year that Wagner, referring to *Parsifal,* exclaimed that he hated the thought of "all those costumes and grease paint! . . . those dreadful artists' balls." He never considered *Parsifal* an opera. He called it a "stage consecrational festival play."

But practical matters intervened. The king's support of Wagner and the resulting financial drain on the treasury created a good deal of hostility in certain quarters of the government and with the public. It had to be dealt with. In March 1878, the king and Wagner signed an agreement granting the Court Theater in Munich production rights to all of Wagner's works, but only after the first production in Bayreuth. For that first production, Munich personnel were to be employed. Proceeds from the Munich performances were to be used to retire Wagner's debt. But as Wagner continued work on the opera, the contract notwithstanding, his determination that *Parsifal* not be abandoned to the theaters was obviously growing in intensity.

On August 25, in a letter to the king, he declares that he wants nothing more to do with the ordinary theater. It would please him, he says, to complete it for his own artistic satisfaction, then to seal the score until his son's maturity. Only the king's desire to hear it, he tells Ludwig, restrains him from such a course. It would be an outrage, he continues, to "hand this work over to the theater public of our towns, with its usual late-coming and early-going, its chatter, its boredom, and all the rest of it."

Repeatedly in her diary, in the latter part of the year, Cosima notes that her husband is very emphatic; he does not wish to stage *Parsifal*. He would return the patrons their money, and have nothing more to do with singers, orchestra, or the Munich theater. He broods over it. Do his patrons want to help? They can do so by paying his debt to Munich. "I should like to produce it," he tells Cosima, "only when we, you and I, feel we want to."

Throughout 1879 and much of 1880 he was haunted by the subject. Desperate to retire his debt to Munich, he sold to his publisher,

Franz Schotts, a number of his treasured personal compositions, including the "Siegfried Idyll," written specially as a present to Cosima in celebration of the birth of their son. He also sold to Schotts certain rights to *Parsifal,* namely publication of the piano score only. Each copy was required to, and did, bear the words: "This copy must not be used for production on the stage." Nonetheless, it was a transaction that, many years later, would cause Cosima much grief.

Matters came to a head in September 1880. In a direct appeal to the king, Wagner invoked his help in the name of religion, by no means Wagner's own reason for wishing to prevent performances by other theaters. But he warned the king, prophetically as it turned out years later, of the possible protest by Church authorities against "representation of the holiest mysteries complacently sandwiched between the frivolity of yesterday and the frivolity of tomorrow, before a public attracted to it only by frivolity." He must have a dedicated stage, he continued, and this could only be in his theater in Bayreuth.

> There alone should *Parsifal* ever be performed. Never must it be put before the public in any other theater whatever as an amusement; and my whole energies are devoted to finding out by what means I can secure this destiny for it.

With the sympathetic king, Wagner's letter carried the day. On October 15 the monarch annulled the contract of 1878, and in a letter to the composer agreed that "*Parsifal,* your solemn stage-dedication-festival-play, shall be given only in Bayreuth, and never be desecrated by contact with any profane stage." The first crisis had been weathered.

The opera was completed in January 1882. In July it was performed sixteen times in the Festival Theater before spellbound audiences from all parts of the globe. On February 13, 1883, while vacationing in Venice, Wagner died of a sudden heart attack in the arms of his wife. For twenty-five hours the emotionally shattered woman sat next to his lifeless body, sometimes cradling him in her arms, sometimes whispering to him, refusing all offers of food. Finally she left on the arm of one of the daughters of her first marriage. When the coffin was brought, she cut off her hair and placed it inside.

Ludwig's word concerning *Parsifal* was kept in spirit, if not to the letter. Within two years of Wagner's death, the crowd-shy king, who did not attend the Bayreuth *Parsifal* despite a special entrance that had been constructed for him, saw eight performances in Munich, which he ordered for his personal viewing only and from which the public was excluded.

Following Wagner's death, Cosima became a recluse. Many of her closest friends and associates believed that she was trying to follow her husband to the grave. But in the summer of 1883 things changed. The Bayreuth Festival again took place, this time with twelve performances of *Parsifal*. Whether by design or fortuitous happenstance, an audience member, now unknown, delivered to her a lengthy memorandum comparing the current performances most unfavorably to those of the preceding year. It contained biting criticisms of these stagings, and they struck a chord in the composer's still emotionally paralyzed widow.

Whatever the purpose of the memorandum, it had an effect on her that was both electrifying and galvanizing. She realized that her self-appointed mission in life was not over. With a vengeance, she now demanded, fought for, and won the right to take charge of the festival. She did so with but one purpose in mind: to carry out the wishes and directions of "the master" to the highest degree. His every utterance, or her recollection of it, whether concerning orchestration, singing, acting, or staging, became immutable law. Any controversy over interpretation or performance was settled by her pronouncement that "the master said," or "the master did, . . ." down to the minutest detail of gesture or nuance.

She was met with hostility. She made enemies, and she was forced to deal with crises. The most acute of those were threats to perform *Parsifal* outside Bayreuth. In 1886, King Ludwig died under circumstances still shrouded in mystery. Shortly prior to his death he had been certified insane by four psychiatrists, not one of whom had ever spoken to or seen him. In matters pertaining to Bayreuth, the new government was less pliable. It dealt with the Wagners through one of its ministers, Baron von Crailsheim. Crailsheim was appointed to office by Ludwig himself in 1879, but was nonetheless instrumental in Ludwig's commitment. He had little regard for any claim of sanctity for *Parsifal* or for the Bayreuth Festival.

In a stormy session involving Crailsheim and six other officials on one side, and Adolph Gross, Cosima's friend and representative on the other, Crailsheim claimed for the government the right to all of Wagner's works, *Parsifal* included, citing the agreement of 1878. Gross responded with documents showing Ludwig's voluntary renunciation of that contract and his recognition of exclusive domain over *Parsifal* by Bayreuth. Referring to Ludwig's alleged insanity, Crailsheim rejected the argument and the validity of the documents as those of an "incapacitated" king. As quoted in George Marek's biography of Cosima, Gross retorted: "My documents were signed a year before you, Excellency, were appointed. If, then, my documents are null and void, so is your appointment." Lengthy negotiations resulted in a full recognition by the government of the exclusive rights of Wagner's heirs to all of his works. The second crisis had been successfully weathered.

The protection granted by German copyright law expired before the end of the century, and Cosima's efforts to persuade the Reichstag to extend the law's coverage failed. But no new threat was posed by German theaters; they had apparently accepted the moral, if no longer the legal, exclusivity of the claim of Cosima and Bayreuth. The new threat came from overseas, in the person of a dynamic director of the New York Metropolitan Opera.

Heinrich Conried, whose directorship was effective from early 1903, had ambitious plans, the most important of which was to perform *Parsifal* at the Met. When Cosima heard of it she was enraged, and determined to put a stop to it at whatever cost. But there was no copyright treaty in existence between the United States and Germany. She lashed out, blindly at first, as she did not seem to know where the blow was coming from. With persuasion and cash, Conried had recruited many Bayreuth artists, and she suspected a conspiracy centered in Munich. She wrote to the famed conductor, Walter Damrosch, in New York. He had given orchestral concerts of excerpts, and she asked him not to give the parts to Conried, assuring him that Schotts would not hand over the score. But, as she would soon learn, Schotts had already caused irreparable damage.

On October 11, Cosima caused the publication in New York of a letter she wrote addressed to a friend in that city. In it she lamented the impracticality of a boycott to thwart the "tramplers on musical etiquette," and, taking her cue perhaps from Wagner's earlier appeal to King Ludwig, she raised the religious question in what seemed to be an invitation to the ministry:

> It is well known that the inhabitants of the United States are deeply religious. I should not be surprised if some American minister of the Gospel should combat the idea that a work of decidedly religious nature like *Parsifal,* wherein the Sacrament of the Lord's Supper occurs, should be performed in public. I am of course not expressing any opinion of my own in alluding to such a contingency.

That, indeed, was not her opinion. Her objections had no more to do with religion than did Wagner's. That Wagner's concern had no religious root is clear from his own utterances as recorded by her in her diary. It had to do with art, the "Bayreuth atmosphere, the Bayreuth spirit, which cannot be transferred to any other place," as she phrased it in her open letter.

She filed suit seeking an injunction. Lacking any claim of copyright in the United States, her suit was based on the common law right of property, the underpinning of which must be that the material sought to be protected has not been published, and is hence not in the public domain. Conried and the Metropolitan defended on the ground that the score was in wide circulation and was being extensively bought and sold.

While the case was pending, the clergy took Cosima's bait and entered the fray. On November 11 one of them claimed to represent a committee resolved to oppose the performance, and, for that purpose, to conduct an "educational campaign." He issued a lengthy statement. Included was a colorful, but hopelessly inaccurate, summary of the story. Kundry was referred to as "a more advanced member of the red light legion." The chief complaints were the depiction of Christ being subjected to temptation and the idea of the Lord's Supper portrayed in a "playhouse." Parsifal, the lead character of the opera, of course, was never meant to depict Christ. When once so asked, Wagner replied: "Christ, a tenor! God forbid."

Other ministers joined in the attack, one of them terming the opera a travesty of things held sacred by all Christian people, another complaining that it would cheapen and degrade the solemn ceremonials of the church. The lawyer for the Wagner family denied having fomented any of the controversy or of having played any part in it. There were a number of long-winded letters to the editor expounding both sides, and much public argument and counterargument over what *Parsifal* did and did not contain, and what it did and did not mean.

In an editorial, the *Times,* after reviewing the protests emanating from the Protestant clergymen, concluded that it must agree with a bishop (denomination not specified) to whom its editors had spoken. The cleric stated that he had no information on which to form an opinion. It may seem cowardly of us, said the *Times,* but for an opinion to have weight, "the opinionator must know what he is talking about." A Catholic priest commented that it was not the practice of his church to take from Protestants its notions of what was and was not sacred.

Even before the circuit court ruled on the request for injunction, tickets were placed on sale, and the scramble for them was so great that dealings by speculators were evident. The line extended "up Broadway," according to the *Times,* "to Fortieth Street and around the corner of the opera house halfway to Seventh Avenue." It was rough and tumble, said the paper, and only the strongest and most insistent got the tickets.

On November 24 the court ruled, the pivotal point of the decision being that Schotts had published an edition of the full score, complete with words and stage directions, "of which several copies were actually sold." True, the title page of each of these contained the words "This copy must not be used for production on the stage." It did not matter, said the court. If publication is complete, "such notice is ineffective to reserve the very right which publication dedicates to the public."

During the month that elapsed between the court decision and the *Parsifal* performance, there were more letters to the editor, more editorials, interviews with artists, and public lectures by well-known musical scholars such as Walter Damrosch. A statement by the New York Wagner Society, lamenting the "shocking" state of affairs that permitted the opera to be "vulgarized and dragged into the dust," drew a rebuke from a newspaper in Frankfort, Germany. The paper regretted the insult to New Yorkers by the intemperate language, but nonetheless went on record as opposing the production. For the vituperative language aimed at him by another German writer, Conried brought a defamation suit even as Cosima herself referred to Conried as "an audacious Barnum from Vienna." Several weeks before the premiere, additional performances were announced.

A piano recital on the New York's East Side, intended to acquaint the public with the *Parsifal* music, played to a standing-room-only audience. And as the big day approached, audiences were warned to be in their seats a few minutes before the 5 P.M. curtain as "after the conductor is at his desk, no one will be admitted to the auditorium." From Chicago came a group of music lovers in a chartered private railroad car. The entertainment en route: piano excerpts from *Parsifal*. Five days before the performance, three-quarters of a column was devoted by the *Times* to a controversy over the appropriate dress. The chief problems raised were the early curtain time and the sacred nature of the representation. The matter was put to rest by incidental mention in an official announcement of "Parsifal Week" at the Met. It was assumed, said the announcement, that the patrons would wear evening dress. Thus was the frivolity of the day "sandwiched between the frivolity of yesterday and the frivolity of tomorrow."

On the evening of the performance, extra policemen were on duty to handle the crush. It was not Christmas Eve in the neighborhood of the Met that night, according to the *Times,* it was *Parsifal* night. There were, according to the cabmen, more than two hundred additional carriages and cabs than on any night except the season opener. This was the opera that Wagner wanted to reserve for himself, Cosima, Ludwig, and a few close friends and supporters.

And when it was over, though the debate about propriety continued, the enthusiasm could hardly be contained. Reactions ranged from extremely favorable to ecstatic. One pundit termed it the "greatest triumph that any operatic manager in this country has ever achieved." Another went him one better: "the most perfect production ever made on the American stage." An editorial in the *Times* concluded that opera had been advanced "from its low estate" to one that raises questions that are "serious and deep." It was performed a total of eleven times that season, and sold out every time. The final performance was decreed by Conried, who personally held the lease on the opera house, as a "manager's benefit," and he pocketed the profits.

Cosima never forgave New York, Conried, or the Munich Court Theater, which she still suspected of complicity. Even many years later, those close to her seemed to feel obliged to apologize to her for any trip they made to the United States. That the popularity of the opera gained as it spread to stages throughout the world meant nothing to her.

Would it have meant anything to Wagner? Probably not. The praise of knowledgeable peers he craved. The acclaim of audiences, however, usually meant little to him. He felt that they did not understand his works, and applauded them too often for the wrong reason. That may well have been the case on Christmas Eve 1903.

The most effusive praise for the music that appeared in the *Times* the next day was not really excessive. For those whose devotion this opera has won, no words could be. But, for those not initiated deeply into Wagner's peculiar musical idiom, *Parsifal* is an acquired taste, and the acquisition is often a slow process. Doubtlessly many of the audience were genuinely entranced by the uniquely shimmering, iridescent, hypnotic quality of the work. And probably many more sensed something deep and enduring in it, though not able to grasp so much at once. In a world without commercially marketed phonographs, how many of the fifty thousand who heard *Parsifal* in New York that season could have been attuned to Wagner's musical language? How many were merely carried away by the increasing frenzy of the publicity, the controversy and artificially heightened expectations?

Perhaps the most perceptive observation, psychologically if not musically, that Christmas Day was by the author of the lead article in the *Times*. After almost two full columns of glowing accounts of the performance, the audience, and the atmosphere, he concluded with a paragraph that may have been little noted at the time:

> Without the newness, the strangeness, the tension of anxiety, and eagerness of desire to test a new thing, it is likely that there will be much to weary the most intelligent, the most open-minded. There are long stretches in Wagner's most didactic manner; long explana-

tions such as Gurnemanz in the first act, and even of Kundry in the second, who intermits her blandishment of Parsifal to instruct him in a specious theory of love, that are meaningless without exact comprehension of the declaimed word, and not alluring even with it.

In his assessment of the musical value and the emotional impact of this opera, he was much wide of the mark. For most who are familiar with the music, there is not a dull phrase in it, and the very parts the writer mentioned often stir the deepest emotional response. As Wagner often suspected about others, however, this audience may have been enthusiastic for all the wrong reasons. The *Times* writer, whatever his error of musical judgment, may have been one of the clearest heads in the house.

23

A MYSTERIOUS FAILURE

MADAME BUTTERFLY

THE PLOT: *Lieutenant Pinkerton, a U.S. naval officer in Japan, marries Cio-Cio-San as a romantic lark, though she is deeply in love. He sails away a few months later, promising to return in the spring. Cursed for renouncing her religion and rejecting offers of marriage from a Prince, she remains confident of Pinkerton's return though three years have passed. When he does, it is with his American wife to ask for the infant son that Cio-Cio-San has borne of their union. She agrees, asking Pinkerton to return in half an hour, but then ceremonially ends her life.*

On the evening of February 17, 1904, Puccini was sitting in the wings of Milan's La Scala opera house, watching the second act of the world premiere of his *Madame Butterfly*. He was also listening, not to sounds coming from the stage, but from the audience. First he was merely stunned, then horrified. He bit his nails, and from time to time was heard to mutter through clenched teeth: "Splendid!—Louder still, you beasts—Shriek, yell, jeer at me! Ruin it all for me—But you'll see it is I who am right—It is the finest opera I have ever written."

Signs of trouble had started early on, but gave no hint of the maelstrom that was to follow. The audience sat in stony silence during the opening scene. During performances that pleased them, audi-

181

ences at La Scala did not usually do that. And they certainly would not sit quietly for very long during a performance that did not please them. Something was in the air, and Rosina Storchio, the first Cio-Cio-San, could sense it.

Even before her first few offstage notes, she was unnerved. Upon her grand entrance, she was met with a dead silence, no applause, no cheers. Shortly after, the first calls rang out from the gallery, "*Bohème, Bohème* . . . we've heard that already . . . give us something new." They were hushed by others on the main floor. The balance of the act was received mostly in silence, broken only, at the end of the love duet, by widely scattered applause and renewed, isolated shouts of "*Bohème*." Obviously some patrons thought, or claimed to think, they detected a similarity to melodies from the earlier opera. They were not paying enhanced prices to hear old music.

At the end of the act, Puccini, still suffering from the effects of a year-old automobile accident, limped out onto the stage with the help of his cane to join the cast. The little applause there was was mixed with boos and hisses. Unable to disguise the shock and the hurt from the unexpected insults, he limped quickly back. No one came backstage to congratulate him. One of the few in the audience voicing enthusiastic approval was Pietro Mascagni, composer of *Cavalleria Rusticana* and Puccini's staunch friend. There were also tears, most of them from Giuseppe Giacosa, one of the librettists, and from Puccini's wife, Elvira, and his three sisters.

They might have saved them for what was to come in the second and final act. *Butterfly* was then in two acts. The second, lasting about an hour and a half, combined the two scenes that today are the second and third acts. They were separated by an intermezzo depicting the passage of the night. That second-act performance was summed up by Giulio Ricordi, Puccini's publisher, in a musical journal published the following month: "Growls, shouts, groans, laughter, giggling . . . pandemonium, throughout which virtually nothing could be heard."

Puccini's sister Romelda was less concerned with the niceties of objective reporting. Only hours after the performance, she wrote a letter to her husband: "Giacomo won't talk about the opera at all . . . We don't know how we got through it . . . and as soon as it was over we fled . . . That disgusting, despicable and rude public!" Puccini himself described it the next day as a lynching. "Those cannibals didn't listen to one single note," he wrote to a friend. "What a terrible orgy of madmen drunk with hate!"

Perhaps the low point was reached during the early part of the act when a gust of wind from the wings caused Storchio's kimono to billow out, prompting a catcall from the audience that "Storchio is pregnant—a little Toscanini." The reference was to a well-known love affair between Storchio and the maestro, who was not conducting that night. She did, in fact, later bear his child. At the beginning of the act's second scene, following the intermezzo, Ricordi had arranged for a chorus of chirping bird sounds, indicative of the breaking dawn. It was an unfortunate stroke of showmanship, as it prompted a thunderous caterwaul of animal sounds and laughter from all parts of the theater.

The final curtain fell to hisses, jeers, and insults that drowned out everything from both the stage and the pit. Puccini's eighteen-year-old son, Antonio, embraced his father and broke into uncontrollable sobbing. "How is it possible the public can be so ferocious?" he demanded. Storchio was in hysterics. Mascagni stood alone on the stage, weeping and haranguing the departing audience for its disgraceful behavior. He dried his tears, kissed Puccini, and whispered encouragement. A scheduled celebration dinner was canceled. Puccini refused to eat at all, and sat in his apartment, across the street from La Scala, banging his fist on the piano. He returned his 20,000 lire advance on royalties and withdrew the opera, vowing to a friend from Rome that "*Butterfly* will rise from the dead."

It had come as a complete shock. Never had Puccini faced a premiere with such confidence. *La Bohème*, eight years previously, after a shaky start had swept triumphantly through the opera houses of the world. *Tosca*, four years after that, had been an instant triumph of equal proportions. Even *Manon Lescaut*, his first success, was still holding its own. Together they were bringing him fame and an income the equivalent of about $150,000 annually that, even in those heydays of royalty, enabled him to live the life of a king. He had approached the premiere of all of them with increasing nervousness, and, in each case, had suffered badly from opening night jitters.

But not this time. Now he had arrived. Unlike those of his earlier works, rehearsals had gone ever so smoothly. During many of them, he was treated to the unusual spectacle of stagehands walking on tiptoe, sometimes stopping their work to listen and wipe tears from their eyes. The cast was superb. The morning of the premiere, Puccini sent an effusive note to Storchio, concluding with the supremely confident words, "Through you I am speeding to victory." Celebrities from distant cities, many from Rome, would be in the audience. Box-office receipts set a record for La Scala openings. Never before had he permitted his family to attend a premiere. He did not want to subject them to the vagaries of opening night audiences, but this time he had no trepidation. He invited not only his wife and son but his sisters, three of whom attended.

It was a tremendous buildup for a smashing fall, and it would be hard to overstate the impact on him. It had hit him in a very vulnerable spot—his true love affair with a fictional Japanese girl. His romances with his operatic heroines seemed to be the deepest and longest-lasting affairs of his life, a life filled with countless sexual liaisons, flings, and flirtations. These he openly avowed to his wife, Elvira; he felt entitled to them, and, in any event, if ever he tried, was unable to resist them.

He and Elvira were married just weeks before the premiere of *Butterfly,* after the couple had lived together for almost twenty years. The ceremony followed, by the legally requisite ten months, the death of Elvira's long-abandoned husband. In 1915, after eleven years of marriage, Puccini wrote Elvira a chastising, and revealing, letter summing up what appears to have been his credo throughout life. "All artists cultivate these little gardens," he pointed out. "You imagine immense affairs. In reality, it is nothing but a sport to which all men more or less dedicate a fleeting thought without, however, giving up that which is serious and sacred; that is, the family . . . The wife of an artist has a mission different from that of wives of ordinary men."

The story of his life bears him out. They were indeed not serious to him. Wherever he went, whatever he did, there were affairs without number. Handsome, famous, wealthy, and romantic—women flocked to him. If he ever gave a thought in advance to the consequences to himself, to the starry-eyed women, or to his deeply embittered wife, irrational and driven half-insane with jealousy, there is little trace of it in his letters or in accounts by those who knew him. These temporary romantic partners seemed to be no more than corporeal surrogates for his ethereal fictional true loves: Manon, Mimi,

Tosca, Cio-Cio-San, and Turandot. And among all of them, Cio-Cio-San, his dainty, delicate Madame Butterfly, was special.

His romance with her began in the summer of 1900 in London when he saw David Belasco's play, *Madame Butterfly*. Its operatic possibilities had been apparent to the stage manager of Covent Garden, who quickly notified Puccini. As with *La Tosca*, Puccini had not understood a word of this play, but, also as with *La Tosca*, he was immediately enchanted. Negotiations with Belasco for composition rights were completed in April of the following year. Into no opera, before or after, did he pour as much of himself as he did into this one.

The accident that left him limping had occurred one year before the premiere as he was being driven home, against a friend's advice, along fog-shrouded roads late at night. The reason for this reckless impatience was his frenzied obsession with *Butterfly*. He could not bear waiting until morning to continue his work. The car skidded off the road, and dropped fifteen feet down an embankment. Puccini, with a broken leg, was trapped under the car and rendered unconscious by fumes from the motor. Taken to a nearby house, he came to, and, with tears streaming down his face, muttered only "Poor *Butterfly*! Poor *Butterfly*!"

By then, the seeds of what may have been one cause of the opening night catastrophe were already planted. The Greeks would have called it hubris. It affects artists no less than statesmen.

The Belasco play was in one act. The original plan among the composer, his publisher, and the two librettists was for a three-act opera, the first act in the consulate, the second and third in the Japanese home. Puccini soon decided that the act in the consulate must be dropped. To that decision, he met with little resistance. But this required a lengthening of the second of the remaining acts. In keeping that second act intact, in failing to cut it between the beginning of the night-long vigil of Butterfly and the appearance of Pinkerton with his American wife, Puccini went stubbornly against the advice of his three collaborators.

Giacosa, in particular, was adamant in his determination to cut the act in two. But against Puccini's supreme confidence in his own judgment, he was unavailing. In January 1903, just weeks before Puccini's accident, Giacosa wrote the composer, angrily withdrawing from the project and warning that the act, as it stood, would be "interminable and too contrived." His remarkably accurate prediction: "I foresee a disaster with the public." Puccini was unyielding, but wooed Giacosa back into the fold. Toscanini, though not conducting, had reviewed the score. He later commented that he thought Puccini blundered badly in casting the opera in only two acts: "I thought at once this length is impossible. For Wagner, yes! For Puccini, no!"

No doubt it contributed to the ultimate fiasco. But was it the only cause? It is almost impossible to think so. Already in the first act, by every account, the air was heavy with hostility. At that point, none in the audience could have known of the inordinate length of the second act, or yet felt any restlessness.

What else, then, lay behind the debacle? Ricordi's article about the premiere in a March musical journal contained a possibly significant comment: "The spectacle given in the auditorium seemed as well organized as that on the stage, since it began precisely with the beginning of the opera." Puccini's letter, written the day after the premiere, describing the "lynching," noted drily: "That first performance was a Dantean Inferno, prepared in advance."

By whom? These are intriguing comments, but no one has ever claimed to know for a certainty who, if anyone, was behind it. But what is certain is that a well-organized claque existed in Milan, which sought full control over who would succeed and who would not, which operas would remain on the boards, which would be consigned to oblivion. Their decisions were not always based on artistic merit. According to the Russian bass Fyodor Chaliapin, who made his Milan debut in 1901, their stock in trade was intimidation and blackmail.

One of Puccini's biographers, Mosco Carner, quotes a London newspaper article, giving Chaliapin's account of this claque, which he termed "an institution" in theaters all over Europe. Members were installed in various parts of the theaters, and would applaud and cheer loudly or create disturbances and shout insults to singers depending on whether they had been paid tribute. Not surprisingly, many singers paid, not as much for the applause as to avoid the mass show of disapproval and possible disruption at important performances. According to Carner, Chaliapin himself was paid a visit at his hotel room in Milan by a claque member demanding payment in return for "goodwill." A few moments later, so Chaliapin claimed, the intruder found himself rolling down the stairs.

With *Butterfly*, there was never any hint of a demand for money. But there has been at least some suspicion that the claque's services that night were paid for by others. The motives? Various biographers have suggested a number of them: jealousy on the part of Puccini's less successful fellow composers, his aloofness from them, private uncomplimentary remarks that were bound to get back to them, and his refusal to fawn or curry favor. According to some, the claque, or many members of it, had not forgiven him for his deception of Alberto Franchetti in connection with the composition rights to *Tosca*. Another writer has suggested that Ricordi's rival, Sonzongo, could not bear another smashing success by his competitor; that after *Manon Lescaut, Bohème,* and *Tosca,* another such triumph would be too much, and that he himself had engaged the claque.

There is no proof of any of it, but these were all matters in the air, and Puccini had aggravated the situation by now ignoring not only the claque members but repeated requests by the press for interviews. The Ricordis, father and son alike, were, if anything, more secretive about the new opera than Puccini, and barred the press, including critics, from rehearsals.

When a crowd turns into a mob, there is often more than one reason. Possibly a combination of all of these factors lit the spark. But Puccini wasted little time with it. He acknowledged his error in failing to divide the second act in two, and set about the changes and rewriting with a vengeance. Apart from the division of the second act, one of the more significant alterations was in the depiction of the American wife, who in the first version had coldly demanded the baby from Butterfly, an unnecessarily callous episode.

In rewriting, Puccini seemed to be driven not only by his determination to bring *Butterfly* to life, but to defy his enemies. One week after the fiasco, he wrote his brother-in-law that he was well except for "a slightly bitter taste in my mouth," and expressed hope that it would soon "pass into many other mouths and in a more poisonous form."

He was determined that the revival would not be staged again before the Milanese "cannibals." It took place on May 17 in Brescia, at the suggestion of Giulio Ricordi's son, fourth in the Ricordi line and named Tito after his grandfather. Unlike his father, Tito always had complete faith in the opera.

The firestorm of enthusiasm for the revised *Madame Butterfly* dwarfed that of any of Puccini's previous works. Every aria and duet was applauded. The entire love duet had to be repeated to quiet the thunderous ovation. So did "Un Bel Di," the letter scene, and the flower duet, and with the humming chorus at the conclusion of the second act, the enthusiasm became hysteria. At the final curtain, the composer was obliged to appear on stage ten times to satisfy the incessant shouts of "Puccini, Puccini!"

The public's favorite Puccini opera today is probably *La Bohème*. But until the end of his life, Puccini's favorite was *Butterfly*. It was, he said, his only opera that he did not tire of hearing again and again. And years later he would write that with the love he harbored for Cio-Cio-San, his love for his other heroines, Mimi and Tosca included, was not to be compared.

OSCAR WILDE AND THE EVIL OF INNOCENCE

SALOME

THE PLOT: *Jokanaan, the Hebrew prophet, is imprisoned in a cistern by King Herod. Herod's beautiful stepdaughter, Salome, rejects Herod's advances, but is fascinated with Jokanaan. She beguiles a Syrian youth into bringing him up from the cistern, then pleads for a kiss, which Jokanaan contemptuously refuses. Herod offers her any wish if she will dance for him. She dances, then demands the head of Jokanaan. The shocked Herod finally agrees, but when Salome kisses, then dances with the severed head, the disgusted king orders her immediately killed by his soldiers.*

One night in late 1891, a tall, robust Englishman with rosy cheeks and protruding teeth dashed into the Grand Café on the corner of Paris's boulevard des Capucines and the rue Scribe. In the midst of small groups and couples talking, drinking, and romancing, he sat at a table, ordered a drink, and motioned over the leader of the orchestra. "I am writing a play," said the Englishman, "about a woman dancing with her bare feet in the blood of a man she has craved for and slain. I want you to play something in harmony with my thoughts." Never one to refuse a reasonable request, the musician led his group in a wild, screeching cacophony that stopped all conversation dead in its tracks. The Englishman, Oscar Wilde by name, then returned to his room on the boulevard des Ca-

Oscar Wilde. His play *Salome,* written in French, probably was intended to be performed by Sarah Bernhardt and undoubtedly to shock the public. It never succeeded until, in a German translation, it was set to music by Richard Strauss. (Broad, Lewis. *The Friendships and Follies of Oscar Wilde.* London: Hutchinson & Co. Ltd., 1954.)

pucines, where earlier that afternoon he had started his play, *Salome*. Later that night, he finished it.

This is not the only evidence of the presence of Euterpe, the muse of music, at the creation of Wilde's *Salome*. In his correspondence and in the posthumously published *De Profundis*, he refers to the recurring motifs of doom that make *Salome* "so like a piece of music and bind it together as a ballad." But in *Salome* his obsession was not with music. It was with hideous evil.

For centuries, Salome had been the subject of painters and authors, but the story as told by Wilde in his play is his own, whatever elements of it he may have taken from others. The sexual obsession of the innocent young virgin, and her lust for blood, are original with him. He intended to depict her as evil incarnate, and nothing, he claimed, is so evil as innocence. The story had come a long way, and through many metamorphoses, from the original few lines in the New Testament.

In the biblical telling she is not mentioned by name, only as the "daughter of Herodias." Herodias was married to Herod Antipas, having divorced his half-brother, Herod Philip. Each of the two brothers ruled part of the former kingdom of their father, Herod the Great. For marrying the wife of his living half-brother, Herod Antipas was rebuked by St. John the Baptist, who, for this audacity, according to the New Testament, Matthew 14:4, was imprisoned by Herod Antipas. Then, according to Matthew, Herod gave himself a birthday party,

> . . . and when the daughter of the said Herodias came in, and danced, and pleased Herod and them that sat with him, the King said unto the damsel, Ask of me whatsoever thou wilt, and I will give it thee . . . And she went forth and said unto her mother, what shall I ask? And she said, The head of John the Baptist. And she came in straightway with haste to the King, and asked, saying, I will that thou give me by and by in a charger the head of John the Baptist. And the King was exceeding sorry; yet for his oath's sake, and for their sakes which sat with him, he would not reject her.

And the head of John was given to Salome to give to her mother. Hence, in the biblical account, it is Herodias who commands the death, and the motive is revenge for John's audacious condemnation of her marriage. The name "Salome" comes from the account by the contemporary historian, Flavius Josephus, which attributes no role to either Salome or Herodias in the death of St. John. According to Josephus, the execution was ordered by Herod Antipas and was motivated by the fear of John's power to incite rebellion.

"You have confused two Salomes," Wilde was told by one Rémy de Gourmont at a dinner during which Wilde discussed his proposed play. One, said Gourmont, citing Josephus as his authority, was the daughter of Herod, but had nothing to do with the dancer of the Bible. But a close reading of Josephus indicates, rather, that Gourmont had confused two Herods. Wilde's genealogy seems to jibe with that of the historian. Not that any of it mattered to Wilde. As he commented later about Gourmont, "What he told us was the truth of a professor . . . I prefer the other truth, my own."

However minor her role in historical accounts, what a spell Salome has cast on the imaginations of creative artists! And by the time of his Paris sojourn of 1891, Wilde was, or would soon become, familiar with all of their finest creations. She had been painted by Rubens, Dürer, Moreau, Stanzioni, and Titian, to name but a few. Wilde had studied them all. She had been written about by French novelist Gustave Flaubert; the German poet Heinrich Heine; the French poet Stéphane Mallarmé, and an American, J. C. Heywood, whose book Wilde reviewed.

One of the more powerful influences must certainly have been a book written in 1884, *A Rebours,* or *Against the Grain,* as it is known in English, by Joris Huysmans, the French novelist and art critic. It contains descriptions of two paintings of Salome by Moreau. In one of these paintings, Moreau shows Salome's horror upon being confronted with the severed head. But it is the description of the other that must certainly have set Wilde's juices flowing. That painting is a depiction of the arousal of desire by the seductive dance of Salome, as evidenced in Herod's lecherous glances. Her movements are described by Huysmans as "the symbolic incarnation of undying lust . . . the catalepsy that hardens her flesh and steels her muscles, the monstrous Beast, indifferent, irresponsible, insensible, poisoning, like the Helen of ancient myth, everything that she touches."

Wilde was not satisfied with the arousal of lust in others. His Salome would herself be consumed with it and the object of her desires would be John the Baptist. Her lust must be infinite, he explained to his lifelong friend, Robert Baldwin Ross, her perversity without limits. In Wilde's *De Profundis*, he spoke of having "entertained at dinner the evil things of life," and having found pleasure in their company. "It was like feasting with panthers," he explained, "the danger was half the excitement. I used to feel as the snake charmer must feel when he lures the cobra. . . . Their poison was part of their perfection."

It started as a prose narrative. Then he decided to make a poem out of it, then to write the play. Why?

On the face of it, there is little that Strauss's *Salome* and Puccini's *Tosca* have in common, dramatically or musically. They are different creative oeuvres, but they share this: They were both based on plays written specially for a legendary, almost mythological, living person, one of the few that Wilde himself held in awe: a mesmerizing French actress named Sarah Bernhardt. Victorien Sardou's *La Tosca* was the third of seven plays he wrote for her over a period of twenty years.

He has denied it, but many of his biographers nonetheless claim as a fact that the motive for Wilde's casting of *Salome* in dramatic form, consciously or otherwise, was the "ethereal elegance," as one critic described it, of the same great actress. In the very letter to the London *Times* in which Wilde denied it, he also denied ever having written a play for any actor or actress, a statement that has been convincingly demonstrated to be untrue.

The play was written in French, which Wilde spoke fluently, but it was not his first language. In 1905, the French writer Romain Rolland was assisting Strauss in adapting the opera, written to a German translation, back to the original French for a Paris production. "When there are mistakes in French, don't hesitate to correct Wilde's original," he wrote to the composer. "However remarkable Wilde's knowledge of French may have been, it is nevertheless impossible to consider him a French poet."

Why then was *Salome* written in French? Wilde's own explanations are very unconvincing. It is a fact, however, that Bernhardt spoke no English. There were, admittedly, possible reasons for using French that had nothing to do with Bernhardt. For one thing, depiction of biblical subjects, under the provisions of a little used sixteenth-century English law, were subject to prohibition by the censor, known as the examiner of plays. The law was seldom invoked, but an author could get away with a good deal more in French than in English. But Wilde could have avoided the entire problem by rendering his story as a novel or a poem, as he started to do. Other than the fact that he would never have experienced the thrill of hearing Sarah Bernhardt declaim his lines, there appears no reason for his not doing so.

His determination to do just that was no passing fancy. In 1879, at the age of twenty-six, he was at Folkstone to greet the great actress upon her first tour of England, to throw an armful of lilies on the ground in front of her and shout, "Vive Sarah Bernhardt!"

He was not alone. The Bernhardt mania had swept France, England, and eventually the United States, and had engulfed many men of great renown. But not to many did she respond as quickly as she did to Wilde, for, as she soon noted, he was one of the few who paid court who did not have an ulterior motive. It was certainly not the usual ulterior motive, but he did have his own agenda. He wanted to write a play for her. In 1892 the friendship had grown, as had Wilde's reputation and the actress's respect for him as a playwright. At a party, she said to him: "You should write a play for me," to which he responded, "I already have."

Describing the *Salome* rehearsals in unaccustomed superlatives, Wilde gloried in hearing his own words spoken by "the most beautiful voice in the world" as "the greatest artistic joy." Hers was "the most splendid acting" he had ever seen, and she "the greatest artist on any stage."

After many rehearsals and much preparation, the play was banned by the examiner. The use of French had not saved it, and it was not heard in London until 1931. The ban precipitated a minor outcry—most of it from Wilde. The voice of George Bernard Shaw was one of the few others to be raised in protest. The play was published in 1893, and was described by the *Times* as "an arrangement in blood and ferocity, morbid, bizarre and repulsive." Bernhardt returned to France with the announced intention of producing the play herself. It never materialized. It was produced in Paris in 1894, and did well, but not with Bernhardt. She had apparently had second thoughts about it.

When the play opened in Paris, Wilde was in prison in England, his reputation ruined. He had been charged, convicted, and sentenced to two years in prison for pederasty, and was emotionally, financially, and, finally, physically destroyed. Imprisoned before the trial, desperately in need of funds, his sources of income having dried up, he asked Bernhardt to buy the play. She wept for her friend, but declined, offering instead to lend "poor Oscar" money. Further attempts to contact her through intermediaries met with evasions and broken appointments. In 1900, just a few months before his death, they met in Cannes, embraced, and, as Wilde said, she "wept and wept and wept."

The play was only a modest, and short-lived, success in France. But in Germany it swept the boards. It was staged first in Breslau in 1902, and a year later in Berlin by the brilliant and innovative twenty-nine-year-old producer Max Reinhardt, then on the threshold of his career. He utilized a translation by Hedwig Lachmann. In Vienna, Anton Lindner wrote an adaptation of it. It was that adaptation that was the introduction to *Salome* for the thirty-nine-year-old Richard Strauss.

Strauss was already internationally acclaimed, mostly, at that time, for his tone poems. His few operas written before that time had not been successful, and today are rarely performed. He immediately recognized Wilde's story as one that "cried out for music" as he later said. The rendering by Lindner was not to his liking, however, and he sought out the original Wilde play, as translated by Lachmann.

Strauss was employed at the time as conductor of the Royal Opera House of Berlin, and was music director of the Berlin Tonkünstler Orchestra. As a court employee, he felt it politic to sound out Kaiser Wilhelm about the proposed stage depiction of a biblical subject. It was unnecessary, however, as the kaiser gratuitously suggested to him another biblical subject, and was in no position to object to Strauss's reply that he was already at work on *Salome*.

Strauss eliminated some of the lines of the play that he felt were not necessary to the drama and unsuitable for music. Otherwise, he set the play to music just as Lachmann had translated it. The work was completed in June 1905 and was first performed in Dresden on December 9. Rehearsals were not altogether smooth. The performer in the lead role found the dance too indecent and others found their roles too difficult. The orchestration, which sounded so strange to the first audiences, sounded no less so to the musicians. "Maybe this passage works on the piano," said one of the oboists to Strauss, "but it doesn't on the oboes." "Take heart, man," replied Strauss, "it doesn't work on the piano either."

It may not have been meant in an entirely humorous vein. Giacomo Puccini attended both a rehearsal and a first performance of the opera in Naples in 1908. In a letter to his publisher, Ricordi, he quotes Strauss exhorting his musicians during rehearsal: "Gentlemen, this is not a question of music, but of a menagerie. Make a noise! Blow into your instruments!" Asked Puccini of Ricordi, "What do you think of that?" What Puccini himself thought of it, he did not say.

Despite a cry of indignation from some quarters, most of Germany was in a state of excitement as the date for the premiere approached. The tension of anticipation was heightened by a number of factors, one of which was the controversy that surrounded the Wilde drama. The other was the prospect of new and possibly excitingly different music from the only living heir of the legacy of Bach, Mozart, Beethoven, Wagner, and Brahms.

The audience was not disappointed. At the final curtain the pent-up tension that built during two hours of nerve-wracking sounds exploded. For composer and artists there were thirty-eight curtain calls. That was Dresden. That was also the scenario in about fifty other opera houses throughout Germany during the next two years. But it was not the case everywhere.

Though the kaiser did not object to Strauss's composition of the work, he refused to permit it in Berlin. He relented only when the director of the opera house placated the ruler by showing the Star of Bethlehem shining on the final scene, signifying the coming of the three Magi. The kaiser expressed the opinion that Strauss was certain to damage himself considerably with the opera. Commented Strauss to a friend: "From this damage I was able to build my villa in Garmisch."

It was a great success in Turin and Paris, but was banned in Chicago. Franz Joseph would not permit it in Vienna, but it was played in nearby Graz. It was attended there by Puccini, Gustav Mahler, and Herr Adolf Hitler, who told Strauss's son, Franz, that he had borrowed the money to attend. Strauss recalled this remark with wry amusement when, in 1939, the opera was banned in Graz by Austrian Nazis as a "Jewish ballad."

And London, the city that would not permit the play? It was performed there in 1910, in German, under certain rather far-reaching conditions imposed by the lord chamberlain: No reference to St. John the Baptist would be allowed. He would be called only the prophet. The severed head would not be shown. A covered platter would be handed up with not the slightest hint allowed that a head was beneath it. The most extensive and disastrous change required that the passion of Salome be distilled into a desire for spiritual help, and the lines were changed accordingly.

According to Sir Thomas Beecham, who conducted the performance, the cast began by singing the watered-down lines. Slowly at first, then more often, they dared to sing the original. Finally, through the second part of the opera, they threw caution to the winds and sang it entirely as first written. Apparently no one, including the representative of the lord chamberlain, was any the wiser.

It was finally heard in New York also, in January 1907, at the Metropolitan Opera House. Heinrich Conried, the director, and lessee of the House, held a special dress rehearsal on the morning of Sunday the twentieth for a thousand invited guests. Among them were the members of the board of directors of the Metropolitan, which included, as one of its most vociferous members, J. Pierpont Morgan. He was revolted and was in a position to do something about it. The first public performance was the following day, Monday the twenty-first. Two days later, led by Morgan, the directors demanded that Conried withdraw the opera as objectionable and detrimental to the opera house. They offered Conried reimbursement for part of the loss resulting from the heavy expenses, but Conried rejected it. He and his backers bore the loss themselves.

The board was not completely out of step with the public. One of the spectators at the performance, described by the *New York Times* as a "distinguished physician," complained to the editors that *Salome* was a "detailed and explicit exposition of the most horrible, disgusting, revolting and unmentionable features of degeneracy that I have ever heard, read of, or imagined." The *Times* itself, despite a balanced and favorable review of the music, reported that many of the women in the house turned away from the dance and that a number of the men decided to go into the corridors and smoke. And from two front-row boxes, the occupants "tumbled precipitously into the corridors," calling an employee to get their carriages.

"In the galleries," continued the *Times*, "men and women left their seats to stand so they might look down on the prima donna as she kissed the dead lips of the head of John the Baptist. Then they sank back in their chairs and shuddered."

The *Tribune*'s H. E. Krehbiel spoke of "smarting eyeballs and wrecked nerves," and found the story "abhorrent, bestial and loathsome." In a volume he published the following year, he approved the board's decision to ban the opera: "Decent men did not want to have their house polluted with the stench with which Oscar Wilde's play had filled the nostrils of humanity." W. P. Eaton, also in the *Tribune*, belittled the applause as scattered and brief. He described the departing crowd as having white faces, "almost as those at the rail of a ship." He wrote of silent women and of men who spoke as if in a bad dream, and let it be known that "The grip of a strange horror or disgust was on the majority."

According to Henry T. Finck, a music critic and historian, the audience was "disgusted but fascinated." Even ten years later, while grudgingly acknowledging that it was a musical masterpiece, he decried it as "horribly, damnably wasted on the most outrageous scene ever placed before a modern audience."

Oscar Wilde would have been pleased.

25

THE TRAGEDY OFFSTAGE

THE GIRL OF THE GOLDEN WEST

THE PLOT: *Minnie is a saloonkeeper. Rance, the sheriff and an unsuccessful suitor, is jealous when she is attracted to Johnson, a stranger. The miners learn that Johnson is really Ramarrez, an outlaw. When he appears wounded at Minnie's cabin, she shelters him. Rance finds him there, but Minnie saves him from being shot by playing cards with Rance, the stakes being herself for the life of Johnson. She wins through trickery, but Johnson is caught by the miners. By her pleas, she saves him from hanging and the two leave to begin a new life in the East.*

$\mathcal{I}$t was early evening of December 10, 1910. The mix of motor cars and carriages tied up at the entrance to New York's Metropolitan Opera House stretched for blocks, while police on the sidewalk pushed back a bulging crowd of elegantly dressed and bejeweled patrons. The cause of the melee was the requirement that before admittance, each ticket be signed by the ticketholder, and the signature compared with the one on the back of the ticket when purchased. The reason for this ritual was the determination by the Met's directors to put an end to the notorious ticket scalping, the speculation in tickets for major events.

And this was certainly a major event. It was the world premiere of a new opera, *La Fanciulla del West*, or, as it is called in English,

199

The Girl of the Golden West, by the composer of *La Bohème, Tosca,* and *Madame Butterfly.* That it was opening in America rather than in Europe was a very exciting novelty, and it had been ballyhooed for six months. The elaborate precautions were not completely successful. Some tickets, prices for which were already doubled by the Met, went for as much as thirty times the box-office price.

The premiere was a smashing success: fourteen curtain calls after the first act, nineteen after the second, twenty after the finale, following which a silver crown, bearing the colors of Italy and the United States, was placed on Puccini's head amid a rain of bouquets. Only the Met's directors were happier than the audience. Prices for the next performance were promptly doubled again, thus quadrupling the usual prices and resulting in some empty seats. At standard prices, it played eight more times at the Met that season, and the success was repeated in Chicago, Boston, London, and Rome.

Few paid attention to the almost uniformly negative opinions of the New York critics, but this time the pundits proved right. Three years later, while *Bohème, Tosca,* and *Butterfly* were still playing to full houses, *The Girl of the Golden West* was performed for the last time at the Met until 1929. It seems likely to remain in the standard repertory and trotted out every so often. It has too many fine moments to disappear entirely, but it has never shared the popularity of Puccini's greatest successes. It is an operatic stepchild of critics and audiences alike.

In the previous fourteen years, Puccini enjoyed three of the greatest triumphs in operatic history. An even earlier success, *Manon Lescaut,* still holds its own to this day, as do other still popular works written after *La Fanciulla.* At fifty-two years of age, he was, presumably, approaching the height of his creative powers. Why then should he have written an opera that survives only because of the sporadic passages and faint traces of the lyrical beauty that fill its three predecessors to the brim?

For once the biographers are in agreement about a matter normally consigned to the realm of guesswork and debate, and lacking in consensus. They blame a shattering episode in the personal life of the composer, one that left him emotionally drained and beaten, and from which he perhaps did not fully recover until his last years. It is true that many of the greatest operatic specimens were written during periods of tremendous stress: Mozart's *Magic Flute*, Wagner's *Tristan*, Tchaikovsky's *Eugene Onegin*, to mention only the most obvious. Was Puccini of lesser mettle? Perhaps, but it would not be fair to conclude that. About this tragedy there was something markedly different. In fact, had it not taken a toll on his creativity, it would have been remarkable.

In January 1907, Puccini and his wife, Elvira, crossed the Atlantic to be present in New York for a run of his operas at the Met. He let it be known that he was looking for a good American western libretto. He stood through a performance of David Belasco's play, *The Girl of the Golden West*, all seats having been sold. They stayed in New York five weeks, then he and Elvira sailed home. It was some time before he decided definitely on Belasco's play and completed the negotiations for it. Tito Ricordi, Giulio's son, successfully urged the retention of a new librettist, Carlo Zangarini, for the somewhat curious reasons that he spoke English and had a Colorado-born mother.

By August 1908 Puccini was at his country home of Torre del Lago, on the shore of a shallow lake near the northern Italian town of Pisa, when he received what he considered a satisfactory working draft of the libretto. He contributed as much to it as did Zangarini, and he still continued to prune it. On September 21, he wrote to Sybil Seligman, a wealthy and attractive English lady, opera devotee, and close friend since 1904, that he was now getting down to serious work, namely, the composition of the music. But on October 4, he wrote, "My life goes on in the midst of sadness and the greatest unhappiness . . . As a result 'The Girl' has completely dried up—and god knows when I shall have the courage to take up my work again."

Between September 21 and October 4, much had happened that he did not yet care to relate to Sybil.

One night, close to midnight, Elvira was awakened by a cough. She heard voices, and was immediately overcome by one of her increasingly frenzied fits of jealousy. She ran downstairs to find Puccini and their twenty-two-year-old servant girl, Doria, in conversation near an open door adjacent to the garden. Apparently, something in Elvira snapped. She began to shriek at both Puccini and Doria, accusing the girl of clandestine relations with her husband. Puccini's attempt to calm her further enraged the hysterical woman and brought forth a stream of invective that sent Doria, trembling and ashen-faced, running to her room.

Doria Manfredi had been working at Torre del Lago since Puccini's injury in an automobile accident in early 1903. She was sixteen at the time, and was hired primarily as a nurse. She had been warned by many in the town of Torre, including her own family, of Elvira's already legendary jealousy and temper. She was one of a long line of domestics, most of whom had been unable to endure the harsh regime of the lady of the house. But Doria seemed happy, perhaps enchanted, to be working for the famous composer. She cheerfully did everything demanded of her, and seemed as devoted to Elvira as to Puccini. Whether Elvira's suspicions about her arose before the night in question or came on suddenly is not clear.

After Doria locked herself in her room, Elvira hammered relentlessly on the door for hours. Her behavior was irrational by any standard. It had become increasingly irrational for the six years of their marriage, and during the twenty years that she and Puccini lived together before marriage. But it was a case of overreaction, not delusion. Puccini's sexual escapades were open and notorious. He saw nothing amiss in them; they were his right as an artist. Secrecy or discretion was only for practical reasons, and one of those reasons was to avoid the wrath of his almost insanely jealous wife.

But for every amorous adventure, affair, or casual fling in which Puccini indulged, Elvira suspected countless others. She became suspicious of his every absence. She could have been busy enough raging at his actual infidelities, none of which could she ever forgive. But she tortured both herself and her husband with innumerable episodes of jealous rage for imagined affairs of such number that they would have been beyond the capability of any man, even Puccini. She was suspicious of his every visit to the doctor for diabetes and a perennially sore throat. She once confronted an attractive young singer, visiting her husband for purely professional reasons, and chased her out of the house with an umbrella. The superstitious woman in later years admitted to having placed camphor in his trouser pockets, and mixing a supposed anaphrodisiac with his drink during many of the not infrequent visits to their home of attractive women.

None of this altered Puccini's lifestyle in the slightest degree. He was indignant when wrongly accused, and pled his entitlement to such diversion when rightly accused. He never saw the former as a consequence of the latter, and there were, of course, as Elvira well knew, many such incidents of which she could have no suspicions at all, such as occurred during a visit to Vienna to attend rehearsals for *Madame Butterfly* while working on the libretto for *La Fanciulla*.

A seductive voice on the phone one morning asked for "an interview," which he quickly granted. The owner of the voice was quite attractive, and Puccini, still in his pajamas, excused himself to dress. When he returned, he found the lady stark naked. As he later explained to a friend who demanded all the details: "I felt too sorry for the lunatic to send her away."

Such was the incendiary background to the explosion that engulfed the badly shaken Doria. It was early in the morning before Doria felt safe in emerging from the sanctuary of her room and fleeing to her mother's home. She found no respite there. Brandishing her standard weapon of choice, a large umbrella, Elvira raged into town, loudly claiming to have surprised the pair in the act, threatening to drown the terrified Doria should she ever come near her husband again. She shouted her accusations at the Manfredi home, and followed Doria through the streets screaming curses and epithets, slut and whore being two of the most frequent. She demanded of the local priest that he persuade her parents to drive the girl from town, which, though not discounting the possible truth of Elvira's accusations, he refused to do.

Despite Puccini's strenuous denials, not many in Torre did discount the story. Puccini's reputation both for attracting and using women of all ages, social strata, and stations was well known. Elvira's distorted perceptions were also well known, but few were ready to doubt her claims of having caught them in flagrante delicto. Rumors soon spread that Doria had had an abortion. Doria's brother was making threats of his own, namely, to kill Puccini. He, too, apparently, did not disbelieve the accusation.

From the threats, the silent contempt of the villagers, and Elvira's unabating accusations, Puccini looked for escape in Paris, writing Sybil that life had become unbearable and that "I have often lovingly fingered my revolver." But sooner or later he had to return to "Hell," for, as he wrote, he was much concerned about his "poor beloved Minnie," his girl of the golden west.

Back in Torre del Lago, he was concerned about more than Minnie. He met Doria secretly once or twice and wrote to Sybil that the sight of her was enough to make him cry. It is little wonder, as she rarely ventured out and persistently refused food. He wrote the girl's mother, assuring her that there was not "a shadow of truth" in the accusations. He wrote Doria herself that he was "desolate to see you thus sacrificed and slandered" and that anyone who accused her of wrongdoing lied. None of it helped. The villagers were aligned behind Elvira as the wronged wife.

One evening, out of doors, he saw Elvira wearing his clothes, obviously spying on him. On more than one occasion, she insisted on repeating her increasingly strident and detailed accusations to their son and to Elvira's daughter from her first marriage. Puccini wrote to Sybil that he no longer wanted to live, "certainly not with her."

Meanwhile, the half-starved Doria wept hysterically. On January 23, after almost four months of continual villification, humiliation, and ostracism, she took three capsules of corrosive sublimate. For five days she writhed in agony before dying a painful death. An autopsy was conducted. She was found to be a virgin. The outraged family brought an action against Elvira for public defamation.

It was all too much for Puccini; he went, first to Rome, then wandered aimlessly. For months, as he later wrote, he could not shake the image of Doria. He was haunted by it. With dramatic, if understandable suddenness, the public sympathy for Elvira turned to contempt, and she fled to Milan. Through their son as an intermediary, Puccini, despite his grief and his anger toward Elvira, tried to counsel her as to the best defense to the suit. She was facing the possibility of prison, and he begged her to admit that she was misled by appearances and never intended the result, deploring it as much as anyone. Elvira grieved, but the shock did not clear her judgment a great deal. She was adamant. She rejected the attorneys he recommended, choosing her own, and insisted that she had proof that would establish the justification for her actions.

In mid-June, with the trial less than a month away, Puccini wrote Sybil that Elvira's lawyers were trying only to run up fees and gain

sensational publicity for themselves. Of sensationalism, there was
plenty. The newspapers filled their pages with lurid details, and at
Torre del Lago, reporters were continually banging on Puccini's door
for interviews. Puccini felt certain that he was finished once and for
all. He tried to persuade Doria's brother, with cash, to cease the pros-
ecution. The brother was no longer hostile to Puccini, but he rejected
the offer out of hand and swore that if the law did not punish Elvira,
he would kill her.

Puccini asked Ricordi to have a suit for separation instituted
against her. Their son Tonio quit his engineering studies and went to
Munich. His threat to leave for Africa brought the couple together in
early May for their first meeting in almost four months, but they
parted in anger. Hers was directed primarily at his plea that her proposed defense would subject him to further bad publicity. Puccini's
self-interest, and his self-pity, never wavered. To his son, he had written in April concerning his proposed emigration: "What have I done
to deserve this treatment?" To Sybil, he wrote in June: "I can't
work—it's a real crime that is being committed, to torture in this way
a poor fellow who has never done anyone any harm—or," he added
as an afterthought, "at least never intended any."

At a second meeting with Puccini in June, Elvira waxed enthusiastically about her "new evidence," namely of Doria's propensity for
hysteria, and about her own lawyer's great powers of oratory, which
would surely save her. Puccini, grimacing in disgust, his hands over
his ears, ran from the room. The last piece of bad advice Elvira got
from her lawyers was to feign illness and stay away from the trial.
Her vaunted defense was woefully inadequate. She was found guilty
of defamation, libel, and threatening life and limb, namely, by saying
that she would drown Doria. She was sentenced to five months' imprisonment and a fine of seven hundred lire. Upon hearing the verdict,
Tonio collapsed.

Her lawyers took an appeal. While it was pending, Puccini again
approached Doria's brother, offering 12,000 lire for abandonment of
the action. This time the Manfredis agreed, and it was dropped in
early October 1909, about a year after that fateful night at the Puccini
home.

Puccini and Elvira reconciled; Puccini obviously could not do
without her. Perhaps, despite his self-pity and air of innocence, he

recognized that he had not been so blameless after all in bringing this tragedy about. Elvira was chastened, but their relationship continued with an icy reserve. Not until late in life, almost ten years later, did any mutual warmth or affection become evident.

Puccini had done practically nothing of the musical composition of *La Fanciulla* when the storm broke. He now resumed work, finishing the first act in January 1910, the second in April, the third on the fifth of August. He dedicated the opera to Queen Alexandra of England in gratitude for her enthusiastic acclaim of *La Bohème*. Puccini sailed for America on the S.S. *Washington* for the premiere, occupying the lavish Imperial Suite, which he exuberantly described to Tito Ricordi in great detail. He enjoyed it alone, having persuaded Elvira not to come.

The matter with Doria had faded into history, and in America never made much of a splash to begin with. More than likely, very few in the audience had ever heard of it. Certainly, as the silver crown was pressed down on his head amid the cheers and flowers, there was not a hint that anything had gone wrong with his fabulous life or had interfered with his artistic creativity. He could keep his scars from the audience that first night. But he could not keep them from the music. They would show in time.

He returned to Europe on the *Lusitania* on New Year's Day. Before departing he wrote to Carla Toscanini, living in New York with her husband the famed maestro. He thanked her for the many courtesies they had shown him, envied them their close family, and, seeming to dread approaching old age, lamented that in contrast, he was so alone, "hankering after something, and never finding it, and I'm always misunderstood."

RICHARD STRAUSS, STEFAN ZWEIG, AND THE NAZIS

DIE SCHWEIGSAME FRAU

THE PLOT: *Sir Morosus's eardrums are damaged and he cannot stand noise. He threatens to disinherit his nephew for marrying a singer and joining her troupe of noisy actors. Morosus's barber convinces him to marry a quiet, retiring woman. But, at the barber's direction, for the purpose of restoring the nephew to Morosus's good graces, the "wedding" is done by the troupe in disguise, the singer playing the shy, virginal wife. After the wedding, as orchestrated by the barber, she turns into a noisy shrew, and the troupe arranges a "divorce." When the charade is revealed to him, he joins in the laughter, makes peace with the nephew, and promises a new outlook on life.*

In 1935 the planned premiere of *Die Schweigsame Frau* became a painfully embarrassing dilemma for the Nazi government of Germany, requiring the personal intervention of Herr Hitler himself. To permit the premiere of an opera with a Jewish librettist was contrary to every stricture by which good Nazis lived, not to mention the vile laws they promulgated. But to prohibit an opera by the most revered German composer of the day was to invite a storm of international protest and ridicule.

The story of *Die Schweigsame Frau*, in English, *The Silent Woman,* is a lighthearted comedy. The background against which it was written and produced was a personal tragedy for the two humanly flawed men of genius who brought it to life. The stage for the creation of the comedy, as well as the tragedy, was set with the sudden, unexpected death of Hugo von Hofmannsthal, Richard Strauss's librettist for over twenty years, beginning shortly after the production of *Salome*. That relationship had been one of the most fruitful in operatic history. A highly skilled and imaginative dramatist, Hofmannsthal furnished Strauss with librettos for six of his most popular operas. After his death in 1929, a despondent Strauss felt certain that his days as an opera composer were over.

But by 1931, at the age of sixty-seven, he was seeking a new librettist, and it was natural that he would want one whose credentials were equal to those of Hofmannsthal. Stefan Zweig, a fifty-year-old Vienna-born author of biographies, plays, poems, and novels, was more widely published and translated than any other author writing in German at the time. He was also a lifelong devotee and connoisseur of music and a great admirer of Richard Strauss.

In October of that year, Zweig's publisher, en route to the author's home in Salzburg, stopped to visit Strauss, an acquaintance of many years, at his villa in the south German resort town of Garmisch. Strauss suggested that he sound out Zweig, whom Strauss had never met, about any ideas he might have for an opera. As it happened, Zweig had ten years previously completed a plan for an opera based on an early seventeenth-century play of Ben Jonson's, *Epicoene, or The Silent Woman*. He would consider no one for it but Strauss, as he later told the composer, but out of consideration for Hofmannsthal had refrained from approaching him earlier.

He was soon exchanging correspondence with Strauss, then meeting with him in Munich, then sending detailed sketches for the opera, which they at first called *Morosus*, the lead character in Jonson's play. Zweig referred to his subject as a "dancing pantomime in grand style." He had already written a play based on another of Jonson's works, *Volpone*, which Strauss had seen and admired.

Strauss was obviously very much taken with Zweig's ideas, referring in his letters to the "delightful opera subject" and the "charming material." In June of the following year, after seeing a draft of the libretto, he wrote Zweig, full of enthusiasm, declaring that "it is enchanting—a born comic opera—a comedy equal to the best of its

Stefan and Friderike Zweig in 1935. The spread of Nazism destroyed Stefan's promising artistic partnership with Strauss and may have contributed to the breakup of his marriage with Friderike in 1938, the year of the German occupation of his native Austria. (*Stefan Zweig: Ein Bildbiographie.* Munich: Kindler Verlag, 1961.)

Richard Strauss, his daughter-in-law, Alice Grab Strauss, and his grandson Richard. To save his Jewish daughter-in-law and her two children from death camps, Strauss may have agreed not to speak out against the Nazis. (Kurt, Wilhelm. *Richard Strauss, an Intimate Portrait.* London: Thames and Hudson, 1989. By permission of the Richard Strauss Archive, Garmisch-Partenkirchen, Germany.)

kind—more suitable for music than even *Figaro* and *Barber of Seville.*" And on September 14, upon receiving a completed portion of the first act, he wrote Zweig that it was "absolutely exquisite."

Such was the beginning of the Strauss-Zweig relationship. It had every promise of being as rich and productive as the combination of Strauss and Hofmannsthal. Strauss and Zweig came from vastly different backgrounds, but they had in common a devotion to their respective arts, an admiration for each other, and a firm belief that as artists they were beyond the reach of mundane events. In other times they might have been. Though history often intrudes in the world of opera, as in all human affairs, rarely has it done so with such brutal force or tragic consequences. What was taking shape in the early days of their acquaintance was one of history's blackest episodes.

On January 17, 1933, the libretto was completed, and Strauss was working on the composition of the first act. On January 30, Hitler was appointed chancellor of Germany. The fact that Zweig was a Jew did not at first seem to them to threaten the Strauss-Zweig partnership, which they naively considered to be above "politics." Zweig had, after all, done nothing to incur the wrath of the Nazis. To frequent requests from Jewish organizations to lend his prestige to protests against the alarming anti-Semitism in Germany, his responses had been few and cautious.

Zweig was very conscious of his Jewish heritage, and unlike many European Jews of the time, prided himself on it. But he considered himself "apolitical." Never did he attack Germans, not even the Nazis; he wrote sparingly, in defense of the persecuted, never to attack the persecutors. In the years to come he would be judged harshly by Jewish publications for his aloofness. In 1930, he had termed the shockingly huge vote garnered by the Nazi party "a laudable revolt" of the young against the stagnation of the past, a lapse of judgment for which he was roundly criticized by Thomas Mann's son, Klaus Mann, among others.

Strauss was not a Jew, but his daughter-in-law and two young grandchildren were. His own father, Franz, a horn player in the Munich Orchestra, was a virulent anti-Semite, and anti-Semitism was part of Strauss's upbringing. He was not immune, but neither was he very receptive to it. In 1924 his son, also named Franz, married a young Jewish woman from Vienna, Alice Grab. It was quipped at the time that the wedding of his son was the funeral of his anti-Semitism. But, in fact, Strauss and his wife, Pauline, had been warm friends of Alice's parents, both Jewish, since 1907. Strauss was very fond of Alice, and was delighted to hear of the young couple's engagement. His attachment to her grew over the years.

Somewhere along the line, he made a deal with the Nazis: He would not speak out against them, and they would leave his daughter-in-law and his two grandchildren alone. The details are sketchy, but it seems clear that, tacit or overt, some such agreement was confected.

In early 1933, as Strauss was composing the music for his new opera, things were happening very swiftly in Germany. Almost immediately following Hitler's appointment as chancellor, a wave of violence against Jews and Jewish businesses by Nazi hooligans spread across Germany. At the end of February, following a fire at the Reichstag building, came a declaration of national emergency, suspension of constitutional rights, and mass arrests of left-wing opponents. In March, there followed seizure of control by Hitler throughout Germany, a sweeping grant of power to him by the Reichstag, and the establishment of the first concentration camps.

In early April came war against "pan-Judaism," beginning with a highly organized boycott against Jewish businesses. Stormtroopers warned patrons not to enter on pain of having their pictures splashed on local cinema screens. There was an order for the dismissal of civil servants not of "Aryan extraction," and restrictions on Jews from practicing law and from acting as jurors.

On April 13, in one of many letters that had been flowing between Strauss and Zweig, Zweig writes:

> Politics pass, the arts live on, hence we should strive for that which is permanent and leave propaganda to those who find it fulfilling and satisfying. History shows that it is at times of unrest when artists work with the greatest concentration.

Zweig, living in Austria, may not have been fully aware of all of the bestial details of the new "politics," but he must have known of many. Strauss, in Bavaria, would have had to be deaf and blind not to know even more.

Later that month came quotas for Jewish students in all schools;

in May, prohibitions against Jewish tax accountants and the burning of books of "un-German" authors. In June, there were restrictions against Jewish dentists and dental technicians. In July, Jewish immigrants from eastern Europe were stripped of their citizenship.

On September 3, Zweig felt obliged to deny to Strauss a Munich newspaper report listing him as a protester against the deprivation of citizenship of certain cultural leaders. His only protest had been months ago, he claimed. "Since Christmas 1932 I have not published a line . . . and I have not collaborated anywhere . . . Politics has always disgusted me and I resist as much as possible being drawn into other people's games." From later correspondence it appears that he had been confused by the Nazis with one Arnold Zweig, not a relative, and, much to Stefan's chagrin, apparently more outspoken than he.

The protests of a growing number of non-Jewish musicians, artists, and authors, including many Germans, a number of whom were leaving their homeland, was a source of intense embarrassment to the regime. It desperately needed a counterforce, namely, compliant artists. It needed Richard Strauss.

In March 1933, the Jewish conductor Bruno Walter was scheduled to conduct the Berlin Philharmonic but was threatened by rowdies that the hall would be wrecked if he did. The government advised him that it would not cancel the concert as it had no wish either to relieve him of an embarrassing situation or of his obligation to pay the musicians. Walter withdrew, and Strauss took his place. He used his fee to pay the musicians.

That summer, Arturo Toscanini was scheduled to conduct the performances of Wagner's *Parsifal* at the Bayreuth Festival. He canceled because of "painful events which have wounded my feelings as a man and as an artist." This was a heavy blow. Toscanini's tremendous stature and popularity were such that no claim of Jewish manipulation would dare be asserted, and a radio ban on his recordings was quickly revoked as a "mistake." His place at the festival, at the urgent request of Wagner's daughter-in-law, the festival's director, was taken by Strauss, for which he would accept no fee. This was the fiftieth anniversary of the death of Wagner, whom Strauss revered above all others, and the "political" situation was secondary.

Shortly thereafter Toscanini met Strauss in Milan, and greeted him with the stinging remark: "As a musician, I take my hat off to you. As a man I put it on again." For this and other open condemnations of the Nazi government, Toscanini received many accolades and expressions of admiration. He deserved every one of them. But he was not living in Germany, nor did he have a Jewish daughter-in-law or Jewish grandchildren living there.

Zweig, in his autobiography, *The World of Yesterday,* is less judgmental. He mentioned Strauss's fear for his grandchildren, "whom he loved above everything else," and aptly says of his friend that "Through his art-egotism . . . he was always indifferent whatever the regime. He had served the German Kaiser as a conductor . . . later he had served the Emperor of Austria . . . and had been 'persona gratissima' likewise in the German and Austrian Republics."

Whatever his reason, the Nazis must have been pleased. On November 15, Joseph Goebbels, propaganda minister, created a State Chamber of Music and, without consulting him, announced the appointment of Strauss as president. Strauss accepted. There is nothing in the existing correspondence of Zweig to Strauss to give a hint of his own feelings about Strauss's seeming collaboration. But, in his *World of Yesterday,* written in exile in Brazil eight years after the fact, he tells us that in addition to the other very practical reasons for his cooperation, Strauss cared about only one thing, a production of *Die Schweigsame Frau,* which "lay particularly close to his heart." He continues:

> That such concessions to National Socialism were extremely embarrassing to me, goes without saying. For how easily might the impression develop that I collaborated secretly or even agreed that in my person a single exception to such a shameful boycott should be made. From all quarters friends urged me to protest publicly against a performance in National Socialist Germany. But fundamentally I loathe public and pathetic gestures; besides, I was reluctant to cause difficulties for a genius of his rank . . . he had spent three years at this work . . . Hence I considered that my course was to wait silently and to let matters develop as they might.

And so he did. Not for another year and a half would there be a hint of dissatisfaction from Zweig. In January 1934 he discussed with Strauss their next project, months before the composition of *Die*

Schweigsame Frau was completed. In the same letter, he complained about attempts to drag him into political arguments, and about "political people" who cannot understand those like himself who find "aggressiveness and onesidedness repulsive."

Throughout that year, Hitler consolidated his power. He was now the führer to whom the army swore a personal oath of allegiance, and who could slaughter without trial his opponents within his own party. He also placed ever more oppressive restrictions on Jews in the press and in the theater. Even as he did so, the correspondence flowed between Strauss and Zweig, filled with discussion about their next undertaking. One subject after another was outlined, analyzed, and abandoned, or put aside as a potential project. They had clearly built, at least in their minds, a fortress against the outside world.

For a while the fortress seemed to function. In late May, concerned about the future of *Die Schweigsame Frau,* Strauss directly asks Goebbels if there are any political objections to Zweig, and Goebbels replies that there are not. But German radio calls Strauss's collaboration with Zweig "scandalous." On July 26, Zweig, who is now working in London, writes to Strauss about a news article concerning growing controversy in Germany with *Die Schweigsame Frau,* and assures him that he will not get Strauss into any such predicament. "Silence and aloofness" are the required keys to success.

But eventually the world starts to close in. On August 2, Strauss writes Zweig that he has learned that Zweig has been shadowed while in London and is pleased that his conduct has been found "politically beyond reproach." Don't let anyone distract you from it, he warns. He invites Zweig to meet with him in Germany on his return. Replies Zweig: "I don't want to go to Germany at this time." Don't worry about *Die Schweigsame Frau,* he tells Strauss. Mozart's *Don Giovanni* is still very popular in Germany, though his librettist, da Ponte, was a Jew. On August 24, Strauss suggests that they not mention they are working on anything new, and "in a few years when all projects are finished, the world will probably look different."

But the opera was now becoming a cause for concern among the top echelon of the Nazi government. They were faced with two terrible choices: Permit an opera with the libretto by a Jew or prohibit one composed by Strauss. "How I secretly enjoyed their great worry and painful headache," wrote Zweig in his autobiography.

At Bayreuth that summer Goebbels discussed the matter with Strauss, who offered to withdraw the opera rather than cause problems for Goebbels or Hitler, but termed the entire controversy "a big disgrace." The text was sent to Hitler, who personally examined it and found no objection, that is, as Strauss was to write later in a private memorandum, "other than being authored by an uncomfortably talented Jew." The memorandum, found after Strauss's death, also lamented: "It is a sad time when an artist of my rank has to ask a brat of a minister what he may set to music and what he may have performed." Through the rest of 1934 Strauss and Zweig discuss possible future operas and plans for *Die Schweigsame Frau*. On September 21, Strauss informs Zweig that he is negotiating with the Dresden Opera for the premiere, and it is ultimately set for June 24, 1935.

Early in 1935, the pressure is forcing a rift. Strauss repeats his suggestion that any future work they do together be kept secret until the time is propitious. Zweig replies bluntly that he will have none of it. Such secrecy is beneath Strauss's dignity as a great composer, he says. *Die Schweigsame Frau* has been an exceptional case. He realizes full well that Strauss will not be permitted to write another opera with a Jewish librettist. He would be glad to assist anyone else whom Strauss chooses as his next partner, but he will not write in secret for works that are to be locked away. The seventy-one-year-old Strauss says that he is deeply saddened, but he is obviously more than saddened. He is depressed. He implores Zweig like an abandoned lover: "By chance I found you, and I will not give up on you just because we happen to have an anti-Semitic government now . . . do a few more beautiful libretti for me." To keep them secret is not undignified, he continues, merely wise.

Through April the dialogue continues. For Strauss there will be no one but Zweig. "Please stay with me and continue to work with me," he pleads. A few days later he writes again, "If you desert me now that you have written . . . 'Die Schweigsame Frau,' I have no choice left but to retire." Through May they continue to talk opera, and all goes well except when Zweig makes it clear that he will not write any more libretti himself. The official measures are becoming harsher, and "They cannot but offend one's sense of honor," says Zweig. It is a pity that he cannot work openly with Strauss but will counsel any of his collaborators. "Don't you recommend any other librettist to me," snaps the composer. "Nothing comes of it. It isn't worth the paper."

In May, new laws discouraged Jews from serving in the military and prohibited their service as officers. Throughout that summer came increased Nazi violence against Jews and Jewish businesses, and new boycotts; in July a ban on "mixed marriages" was announced.

On June 15 Zweig wrote a letter to Strauss that has now been lost. At least one biographer suggests that in a fit of his well-known temper, Strauss may have torn it up. Its contents can be surmised from Strauss's reply of the seventeenth from Dresden, where he is overseeing the final rehearsals for the opera.

> Your letter of the 15th is driving me to distraction! This Jewish obstinacy! Enough to make an anti-semite of a man! This pride of race, this feeling of solidarity! Do you believe that I am ever, in any of my actions, guided by the thought that I am German? Do you believe that Mozart composed as an "Aryan"? I know only two types of people: those with and without talent . . . Whether they are Chinese, Bavarians, New Zealanders, or Berliners leaves me cold . . . Who told you that I have exposed myself politically? Because I have conducted a concert in place of Bruno Walter? That I did for the orchestra's sake. Because I substituted for Toscanini? That I did for the sake of Bayreuth. That has nothing to do with politics . . . I would have accepted this troublesome honorary office under any government, but neither Kaiser Wilhelm nor Herr Rathenau offered it to me . . . the show here will be terrific, and with all this you ask me to forgo you? Never ever!

Perhaps in London Zweig was getting a clearer picture than he had in Austria of the calamity that was befalling Hitler's Germany. As early as 1933 a book by Joseph King, *The German Revolution*, published in London, narrated in ugly detail the atrocities up to that time. Whether such information was available in Zweig's Austria is extremely doubtful. Whatever the reason, Zweig obviously had had enough of working according to the whims of the racist German bureaucrats and butchers. It is not very likely that Strauss's myopic letter would have helped Zweig's growing apprehension—even if he had received it. But he never did.

It was intercepted by Gestapo agents, who had obviously been monitoring the correspondence between the two men. It was deemed of sufficient import to be sent directly to Hitler. Five days later, on the twenty-second, Strauss wrote Zweig, apologizing for his outburst of the seventeenth and assuring him of the magnificence of the performance that would take place on the twenty-fourth, that Goebbels would attend, and that a state subsidy would be forthcoming. "As you see," he continued, "the nasty Third Reich has its good aspects too." In fact, it had also been anticipated that Hitler would attend the premiere. But on the same day, an emissary from Goebbels came to Strauss and suggested he resign as president of the Chamber of Music for reasons of "ill health." He did so at once.

Later that same day, Strauss played skat in his hotel room with two companions, the son of the conductor of the Dresden Opera, and the theater stage designer, but his mind was not entirely on the game. Suddenly, the two companions were shocked to hear the composer loudly demand: "I want to see the program." After consultation with the general manager, arrangements were made for him to see the printer's proofs. As Strauss had suspected, Zweig's name was not on it. The program stated only, "From the English of Ben Jonson." Strauss's face flushed. "You can do this," he declared, "but I will leave tomorrow and the show can take place without me." With his own hand he restored Zweig's name. The next day, the program was changed to include it.

Zweig did not attend the performance. He anticipated that Hitler and Goebbels or, in any event, a swarm of brownshirts would be there. Neither Hitler nor Goebbels attended, citing bad weather that prevented their flight. The more likely cause for their absence was the intercepted letter. There were four performances. Reviews, including critiques of the libretto, were very favorable. After that the opera was banned and was not heard again in Germany until after the war, though there were performances in 1936 in Graz, Milan, and Zurich. There is evidence that until the end of his days, Strauss considered it, not *Der Rosenkavalier*, the "finest operatic comedy since *The Marriage of Figaro*," an opinion not shared by many.

It was on the third of July that he wrote the private memorandum found in his notebooks. He concluded it with these words:

I almost envy my friend Stefan Zweig, persecuted for his race, who now definitely refuses to work with me in public or in secret because, he says, he does not want to have any "special privileges" in the Third Reich. To be honest, I don't understand this Jewish solidarity and regret that the "artist" Zweig cannot rise above "political fashions." If we do not preserve artistic freedom ourselves, how can we expect it from soapbox orators in taverns?

With "Die Schweigsame Frau" my life's work definitely seems to have come to an end. Otherwise I might have been able to create other works not entirely without merit. It is regrettable.

About a week later, Strauss wrote another private memorandum, also found in his notebooks after his death. The interception of his letter seems to have been a stunning blow. To him also, events were finally coming into focus:

Now I might examine the price I had to pay for not keeping away, from the beginning, from the National Socialist movement . . . I was slandered as a servile, selfish anti-semite, whereas in truth I have always stressed at every opportunity . . . that I consider the Streicher-Goebbels Jew baiting as a disgrace to German honor, as evidence of incompetence, the basest weapon of untalented, lazy mediocrity against a higher intelligence and greater talent. I openly testify here that I have received so much support, so much self-sacrificing friendship, so much generous help and intellectual inspiration from Jews that it would be a crime not to acknowledge it all with gratitude . . . True, I had adversaries in the Jewish press . . . But my worst and most malicious enemies were "Aryans."

There appears no good reason to doubt the sincerity of any of it. But that was a purely private memo. There was still the matter of self-preservation. Fully cognizant now of the nature of the beast he was trying to ignore, and perhaps more than a little frightened, he wrote directly to "Mein Führer." He explained the language of his intercepted letter, acknowledging that it could easily have been misinterpreted, and appealed to Hitler as "the great architect of German social life" for a personal discussion of the matter. His letter was never answered.

Correspondence continued between Strauss and Zweig, who was again in London, through the fall of 1935, the composer still beseeching his librettist to continue to write for him secretly and promising discretion. The last extant letter to him from Zweig was in December, and it was signed "Morosus."

Strauss wrote four new operas between 1935 and the end of the war, but life under the Nazis was not pleasant. Too important to treat too harshly, he was tolerated but was regarded with suspicion and was treated with contempt. In 1942, summoned before Goebbels for a minor act of defiance, he was insulted and screamed at by the hysterical propaganda minister until Strauss was at the point of tears. In 1943, a local bureaucrat demanded that Strauss make his Garmisch villa available for bombing victims. Everyone must make sacrifices, the bureaucrat declared, when thousands of Germans were falling at the front. "No soldier needs to fall on my account," was Strauss's testy reply. "I didn't want this war." The official reddened, shouted that other heads had rolled, and reported the matter to Hitler. The following year the villa was commandeered.

And what of Zweig, the friend that he "almost envied"? He traveled extensively throughout Europe, the United States, and South America, writing, lecturing, and meeting with heads of state. His plans to resettle with his first wife in Austria were dashed by the German occupation of 1938. The couple was divorced later that year. He sought a new beginning, in England, the United States, and, finally, in Brazil, where he and his second wife, Lotte, lived in the town of Petrópolis. In October 1941 he completed his autobiography. On February 22, 1942, after painstaking preparations, he wrote a two-paragraph declaration. He gave thanks to Brazil for its hospitality, and he said that he would have preferred to rebuild his life there,

> But after one's sixtieth year unusual powers are needed in order to make another wholly new beginning. Those that I possess have been exhausted by the long years of homeless wandering. So I hold it better to conclude in good time and with erect bearing a life for which intellectual labour was always the purest joy, and personal freedom the highest good on earth.
>
> I salute all my friends! May it be granted them yet to see the dawn after the long night! I, all too impatient, go on before.

The Strauss Villa in Garmisch, Bavaria, completed about 1905. Kaiser Wilhelm warned that Strauss would damage himself with *Salome*. Strauss later exulted that it was with such "damage" that he built this villa. (Kurt, Wilhelm. *Richard Strauss, an Intimate Portrait.* London: Thames and Hudson, 1989. By permission of the Richard Strauss Archive, Garmisch-Partenkirchen, Germany.)

Then he and Lotte took massive doses of Veranol, lay down together, and died.

In April 1945, Strauss was back in his home in Garmisch. He was told that his villa was being commandeered again, this time by the Americans. When an American soldier knocked on his door, Strauss answered. "I am the composer of *Der Rosenkavalier* and *Salome*," he barked. "Leave me alone." Strauss was in luck. The soldier was a former musician with the Philadelphia Orchestra. Strauss and his family were allowed to remain in the home. He was later investigated by an allied commission and exonerated of collaboration with the Nazis.

After the war one of the first of his operas to be produced in Dresden was *Die Schweigsame Frau*. On October 12, 1946, he wrote to the conductor:

> So now, after ten years the honorable Sir Morosus has been liberated from the concentration camp of the Reich Theater Chamber and been brought back to his birthplace, where twelve years ago I had great trouble getting the name of the librettist on the program.

Strauss, too, was liberated, as was the much harassed, but still living, Alice Grab Strauss and her children. Some biographers see Strauss's agonizingly difficult position in Nazi Germany in simple terms, and condemn his conduct. It is always simple to prescribe heroics for others to perform. Strauss was no martyr. But to presume to stand in judgment on anyone for not choosing martyrdom is a useless exercise in arrogance. Such writers do him a great injustice.

AFTERWORD

*S*trauss died in 1949, but he was very much a "nineteenth-century" composer. He has, in many respects, more in common with Mozart and Wagner than with composers who are his contemporaries. Nineteenth-century opera may have died with him, but opera, of course, did not. We are approaching the year 2000, at which time, according to the generally accepted date for the birth of this art form, opera will celebrate its four hundredth birthday. New operas appear now with healthy regularity, and many have been well received, maintaining their popularity through the decades. They may herald the beginning of a new golden age. Only time can tell and not enough of it has passed. If we are in fact witnessing another fluorescence it will be a different one. The line that began with Mozart ended with Strauss. He has no successor.

Modern composers have their own hall of minstrels. With history still ridiculing the premature judgments of yesterday, no one can say that they will not rival that prodigious outpouring of enduring passion so recently ended. I predict nonetheless that neither they nor anyone else will ever surpass it.

REFERENCES

Aalholm, O. A. *South Coast Impulses to the Wagner Opera: The Flying Dutchman,* in Aust-Agder-Arv. Arendal, Norway: P. M. Danielsens Trykkeri, 1972.

Abel, Theodore. *Why Hitler Came to Power.* Cambridge: Harvard University Press, 1986.

Beecham, Sir Thomas. *A Mingled Chime.* New York: G.P. Putnam's Sons, 1943.

Bleiler, Ellen H. "The Composer," *Aida,* translated and introduced by Ellen H. Bleiler. New York: Dover Publications Inc., 1962.

Bowen, Catherine Drinker, and Barbara Von Meck. *Beloved Friend, The Story of Tchaikowsky and Nadejda Von Meck.* New York: Random House, 1937.

Branscombe, Peter. *Die Zauberflöte.* Cambridge: Cambridge University Press, 1991.

———. "Emanuel Schikaneder," *New Grove Dictionary of Opera,* edited by Stanley Sadie. London: MacMillan Press Limited, 1992.

Broad, Lewis. *The Friendships and Follies of Oscar Wilde.* London: Hutchinson and Co. Ltd., 1954.

Broder, Nathan. *The Great Operas of Mozart.* New York: W.W. Norton and Company, 1962.

Brown, David. *Tchaikovsky: The Crisis Years, 1874–1878.* New York: W.W. Norton and Company, 1983.

Brugsch-Bey. *Egypt Under the Pharaohs.* New York: Charles Scribner's & Sons, 1891.

Budden, Julian. *The Operas of Verdi* (3 vols.). New York: Oxford University Press, 1979.

———. "Puccini," *New Grove Dictionary of Opera,* edited by Stanley Sadie. London: MacMillan Press Limited, 1992.

———. "La Fanciulla del West," *New Grove Dictionary of Opera,* edited by Stanley Sadie. London: MacMillan Press Limited, 1992.

Bulwer-Lytton, Edward George. *Rienzi: The Last of the Roman Tribunes.* London: George Routledge and Sons, 1874.

Cappon, James. *Victor Hugo.* Edinburgh and London: William Blackwood and Sons, 1885.

Carleton, George W. *Hugo, Witness of His Life.* Translated from the French by Charles Edwin Wilbour. New York: Carleton, Publisher, 1863.

Carner, Mosco. *Puccini, A Critical Biography.* New York: Holmes and Meier Publishers, Inc., 1958.

Cohen, Rosi: "Emigration: a Contributing Factor to Stefan Zweig's Suicide," *The World of Yesterday's Humanist Today,* edited by Marion Sonnenfeld. Albany: State University of New York Press, 1983.

Conati, Marcello. *Encounters with Verdi.* Ithaca and New York: Cornell University Press, 1984.

Cook, Deryck. *I Saw the World End.* London: Oxford University Press, 1979.

Cotterell, Arthur. *The Macmillan Illustrated Encyclopedia of Myths and Legends.* New York: Macmillan Publishing Company, 1989.

Cox, Cynthia. *The Real Figaro: The Extraordinary Career of Caron de Beaumarchaise.* New York: Coward-McCann, 1963.

Cross, Milton J. *The New Milton Cross' Complete Stories of the Great Operas.* Garden City, New York: Doubleday and Company, Inc., 1942.

Curtiss, Mina. *Bizet and His World.* New York: Alfred A. Knopf, 1958.

D'Orliac, Jehanne. *Francis I, Prince of the Renaissance.* Philadelphia and London: J. B. Lippincott Company, 1932.

Davies, Peter J. *Mozart in Person.* Westport, Connecticut: Greenwood Press Inc., 1989.

De Bovet, Marie Anne. *Charles Gounod, His Life and Works.* London: Sampson Low, Marston, Searle & Rivington Limited, 1891.

De Loménie, Louis. *Beaumarchaise and His Times, Sketches of French Society in the Eighteenth Century from Unpublished Documents.* New York: Harper & Brothers, 1857.

Dean, Winton. *Georges Bizet, His Life and Work.* London: J. M. Dent and Sons Ltd., 1965.

Dent, Edward J. *Mozart's Magic Flute.* Cambridge: W. Heffer and Sons, Ltd., 1911.

Deutsch, Otto Erich. *Mozart: a Documentary Biography,* translated by Eric Blom, Peter Branscombe, and Jeremy Noble. Stanford, California: Stanford University Press, 1965.

Durant, Will. *The Reformation (The Story of Civilization,* Part VI). New York: Simon and Schuster, 1957.

Edwards, Gwynne. *Tirso de Molina, The Trickster of Seville and the Stone Guest.* Warmister, Wiltshire, England: Aris and Phillips Ltd., Teddington House, 1986.

Edwards, Sutherland H. *Rossini and His School.* London: Sampson Low, Marston, Searle and Rivington, 1881.

Ellman, Richard. *Oscar Wilde.* New York: Vintage Books, 1984.

Finck, Henry T. *Richard Strauss: The Man and His Works.* Boston: Little Brown, and Company, 1917.

Gatti, Carlo. *Verdi, the Man and His Music.* New York: G. P. Putnam's Sons, 1955.

Glanville, S.R.K. *The Legacy of Egypt,* edited by S. R. K. Glanville. London: Oxford University Press, 1942.

Gold, Arthur, and Robert Fizdale. *The Divine Sarah.* New York: Vintage Books, 1991.

Gould, Robert Freke. *The Concise History of Freemasonry.* London: Gale & Polden Ltd., 1903.

Gounod, Charles. *Charles Gounod: Autobiographica: Reminiscences, with Family Letters and Notes on Music,* translated from the French by Hon. W. Hely Hutchinson. London: H. Heinemann, 1896.

Graml, Hermann. *Antisemitism in the Third Reich.* Cambridge and Oxford: Blackwell Publishers, 1992.

Gregor-Dellin, Martin. *Richard Wagner, His Life, His Work, His Century,* translated by Maxwell Brownjohn. San Diego, New York, London: Harcourt Brace Jovanovich, Publishers, 1980.

Hemmings, F. W. J. *Alexandre Dumas: The King of Romance.* New York: Charles Scribner's & Sons, 1979.

Hildesheimer, Wolfgang. *Mozart,* translated from the German by Marion Faber. New York: Farrar, Straus & Giroux, 1982.

Hobson, Christine. *Exploring the World of the Pharaohs.* London: Thames and Hudson, 1987.

Hodson, Philip. *Who's Who in Wagner.* New York: Macmillan Publishing Company, 1984.

Howarth, W. D. "Hugo and the Romantic Drama in Verse," in *Victor Hugo,* edited by Harold Bloom. New York, New Haven, and Philadelphia: Chelsea House Publishers, 1988.

Hughes, Spike. *Famous Verdi Operas.* Philadelphia, New York, London: Chilton Book Company, 1968.

Hugo, Victor. *Dramatic Works of Victor Hugo,* translated by Frederick L. Slous, and Mrs. Newton Crosland. New York: Peter Fenlon Collier and Son, 1901.

———. *Letters of Victor Hugo.* Cambridge: Houghton, Mifflin and Co., 1896.

Jackson, Stanley. *Monsieur Butterfly.* New York: Stein and Day, 1974.

Jacob, Margaret C. *Living the Enlightenment.* New York and Oxford: Oxford University Press, 1991.

Jahn, Otto. *Life of Mozart,* translated from the German by Pauline Townsend. New York: Cooper Square Publishers, 1970.

Josephus, Flavius. *The Works of Flavius Josephus,* translated by William Whiston, A.M. Cincinnati: E. Morgan and Co., 1850.

Kamil, Jill. *Upper Egypt, Historical Outline and Descriptive Guide to the Ancient Sites.* London and New York: Longman, 1983.

Kapp, Julius. *Richard Wagner, Sein Leben, Sein Werk, Seine Welt,* Berlin-Schöneberg: Max Hesses Verlag, 1933.

Kendall, Alan. *Gioacchino Rossini, The Reluctant Hero.* London: Victor Gollancz Ltd., 1992.

———. *Tchaikovsky.* London: The Bodley Head, 1988.

Kennedy, Michael. *Richard Strauss.* London: J. M. Dent and Sons, Ltd., 1976.

Kinder, Hermann, and Werner Hilgemann. *The Anchor Atlas of World History* (2 vols). Garden City, New York: Anchor Books, 1978.

King, Joseph. *The German Revolution: Its Meaning and Menace.* London: Williams & Norgate Ltd., 1933.

Kinross, Lord. *Between Two Seas: The Creation of the Suez Canal.* New York: William Morrow and Company, Inc., 1969.

Koenigsberger, Dorothy. "A New Metaphor for Mozart's Magic Flute," *European Studies Review,* vol 5, no. 3, July 1975. London and Beverly Hills: Sage Publications Inc.

Kolb, Annette. *Mozart.* Chicago: Henry Regnery Company, 1956.

Kolodin, Irving. *The Story of the Metropolitan Opera.* New York: Alfred A. Knopf, 1953.

Krehbiel, Henry Edward. *A Book of Operas.* New York: The Macmillan Company, 1946.

Kupferberg, Herbert. *A History of Opera.* Mondadore, Verona, Italy: Europa Verlag 1975.

Kurt, Wilhelm. *Richard Strauss, an Intimate Portrait.* London: Thames and Hudson, 1989.

Lafont, Robert, editor. *The Illustrated History of Paris and the Parisians.* Garden City, New York: Doubleday and Company, Inc., 1958.

Landon, H. C. Robbins. *Mozart's Last Year*. New York: Schirmer Books, A Division of Macmillan Inc., 1988.

Landon, Robbins, editor. *Beethoven: A Documentary Study,* abridged edition, New York: Collier Books, 1974.

Lepsius, Richard. *Letters from Egypt, Ethiopia, and the Peninsula of Sinai.* London: Henry G. Bohn, 1853.

Lippert, Woldemar. *Wagner in Exile,* translated by Paul England. London, Bombay and Sydney: George G. Harrap and Co. Ltd., 1930.

Mandel, Oscar. *The Theatre of Don Juan: A Collection of Plays and Views.* Lincoln, Nebraska, and London: University of Nebraska Press, 1963.

Mander, Raymond, and Joe Mitchenson. *The Wagner Companion.* New York: Hawthorn Books, 1977.

Marek, George R. *Cosima Wagner.* New York: Harper and Row, 1981.

———. *Puccini.* New York: Simon and Schuster, 1951.

Mariette, Francois Auguste Ferdinand (Mariette Bey). *Monuments of Upper Egypt,* a translation by Alphonse Mariette of *Itinéraire de la haute Égypte.* Boston: J. H. Mansfield & J. W. Dearborn, 1890.

Mason, Steve. *Josephus and the New Testament.* Peabody, Massachusetts: Hendrickson's Publishers, 1992.

Maurois, André. *The Titans: A Three-Generation Biography of the Dumas,* translated from the French by Gerard Hopkins. Harper & Row, Publishers, 1957.

McCarthy, Mary. *La Traviata.* New York: Metropolitan Opera Classics Library, 1983.

Meilhac, Henri, and Ludovic Halévy. *Carmen: An Opera in Four Acts.* New York: Fred Rullman Inc., nd.

Mérimée, Prosper: *Carmen and Columba,* translated from the French by Eric Sutton. London: Hamish Hamilton, 1949.

Morris, William, trans. *Song of the Volsungs and the Nibelungs,* Chicago: Henry Regnery Company, 1949.

Mozart, Wolfgang Amadeus. *Letters of Wolfgang Amadeus Mozart,* selected and edited by Hans Mersmann, translated from the German by M. M. Bozman. New York: Dover Publications Inc., 1972.

Newman, Ernest. *The Life of Richard Wagner* (4 vols.). Cambridge and New York: Alfred A. Knopf, 1946.

———. *Stories of the Great Operas and Their Composers.* Garden City, New York: Garden City Publishing Co., Inc., 1928.

Osborne, Charles. *Verdi, A Life in the Theatre.* New York: Alfred A. Knopf, 1987.

Osborne, Richard. *Rossini.* London: J. M. Dent & Sons Ltd., 1986.

Pardoe, Julia. *Francis the First: King of France,* (2 vols.). Philadelphia: Lea and Blanchard, 1849.

Perry, Marvin, et al. *Western Civilization: A Concise History,* (Vol. II). Boston: Houghton Mifflin Company, 1981.

Pougin, Arthur. *Verdi: an Anecdotal History of His Life and Works.* New York: Scribner & Welford, 1887.

Powell, Kerry. *Oscar Wilde and the Theatre of the 1890s.* Cambridge: Cambridge University Press, 1990.

Prater, D. A. *European of Yesterday.* Oxford: Oxford University Press, 1972.

Puccini, Giacomo. *Letters of Giacomo Puccini,* edited by Giuseppe Adami, translated from the Italian and edited for the English edition by Ena Makin. Philadelphia and London: J. B. Lippincott Company, 1931.

Pushkin, Alexander. *Eugene Onegin,* translated by Charles Johnston. New York: The Viking Press, 1977.

Raby, Peter. *Oscar Wilde.* Cambridge: Cambridge University Press, 1988.

Reinhardt, Kurt F. *Germany: 2000 years* (2 vols). New York: Frederick Ungar Publishing Co., 1950.

Rivers, John. *Figaro: The Life of Beaumarchais.* New York: Dutton, 1923.

Ross, Michael. *Alexandre Dumas.* Newton Abbot, London, and North Pomfret, Vermont: David and Charles, 1981.

Rushton, Julian. "Die Zauberflöte," in *New Grove Dictionary of Opera,* edited by Stanley Sadie. London: MacMillan Press Limited, 1992.

Schenk, Erich. *Mozart and His Times,* edited and translated from the German by Richard and Clara Winston. New York: Alfred A. Knopf, 1959.

Schopp, Claude. *Alexandre Dumas, Genius of Life.* New York and Toronto: Franklin Watts, 1988.

Skinner, Cornelia Otis. *Madame Sarah.* Boston: Houghton Mifflin Company, 1967.

Smith, Hugh Allison, and Robert Bell Michell. "Introduction" to *La Dame aux Camélias.* London, Toronto, Melbourne, and Bombay: Oxford University Press, 1924.

Solomon, Maynard. *Beethoven,* New York: Schirmer Books, 1977.

Specht, Richard. *Giacomo Puccini: The Man, His Life, His Work,* translated by Catherine Alison Phillips. New York: Alfred A. Knopf, 1933.

Steinberg, Michael P. *Politics and Psychology of "Die Schweigsame Frau," The World of Yesterday's Humanist Today,* edited by Marion Sonnenfeld, Albany: State University of New York Press, 1983.

Strauss, Richard, and Stefan Zweig. *A Confidential Matter: The Letters of Richard Strauss and Stefan Zweig,* translated from the German by Max Knight. Berkeley, University of California Press, 1977.

Strauss, Richard, and Romain Rolland. *Richard Strauss & Romain Rolland, Correspondence, Diary & Essays,* edited and annotated with a preface by Rollo Myers. Berkeley and Los Angeles: University of California Press, 1968.

Taranow, Gerda. *Sarah Bernhardt: The Art Within the Legend.* Princeton: Princeton University Press, 1972.

Taylor, Ronald. *Richard Wagner,* New York: Taplinger Publishing Company, 1979.

Till, Nicholas. *Rossini, His Life and Times.* New York: Hippocrene Books Inc., 1983.

Thayer, Alexander Wheelock. *Life of Beethoven,* Revised and Edited by Elliot Forbes, Princeton, New Jersey: Princeton University Press, 1967.

Toye, Francis. *Giuseppi Verdi, His Life and Works.* New York: Alfred A. Knopf, 1946.

Turner, W. J. *Mozart, The Man and His Works.* London: Methuen and Co. Ltd., 1965.

Verdi, Giuseppe. *Letters of Giuseppe Verdi,* selected, translated, and edited by Charles Osborne. New York, Chicago, and San Francisco: Holt, Rinehart and Winston, 1971.

———. *Verdi: The Man in His Letters,* as edited and selected by Franz Werfel and Paul Stefan, translated by Edward Downes. New York: Vienna House, 1942.

Verneuil, Louis. *The Fabulous Life of Sarah Bernhardt,* translated from the French by Ernest Boyd. New York: Harper and Brothers, Publishers, 1942.

Viaud, J. "Egyptian Mythology," *New Larousse Encyclopedia of Mythology,* new edition. New York: Prometheus Press, 1968.

Wagner, *Cosima. Cosima Wagner's Diaries,* edited and annotated by Martin Gregor-Dellin, and Dietrich Mack; translated and with an introduction, postscript, and additional notes by Geoffrey Skelton (2 vols.). New York and London: Harcourt Brace Jovanovich, Inc., 1977.

———. *Das Zweite Leben, Briefe und Aufzeichnungen 1883–1930,* edited by Dietrich Mack. Munich: R. Piper and Co. Verlag, 1980.

Wagner, Richard. *The Diary of Richard Wagner, The Brown Book, 1865–1882,* presented and annotated by Joachim Bergfeld, translated by George Bird. London: Victor Gollancz Ltd., 1980.

———. *Family Letters of Richard Wagner,* translated by William Ashton Ellis. New York: Vienna House, 1971.

———. *Letters of Richard Wagner, The Burrell Collection,* edited with notes by John N. Burk. New York: Vienna House, 1972.

————. *My Life.* New York: Dodd, Meade and Company, 1911.

————. *Richard Wagner, Letters to Anton Pusinelli,* translated and edited with critical notes by Elbert Lenrow. New York: Vienna House, 1972.

————. *Richard Wagner, Letters to Minna Wagner* (2 vols), translated, prefaced, etc., by William Ashton Ellis. New York: Vienna House, 1972.

————. *Richard Wagner, Sämtliche Briefe,* herausgegeben im Auftrage der Richard Wagner Stiftung Bayreuth von Gertrud Strobel und Werner Wolf (4 vol.). Leipzig: Veb Deutscher Verlag Für Musik, 1979.

————. *Richard Wagner's Letters to August Roeckel,* translated by Eleanor C. Sellar, with an introductory essay by Houston Stewart Chamberlain. Bristol and London: J. W. Arrowsmith, 1914.

————. *Richard Wagner's Letters to His Dresden Friends,* translated and with a preface by J. S. Shedlock. New York: Vienna House, 1980.

Walker, Frank. *The Man Verdi.* New York: Alfred A. Knopf, 1962.

Weaver, William: *Piave, Francesco Mario, New Grove Dictionary of Opera,* edited by Stanley Sadie. London: MacMillan Press Limited, 1992.

Weaver, William, compiler, editor, and translator. *Verdi, A Documentary Study.* Golborne, Lancs, Great Britain: Keyspools, Ltd., (n.d.).

Wechsberg, Joseph. *Verdi.* New York: G. P. Putnam's Sons, 1974.

Weinstock, Herbert. *Donizetti.* New York: Pantheon Books, 1963.

————. *Rossini.* New York: Alfred A. Knopf, 1968.

————. *Tchaikovsky.* New York: Alfred A. Knopf, 1944.

Wilde, Oscar. *Salome, A Tragedy in One Act,* translated from the French by Lord Alfred Douglas. New York: Dover Publications Inc., 1967.

Wilhelm, Kurt. *Richard Strauss, An Intimate Portrait,* translated by Mary Whittall. London: Thames and Hudson Ltd., 1989.

Zweig, Frederike M. *Stefan Zweig.* London: W. H. Allen and Co. Ltd., 1946.

————. *Stefan Zweig, Eine Bildbiographie.* Munich: Kindler Verlag, 1961.

Zweig, Stefan. *The World of Yesterday.* New York: The Viking Press, 1943.

INDEX

233